# Cahokia

# Cahokia

## Mirror of the Cosmos

**SALLY A. KITT CHAPPELL**

*William R. Iseminger and John E. Kelly, Consultants*

The
University
of Chicago Press
Chicago and
London

SALLY A. KITT CHAPPELL, professor emerita in the
Department of Art at DePaul university, is the author of
*Architecture and Planning of Graham, Anderson, Probst,
and White, 1912–1936,* also published by the University of
Chicago Press, and a contributor to the Travel section of
the *New York Times.*

The University of Chicago Press, Chicago 60637
The University of Chicago Press, Ltd., London
©2002 by Sally A. Kitt Chappell
All rights reserved. Published 2002
Printed in China

11 10 09 08 07 06 05 04 03 02     1 2 3 4 5
ISBN: 0-226-10136-3 (cloth)
ISBN: 0-226-10137-1 (paper)

Library of Congress Cataloging-in-Publication Data
Chappell, Sally Anderson
  Cahokia: mirror of the cosmos / Sally A. Kitt
  Chappell ; William R. Iseminger and John E. Kelly,
  consultants.
      p.  cm.
  Includes bibliographical references and index.
  ISBN 0-226-10136-3 (cloth : alk. paper) —
  ISBN 0-226-10137-1 (paper : alk. paper)
  1. Cahokia Mounds State Historic Park (Ill.)
  2. Mississippian culture.  3. Indians of North
America—Illinois—Antiquities.  I. Title.
  E99.M6815 C55 2002
  977.3'89—dc21                    2001027511

This book is printed on acid-free paper.

# Contents

List of Illustrations  vii
Acknowledgments  xi
Prologue  xiii
Introduction: A Deep Time Study  2

Epilogue  189
Notes  193
Bibliography  203
Credits for Illustrations  207
Index  211

1  Cahokia in Its Natural Setting: A Special Place within a
Special Place  7

2  Human Beings Enter the Americas: Paleo-Indians, Archaic and
Woodland Groups, and Emergent Mississippians  27

3  Cahokia: Cosmic Landscape Architecture  51

4  French Explorers, Trappers, Priests, and Monks  77

5  Nineteenth-Century Turmoil  95

6  Early Twentieth-Century Cahokia: Setting the Stage  125

7  Modern Cahokia: A Critical Mass at a Critical Time  153

# Illustrations

1.  Star-forming region, xv
2.  Our star—the sun, xvi
3.  Craters on Venus, xvii
4.  Earth, xix
5.  Dawn at the equinox in Cahokia, 6
6.  Mississippi River system, 8
7.  Coal forest diorama, 10
8.  Glacial map of Illinois, 11
9.  Root systems of prairie plants, 13
10. Geologists examining road cut, 13
11. Loess map of Illinois, 14
12. Earthquake centers and fault zones in Illinois, 16
13. Satellite map of Illinois, 20
14. Prehistoric American Bottom, 21
15. American Bottom about 1800, 21
16. American Bottom physical region, 22
17. Vegetation map of Illinois, 24
18. Cahokia café mural, 26
19. Clovis points, 28
20. Paleo-Indians hunting the mastodon, 29

21. Throwing an atlatl, 30

22. Late Archaic bannerstone of banded slate, 31

23. Late Archaic bannerstone of chalcedony, 31

24. Constructing a dugout canoe, 32

25. Middle Archaic life in the Illinois Valley, 33

26. Grinding corn, 35

27. Adena-Hopewell and related cultures, 37

28. Aerial photograph of Poverty Point, 38

29. Plan and reconstruction of Poverty Point, 39

30. Locust-shaped bead, Poverty Point culture, 40

31. Beaver effigy platform pipe, 41

32. Swan comb of turtle shell, 41

33. Eagle talon of mica, 41

34. Newark Works, Licking County, Ohio, 43

35. Hopewell Mound City, Chillicothe, Ohio, 44

36. Effigy mounds, Dade County, Wisconsin, 44

37. Great Serpent Mound, Peebles, Ohio, 47

38. Missisisippian sites map, 47

39. Notched hoe blade, 48

40. View of Cahokia with four plazas, 50

41. Central Cahokia about A.D. 1100, 52

42. Map of central Cahokia showing four plazas, 53

43. Cahokia mounds on cardinal axes, 53

44. Cahokia mounds on the 47.5 meter module, 53

45. Celestial orientations, 53

46. Greeting the rising sun, 54

47. Plan of McKeithen Mounds, 55

48. Community life in Cahokia, 56

49. Ceramic beaver bowl, 60

50. Water spider motif, 60

51. Chunkey players, 61

52. Changes in stockade construction, 62

53. Woodhenge construction, 63

54. Typical Mississippian pole-and-thatch construction, 66

55. Principal Mississippian mound types, 67

56. Cahokia site with Fowler's layout, 68

57. Flaying of deer, 69

58. Making pottery, 70

59. Reconstruction of a ramada and two houses, 71

60. A Cahokia market, 72

61. Late Mississippian gorget showing two birdmen, 74

62. *Henri de Tonti, Founder of Peoria,* 76

63. Map of the Illinois country and New France, 78

64. Father Marquette's map, 1673, 79

65. Jolliet's map, 1674, 80

66. The first hospital in the Illinois country, 82

67. Courtyard of Fort de Chartres, 83

68. Artist's reconstruction of French chapel, 84

69. French chapel ground plan, 85

70. *George Rogers Clark Addressing the Native Americans at Cahokia,* 87

71. Detail of a map by Georges-Henri-Victor Collot, 92

72. Ste. Anne's Militia reenactors at Fort de Chartres, 93

73. Reenactors Margaret Kimball Brown and Marvin Hilligoss, 93

74. Detail of Hilligoss costume, 93

75. *Panorama of the . . . Mississippi Valley,* by John J. Eagen, 94

76. Sketch of St. Louis mounds by Titian R. Peale, 1861, 100

77. *View of Monk's Mound,* by Karl Bodmer, 102

78. *View of Twin Mounds,* by Karl Bodmer, 102

79. *Old Bear, a Medicine Man,* by George Catlin, 104

80. *Monk's Mound, St. Clair County,* by J. C. Wild, 105

81. Early pioneers, 107

82. View of Alton, Illinois, 107

83. *Homes for the Industrious,* 109

84. *Prairie Scene in Illinois,* 110

85. *View of Monks Mound,* 111

86. Drawings of ceramics by Charles Rau, 112

87. Locomotive near Monks Mound, 113

88. Map of railroads in East St. Louis and suburbs, 114
89. Drawings of artifacts from Illinois River mounds by John Francis Snyder, 116
90. Birthplace of John Francis Snyder, 116
91. Schematic drawing of Monks Mound by Dr. John J. R. Patrick, 118
92. Drawing of Monks Mound in 1882 by William McAdams, 118
93. Birdman Tablet found on Monks Mound, 119
94. Destruction of Big Mound, St. Louis, 120
95. Destruction of Big Mound, St. Louis, later stage, 120
96. Ceramic frog, 122
97. Map of central Cahokia in Amerindian times and the same terrain in 1966, 124
98. Electric interurban trains to Cahokia, 126
99. Horse-drawn slip by trench face of Harding, (later Rattlesnake) Mound, 131
100. Digging a trench, Moorehead excavation, 132
101. Augur tests during Moorehead excavation, 132
102. Ku Klux Klan rally in Cahokia, July 1923, 133
103. Moorehead's letterhead and calling card, 135
104. Morehead's calling card (reverse) and insert in published works, 135
105. Section of map showing location of houses, 138
106. Aerial photo of housing development, 139
107. Aerial photo of Powell Mound in 1922, 139
108. Destruction of Powell Mound, 139
109. Aerial photograph showing surface traces of stockade built eight hundred years earlier, 141
110. Map of Monks Mound quadrant in 1974, 143
111. Plan and isometric of Murdock Mound 1941, 145
112. Aerial photo showing drive-in movie and airstrip, 147
113. Aerial photo of contemporary Cahokia, 152
114. Land acquisition at Cahokia Mounds State Historic Site, 1925–85, 156
115. Vegetation cover on Monks Mound, 157
116. Beaker fragment found near winter solstice pole of Cahokia woodhenge, 159
117. Mississippian stockade construction methods, 161
118. Aerial view of Cahokia with enclosing stockade wall, 162
119. Workforce building the stockade, 163
120. Schematic drawing of Cahokia city plan, 164
121. Excavators at work on Mound 72, 165
122. Mound 72 cross section, 166
123. Re-creation of the burial of a leader in Mound 72, 166
124. Master Plan for Cahokia Mounds State Historic Site, 172
125. Archaeologists mapping different houses on the same site, 175
126. Native American dancer Jay Mule performing in Cahokia, 179
127. Cahokia Mounds Interpretive Center, 183
128. Halley's Comet crossing the Milky Way, 188

# Acknowledgments

From the day I first saw Cahokia to the day, five years later, that I turned in the manuscript to the University of Chicago Press, I have been helped by others. Nearly every time I asked for assistance I was met with a hearty willingness to share, to welcome another worker to the field where there is still so much to do.

I was in the small library of the interpretive center on the Cahokia site when I said to William R. Iseminger and John E. Kelly, the archaeological consultants on this book, "What this place needs is an illustrated history." They replied, "When do we start?" Thereafter they spent days with me, going over the text in line by line critiques, correcting and refining my interpretations. Many of the ideas are based on their original work, both in the field and in publications. Some plans came directly from their drawing boards. Their insights about city planning at Cahokia were a breakthrough for me. Iseminger was indispensable in securing illustrations and other graphic materials. As an architectural historian, I conceived the themes and wrote the text, but during this long period neither of them ever failed to answer a call.

In addition to their extensive publications, many other archaeologists helped me directly. William I. Woods, Rinita Dalan, George Holley, and H. W. Watters were my teachers in the course in archaeological cartography I took at Southern Illinois University at Edwardsville. They demonstrated the importance of hands-on work in the field, in the laboratory, and at the library and patiently answered my many questions. William I. Woods helped me secure pleasant housing, offered me the use of the vast library at the Contract Archaeology Office, and let me photocopy whatever I needed. His online bibliography is an invaluable tool, an immeasurable time- and laborsaving device for all investigators of this subject. James A. Brown, Melvin L. Fowler, and Mary Beth Trubitt let me observe and sometimes participate in their ongoing excavations. I spent many hours with Margaret Brown in illuminating conversation.

In the beginning I feared that interdisciplinary work would mean not only crossing boundaries but stepping on toes. On the contrary, I found that the scientists I encountered were team workers by discipline and by nature. Among those who rolled up their sleeves to find things for me or who offered valuable insights were Michael McNerney, astronomers Phyllis Pitluga and Lynn Albaugh, anthropologist Robert L. Hall, biologist Alan Rester, cultural geographer Geri Weinstein-Bruenig, geologist Christopher J. Schuberth, Cahokia Mounds Museum Society executive director Chris Pallozola, and many others.

Architect Charles C. Morris and designer Gerard Hilferty generously sent me slides and discussed the creative processes and technical problems involved in erecting a building for a UNESCO monument on a prehistoric site rich in artifacts.

I kiss the hems of librarians in gratitude for their never-failing assistance. The privileges I have enjoyed as a professor emerita at DePaul University include the indispensable help of interlibrary loan librarian Denise Rogers and reference librarians Margaret Powers, Susan Clarke, Rosemarie Cooper, and Karen Malenfant. Mary Woolever, at the Burnham Library of Architecture of the Art Institute of Chicago, solved many research problems in a flash and found pathways to materials in obscure rare books. The staff at the Newberry Library, Northwestern University, and the University of Chicago were unfailingly helpful. Special mention is due the Collinsville, Illinois, Memorial Public Library, the smallest of my sources but one of the most important.

Here I was aided over a period of several weeks as I read local materials on the microfilm reader. In a tidy basement room Arvil Wrigley and Floyd Sperino helped me find original works in their carefully preserved archives, proving once again that history is in large part local history. Important aspects of this story would have been lost had it not been for their efforts.

The benefits of friendships in the humanist circles I am privileged to inhabit in Chicago are sustaining beyond measure. I cannot find words adequate to express my gratitude to my friends and colleagues who know what it is to write a book. Some of them listened to or read large sections of the text, and their encouraging suggestions at various stages gave me the energy to carry on. Thank you Robert Bruegmann, Florence Cohen, Kevin Harrington, Wadad Kadi, Sarah Bradford Landau, Stephen Luecking, Joan and Harold Perkin, Ingrid Rowland, Barbara Stafford, and Tilde Sankovitch.

Unconventional as it is, I also want to thank the two anonymous reviewers solicited by the University of Chicago Press. Their diligent reading and insightful criticism helped me find the path to deeper truths and raised the level of the text. Susan Bielstein, the acquisitions editor at the Press, steered the manuscript through this process, selecting the readers and providing the support needed at crucial stages. Later the manuscript editor and designer contributed their skills, attesting to the civilizing quality of the publication process at the University of Chicago Press.

My sons Jonathan and David are both writers, and their interest and help warmed my heart often during the otherwise lonely work of writing. My daughter-in-law, Mary McGee Chappell, and my four grandchildren—Jennifer, Katherine, Lauren, and Ryan—lightened my spirits at every stage over the long road I took to complete this work. At the heart of all my endeavors is the support I receive from my husband, Walter Kitt. His tireless patience, gentle criticism, and love are part of this book.

# Prologue

It is nearly 1:00 A.M. as I stand on the top of Monks Mound looking up at the stars, scattered to infinity. At my feet are countless motes of dust, finite perhaps here in the central Mississippi Valley, but an intimate part of the vast cosmos beyond. They had the same origin, those stars and this dust.

A long time ago, before the Big Bang, none of this existed: nothing in the sky above me or the space below. All was blackness and void. I pick up a handful of dirt and let it slip through my fingers. The components of this dirt, these vital substances of the future earth, were yet unmade. After the Big Bang the primal matter would undergo eons of metamorphosis and geological change before it turned into the dust that settled in Cahokia.

After that first cosmic explosion we call the Big Bang, there was light; there was movement; there were atomic particles. And these were everything. It took billions of years, but these particles, moved by gravity and heated by light, eventually combined and recombined into the universe we know today.

The components of the future earth and of Monks Mound were once bits of matter, created in the cauldrons of exploding stars, moving with great, swirling gravitational forces, like the stars still forming near the Cone Nebula today (fig. 1). Atoms in a crucible of gas and fire.

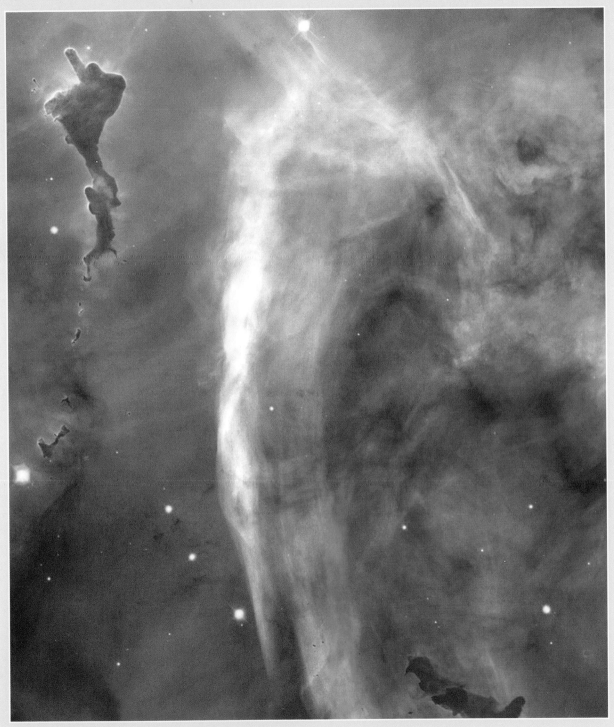

FIG. 1. OUT OF NOTHINGNESS—EVERYTHING!

Among the infinite stars was one fiery newborn—our sun—sharing a vast space with countless other

celestial bodies (fig. 2). Its external temperature is over 6,000°F. High-speed solar winds emanating from

the dark areas on the sun flow past the earth at over four hundred miles a second.

Earth then was like the planet Venus now (fig. 3). Boiling volcanoes everywhere blasted through

its crust and covered the young earth with fiery magma. When the earth at last began to cool the lava

formed into the black basalt that lies deep beneath the surface southwest of Monks Mound today.

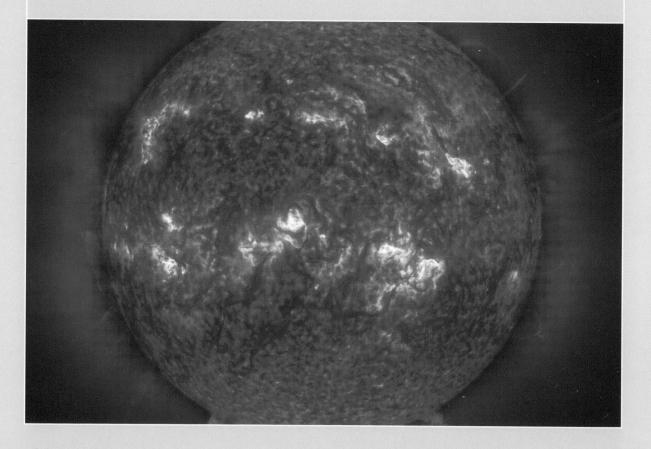

FIG. 2 (OPPOSITE) OUR STAR—THE SUN          FIG. 3 FIERY VOLCANOES AND CONSTANT EARTHQUAKES

Eventually the heat from the volcanoes met the cold air of space, and white clouds were born. When the clouds rose to meet even colder air, raindrops fell earthward to form blue puddles, streams, lakes, and oceans (fig. 4).

The earth is the third planet out from the sun, the only planet in the solar system with surface water. Venus, closer to the sun, is now too hot for water. Its daytime temperature of 800°F turns its atmosphere to steam. Mars, farther from the sun, is now too cold—doomed to ice. Liquid water is possible only in the narrow temperature range between 32°F and 212°F. In our lucky position in the solar system, between steam and ice, we are awash in water.

Tilted, orbiting, and spinning, the earth moves continuously in two different ways: orbiting in space in an elliptical path around the sun once a year, and spinning around on its tilted axis every twenty-four hours. In the temperate zones our lives move to two different but synchronized rhythms: four seasons a year, two light/dark beats every twenty-four hours.

Later we will see how the builders of America's great terraced pyramid at Cahokia hailed the change from winter to spring and summer to fall—when day and night are equal—with elaborate celebrations, and how they patterned their great mound city to echo the rhythms of the cosmos.

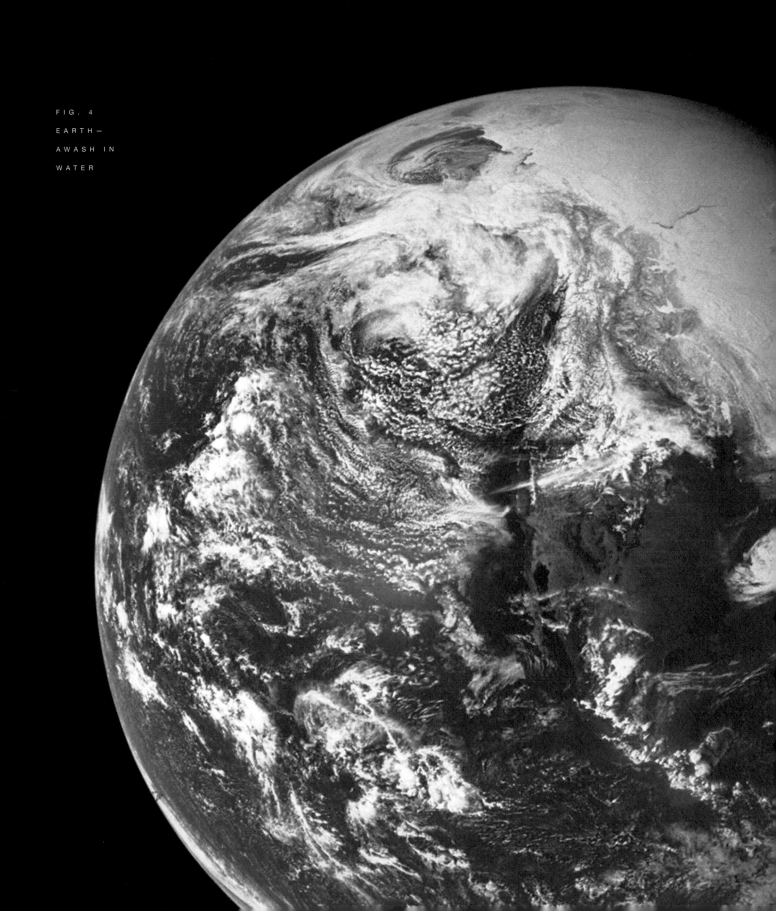

FIG. 4
EARTH—
AWASH IN
WATER

# Cahokia

# Introduction

A Deep Time Study

From the top of Monks Mound the horizon of the wide world beyond forms a perfect circle. At dawn the rising sun embraces this cosmos with an arc of gold, a reminder of the past once cradled in this land on the broad shores of the Mississippi.

At the beginning of the second millennium, a civilization more sophisticated and powerful than any other in the Western Hemisphere north of Mexico emerged and flourished in the Midwest. The center of communal life for these Native American "Mississippians" was in the place we now call the Cahokia Mounds, in southwestern Illinois. At the turn of the millennium, about A.D. 1050, the population of Cahokia and its environs was larger than that of London.[1] Their technology was of the Stone Age, yet without the wheel, beasts of burden, or metallurgy, their stratified society fostered widespread commerce, refined artistic expression, and monumental architecture.

The center of this six-square-mile area, the climax of this Native American world, was a great four-tiered pyramid covering fourteen acres and rising one hundred feet into the sky—the tallest structure in the United States until 1867.[2] All archaeologists know about Cahokia, and in 1982 it was designated a World Heritage Site by UNESCO, one of only eight cultural sites in the United States (in addition to fourteen natural sites, four of them shared with Canada).[3] In spite of this world recognition, surprisingly few people are familiar with its extraordinary history. Even professors who teach in Illinois universities have confessed that they know little about the Cahokia Mounds State Historic Site or the city that flourished there.

2

Most scholars think of prehistoric civilizations in the context of an arid climate such as Mesopotamia or Egypt, but the Mississippian culture developed in a southern position in a temperate climate, one of the richest agricultural regions on earth. A wide variety of indigenous plants thrived there in the days before agriculture, and wildlife was bountiful—a stable, nearly year-round food supply.

How did this land became so fertile, so amenable to human life? Who were the powerful, remarkable people who lived here before the Europeans came? Why did such a complex, thriving metropolis flower in the swampy bottomland of the Mississippi? Why did the whole civilization disappear? What became of the land in the centuries after the Mississippians abandoned it? Why did it lend itself so readily to immense man-made changes such as cultivated fields, borrow pits, mounds, dams, drainage canals, levees, and industrial development? What influences from other countries changed the character of the site? What is it like today? And what can we learn about ourselves as we trace the changing meanings of the site?

## A Sophisticated City from Elemental Means

The visible forms of architecture embody multilayered values: human meaning, social intention, political ideology, religious beliefs, and aesthetic fulfillment, to name a few. In my previous books I dealt with twentieth-century architects and city planners who had at their disposal a dazzling choice of materials and building techniques: steel, concrete, brick, aluminum, copper, glass, stone, and countless other materials from all over the world. Their repertoire of construction techniques ranged through walls, arches, steel cages, cantilevers, portals, and tubes, with computer programs to aid in the design and robots to help with the work.

The Mound Builders had only primitive construction techniques, yet I was more profoundly moved by my first day at Cahokia than by most of the structures of my own time. The Native Americans who lived in what is now Illinois, my home state, had elevated earthworks to a high level of artistic achievement, and they had done it with the irreducible minimum of construction material: dirt. Using the most basic of the basic—dirt carried in baskets on the backs of human beings—they had developed a sophisticated means of architectural expression.

Native American earthworks created an exterior landscape environment, by marking, setting off, bordering, and ordering their world just as streets, parks, and monuments delineate the modern world. The Amerindian natural world was enhanced by a handmade world, and the two were meant to be seen as part of each other. The given and the created had and still have a reciprocal, dynamic relationship. The mounds are an integral part of a larger whole that includes rivers, hills, forests, and overarching sky. But the two worlds are also kept consciously distinct. The handmade is regular, geometric, bilaterally symmetrical, limited. The natural world is irregular, meandering, boundless. Complementary and mutually affecting, the two environments ultimately are mutually transforming. Each becomes more significant because of the other. Nature and culture have been placed in relation to each other in a way that seems to symbolize the powerful meaning the Amerindians attributed to their cooperative, reverential acts of mound building. Earth of the earth in the hands of earth's creatures, shaped in a ritual shrine to express this reciprocity.

Although in ruins for over five centuries, the Cahokia Mounds have inspired successive waves of the many very different human cultures that have flourished there.

Recent theoretical writings in the history of art have emphasized that meaning is assigned to form by cultural convention. This book will examine the changing meaning and changing values assigned to the Cahokia Mounds group, but it will also analyze the site from a more traditional point of view, centered on the idea that the physical characteristics of form have certain innate evocative powers, independent of any a priori cultural assignment of meaning. In other words, all human beings, of whatever culture, are likely to respond in similar ways to certain formal qualities. Siting on a great height, for example, and using structures of enormous scale both tend to inspire awe, a desirable factor in architecture intended for a religious ceremony or as a setting for sacred rituals. The modern and traditional approaches, I believe, are not mutually exclusive; each one highlights a different aspect of the subject and increases our understanding. I am a traditionalist, a modernist, and a postmodernist at various points in this book. If we think of these approaches as three spotlights shining on the same stage, there will be places, for example, where only the postmodernist light reaches. There there will also be places where the three circles overlap, each lighting a different area but focusing on a shared section of inquiry.

In looking at the Mississippian site I found many of the traditional tools of the architectural historian helpful. Formal considerations such as the variety in the shapes of the masses, the disposition of public spaces, and settlement patterns were useful analytic concepts. Mississippian designers employed many of the standard devices of symmetry and balanced asymmetry, unity and variety in massing, alignment, and order. They used forced perspective to dramatize their vistas, ordering the parts of their city to focus on a climactic pyramid, with other masses duly subordinated in scale. By contrasting their negative plaza spaces with their positive earthen mound shapes, they charged both with expressive power. All these factors together demonstrate community planning and social organization on a highly artistic and civilized plane.

To understand the relation of these elements to each other and to changing expressive purposes over time required the help of many other experts outside my own field. For example, the Native Americans arranged their mounds with careful regard to creating a special sense of place, and this was nothing less than the place of human beings in the cosmos. To understand that, I had to traverse many disciplinary boundaries and cross many time barriers.

To find at least partial answers to my questions, I decided on a multilayered approach, a "before, during, and after" study of Cahokia. To probe deeply into the character of the land, I pushed this "deep time" study back as far as possible, to the origins of its very matter—the Big Bang. To begin, I needed the insights of the astronomers. Following them were the geologists and geographers who helped me understand the rich setting that let a civilization flourish with Stone Age technology.

Historians, archaeologists, and anthropologists have been studying the site for nearly two centuries, and their reports formed my sources for the Native American period. The site has received little attention from architectural historians and has been neglected by historians in general.[4]

For the modern chapters I used standard materials—maps, images, charts, hundreds of thousands of lines of books, newspaper accounts, manuscripts, archives, photographs, and drawings. To bring the story up to the present I interviewed staff members, volunteers, Native Americans on their annual pilgrimage to Cahokia, and other visitors to the site.

Each one of these people looked at Cahokia from a different perspective or examined its past with different tools and gave a different account. My aim was to use the historical approach to bring together the many threads of this interdisciplinary fabric. By holding the land area constant, I hoped to eliminate many variables and concentrate solely on how time has affected this space. After the arrival of human beings, I needed to focus on how people had changed the land and how the land had in turn influenced people. This dynamic reciprocity—the conferring of different values on the same piece of land while the land, in turn, continued to inspire different values, is the main theme of this book.

The captions accompanying the illustrations are designed to give readers an overview, a superficial telling of the whole story, or a précis of the book. The prologue deals with the time from the Big Bang to the Precambrian Era. Chapter 1 is a physical history of the land, its geology and geography before human occupation. Chapters 2 to 7 recount the human occupation and its consequences: a hunters' camp by the side of a creek eventually grows into a teeming metropolis, diminishes to a tiny French missionary settlement, then expands to plowed fields dotted by farm buildings, later becoming an Illinois state park, then an Illinois State Historic Site, and finally a UNESCO World Heritage Site. The epilogue is my own reflection on the changing values of the site and its shifting symbolic and personal meanings.

Readers should be aware that prehistory is of necessity approached differently from history. As often as possible I have relied on the hard evidence of the physical sciences or of archaeology, but the informed speculations of observers with years of field experience about what life was like long ago add a valuable dimension to the story. Sometimes I have included their speculations, but to alert readers to the shift in my evidentiary basis, the book's design sets these speculations apart as boxed features.

Whenever an author crosses disciplinary boundaries, vexing problems of vocabulary arise. Archaeologists, for example, see Cahokia as a chiefdom. I agree, but in most instances chiefdoms are not associated with cities, so some archaeologists refuse to call the Cahokia of 1050 a city. Here, as an architectural historian, I part company with them. Given that Catal Huruk and Jericho are often referred to as cities, or as urban centers, and that Cahokia is certainly in their league, I think the use of the word city is completely justified in the wider context of world history.

Another unavoidable difficulty is the word Cahokia itself. It has four meanings. First, it refers to the central place of this study, the Cahokia Mounds State Historic Site just across the Mississippi River from St. Louis, Missouri. Second, it is also the name of a French colonial settlement, a small town still in existence about twelve miles southwest of the site. Third, the term Cahokians (or Cahokia) is used for the Native Americans who inhabited the region for a few hundred years before and after the beginning of the second millennium. These Cahokians were a branch of a larger tradition of people called the Mississippians. Fourth, the term Cahokia also refers to a later group of Native Americans, the Cahokia tribe, one of the subtribes of the Illini or Illiniwek, who lived in the area during the historical period and belonged to the Algonquian language family. Usually the appropriate meaning is clear from the context.

FIG. 5  DAWN AT THE
EQUINOX — AN AURA OF
GOLD

# Cahokia in Its Natural Setting

A Special Place within a Special Place

Against immense odds, the central Mississippi Valley emerged eons after the Big Bang with a kind of cosmic equitableness. Because our planet turns, all the earth's terrestrial creatures respond to the rhythm of days and nights. But the planet's tilt adds another rhythmic beat for those living in temperate zones: four roughly equal seasons. Within this valley, southwestern Illinois itself is halfway up the northern half of the Western Hemisphere of the globe. It is also halfway between the forests of the East and the treeless expanses of the West, nestled between the Appalachians and the Rocky Mountains. The rivers and streams of Illinois spread out in a broad fan across the state, through forests and prairies that alternate in broad ribbons, and the largest waterways converge around Cahokia, near Collinsville, Illinois, and across the Mississippi River from St. Louis,

Missouri. Here one is never far from the bountiful benefits of water and land that interlace so closely.

In the broader context of the central Mississippi Valley, the agriculturally rich soil borders on the mineral-rich hills of the Ozarks. Four ecologies—forest, prairie, valley, and hilltop—meet, intertwine, and thrive together here in the Midwest. Fingers of forested waterways penetrate the broad expanses of prairie in a dense mosaic of green, blue, and tan. The Mound Builders' territory was also within the borders of the wider region known as the Eastern Woodlands, extending eastward from the Great Plains to the Atlantic coast. Cahokia was at the center of this unique environment. Ecologically, it occupied a special place within a special place.

## An Ecological Setting Unlike Any Other

Rivers and their tributaries were essential to the growth of early civilizations—the Nile, the Tigris-Euphrates, the Indus, and the Yellow River. Like the Mississippi, these rivers are in the temperate zone, between 30° and 40° north latitude. But there is one significant difference: a relatively steady and moderate amount of rain reliably falls over the Eastern Woodlands, whose tributaries flow into the Mississippi, whereas the other rivers flow for most of their courses through arid lands, deserts, or grasslands.[1] In the whole Western Hemisphere the Mississippi is the only major river that flows through a temperate zone. The great civilizations in Mesoamerica and the Andes had their origins in tropical or subtropical climates and were not identified with major river basins.

The rainfall in the eastern part of North America accounts for yet another extraordinary feature of the region. The Mississippi has a truly unique network of tributaries (fig. 6). Its total drainage area is nearly 1,250,000 square miles, an area the size of India. The countless rivulets and streams that gather to form the rivers of the mighty river are fed by the ample rains.

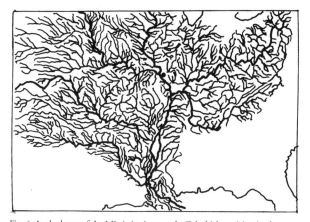

Fig. 6. At the heart of the Mississippi network. Cahokia's position in the center of a great riverine system made it a natural nexus for trade and transportation.

Over the course of time, half of Illinois's days are cloudy, half are sunny—just the right balance for vigorous crops. True, there are droughts, floods, blizzards, tornadoes, and freezing winters, for that is the excitement of the state's changeable weather. But on average our years have just the right amount of rain and sunshine, for that is the dependability of Illinois's climate. And you can also depend on the difficulties: there have always been and will always be the hardships of severe weather. Only people who can look forward, plan, and organize themselves for communal effort are able to survive in such a place.

From the days when the Native American farmers needed to store corn for months and distribute it to a thriving metropolitan population to today when highway plows move tons of snow and scatter salt over vast areas in an hour or two, midwesterners have needed to be socially fit and socially well organized.

Psychologically, the Midwest's vigorous people seem to believe there will be some sunny times, some sad times, and that it is fitting to cope gracefully with both. Over time most people who have lived in this land would agree that this spot on earth is bountiful—on average, that is—and that that balance is sufficient, for it generates hope and the belief that optimism is justified. Bad times will not endure forever: good times will follow as spring follows winter, as sunshine follows the rain. A great civilization can flourish in such an atmosphere. The stage was set long ago.

## Geology Is Destiny

Illinois has been geologically lucky. Eons of titanic geological action gave it fertile soil, gently undulating, arable terrain, and good drainage. Shaping this extraordinary landscape, one of the most productive areas of farmland in the world, took more than a billion years.[2]

About 1.5 billion years ago, in the Precambrian Era, Illinois was blanketed by countless majestic volcanoes, each terrifying in scale, symmetry, and fuming potential for violence. Cataclysmic eruptions continually seared the land with flowing rivers of red-hot lava. In those days the earth was divided into two distinctive parts—land and sea. The land was a red-and-black wasteland, barren and forbidding: "Only the ferocious blasts and powerful shock waves from the erupting volcanoes shattered the unearthly stillness . . . .Nothing lived on the lands. No plants nor animals, not even insects."[3]

Although this Precambrian land was devoid of life, rich minerals, important to the life that was to come later, were deposited on the gradually cooling plains. At the same time, life was beginning far away in the waters of the ocean deep. Slowly, single-celled animals, simple jellyfish, algae, and wormlike forms evolved, diversified, and became more complex. Gradually the waters overflowed and expanded.

UNDER THE WATERS OF THE DEEP

As the seas invaded, the once majestic volcanoes of Illinois, already reduced by wind erosion to merely rugged hills, eventually became surrounded by water. About 525 million years ago the deepening sea again encroached on these islands, and soon they disappeared, completely submerged. Sand settled in ever-thickening layers, covering what was left of the old volcanoes. Deep beneath our feet, however, their cones and the cooled lava remain buried in the bedrock of Illinois.

The waters of this broad sea receded and returned again and again and again. For eons, hundreds of millions of years, the waters came and went, inundating the land and departing only to come again. Each time they brought with them countless fish and other marine life. When these living organisms died and sank to the bottom, their bones and shells eventually formed the successive layers of limestone that underlie Illinois. Better than diamonds or gold or silver, these deposits provide many of the minerals we need to sustain life, as well as the stones for our contemporary buildings. But this comes later in our story.

In time the waters receded, becoming shallow and murky. During this geologic period, before the northern continent had separated from the Eurasian mass and the Atlantic Ocean had opened, the land that is now Illinois was near the equator. The relentless heat of the sun on the tropical vegetation turned the land into a vast swamp, like the Everglades today.[4] When the lush growth of this jungle (fig. 7) died, it fell on waterlogged soil and was rapidly covered by falling fronds that prevented complete decay. This accumulation gradually turned to peat and eventually to coal—another rich stratum, along with oil and gas, created by the bending and folding of the underlying bedrock. Future settlers mined this black gold of the Illinois basin.

Throughout these long geological periods, the rain and the wind continued to erode the multilayered crust of Illinois's surface, carving deep ravines and valleys, leaving magnificent hills, ridges, and bluffs above. Remnants of this dramatic preglacial landscape still rise in a small pocket of the driftless area in northwestern Illinois and in the Shawnee Hills of southern Illinois. But the rest of the state succumbed to an invasion of thousands of years of scraping by yet another powerful geological force: ice.

THE ICE AGE: THREE MILLION YEARS AGO

No one knows for certain when the snow began to fall in the north, but when it did it fell year after year after

Fig. 7. Luxuriant plant growth. Before our continent separated from the Eurasian landmass, Cahokia was near the equator. The lush growth of the tropics eventually turned into the rich coal deposits now lying deep beneath the surface in Illinois.

year, until it was so deep from the winter storms that the sunshine of summer could not begin to melt it all. Gradually the buildup—in places over a mile thick—and the stupendous weight formed glaciers that grew ever larger and expanded southward.

Over the millennia, four of these ice sheets formed in the arctic regions and spread down over the Northern Hemisphere. The third ice sheet (about 150,000 years ago) came so far south that geologists named it the Illinoian (fig. 8). It covered nearly the whole state, reaching as far south as 37°30′ north latitude, and stopped only at the northern reaches of the Ozark Mountains. This glacier left two legacies—a gentle to-

pography and generous finely ground, mineral-rich deposits.[5] As the heavy ice advanced, its sharp edges planed down the hills. Later the dirt of its meltwaters filled in the ravines and valleys of the old landscape, like a planetary plasterer mending cracks. The land emerged as nearly flat, arable terrain—a glacial till plain in geological terms—easy to plant and plow in farmers' language. The Illinois till plain is so flat that the relief changes height on average by only two and a half feet per mile.[6]

Although the flatness of central Illinois is notorious, the state is not the dull tabletop it appears from an airplane window. On foot, in a canoe, on horseback, be-

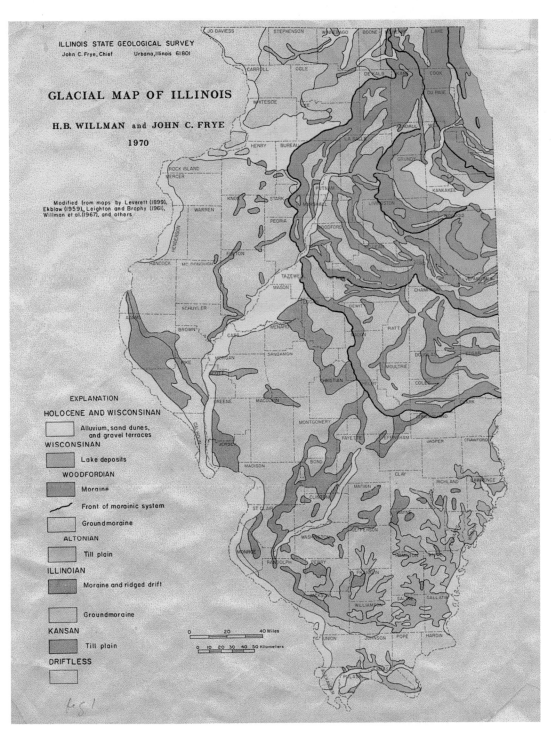

Fig. 8. Gifts of the glaciers. With a gentle landscape, rich in nutrients and easy to farm, after the Ice Age Illinois emerged as one of the richest agricultural areas on earth.

hind a plow, or in a car, the subtle variations in the glacial terrain become apparent. Small ridges and depressions weave a fabric of soft ups and downs, gently rising and falling.

## A NATURAL DRAINAGE SYSTEM

The landscape undulates. Geographers call it a "ridge and swale" topography, a descriptive term ironically recalling the ebb and flow of the waters of the inland sea that was the Mesozoic ancestor of this midcontinental landscape. Even today, coming upon the Springfield Plain from the east, it seems the fields stretch from horizon to horizon, the crops also echoing the ancient waving seas.

The slight overall tilt of the plain toward the southwest is ideal for the slow movement of water through oceans of grasses and down to the waterways, as gravity pulls every drop toward its destiny—the Mississippi and the Gulf of Mexico—where the land particles it carries are once again absorbed in ancestral seas. What is left behind is usually just the right amount of water for plant roots.

When prairie lands are too flat and water accumulates, as in wet prairies, drainage can be encouraged by artificial means such as tiles and pipes. Cultivating the Illinois landscape on the vast scale of modern times, which includes the dry prairies, also had to await the invention of the steel plow to cut through the deep, tough roots of prairie grasses (fig. 9) and of barbed wire to keep maurauding animals away from the tender shoots of young plants.

In their time the Cahokians depended on the wider prairies as a browsing grassland for the animals they hunted. For farming they depended on the immediately surrounding alluvial, silt-textured soil of the American Bottom and on the loess of the bordering bluffs and uplands. As long as there was no flooding after mid-May, which would drown the corn, and enough rain thereafter, their crops would be bountiful. According to William I. Woods, "Cahokia is in an area that has proportionally more of this kind of soil than any other area of a five-kilometer radius in the American Bottom, maybe even in the Midwest."[7]

In addition to relative flatness and good drainage for most of the surrounding dry prairies, another geological gift was a rich blanket of loess over the land. Loess is a fertile, mineral-rich windblown dust of clay and silts that covers upland surfaces. In a railroad cut in Illinois the depth of the loess layer dwarfed the geologists who came to examine it (fig. 10). At the time of Cahokia, loess covered nearly 90 percent of Illinois. Today its depth varies from over twenty-five feet at the bluffs overlooking the Mississippi to one or two feet in areas farther away. This glacially carried, windblown loess supported the variety of plants and grasses that nourished the bountiful life of the prairies, including the thatch and trees the Indians brought back for their fuel, houses, and palisades.[8] The same loess continues to be a source of agricultural wealth for Illinois today. The deep roots of prairie plants and trees make vertical cleavages, drawing water and minerals from below. Loess is thus

*highly desirable as productive agricultural soil. It is friable and permeable to water with good moisture-holding capacity; has a moderate density, medium texture, and a balanced mineral content; and contains no rocks that might interfere with extensive and large-scale mechanized cultivation. Indeed, without it and the presence of nearly level depositional till plains, as well as a favorable climate, it is doubtful that Illinois, heart of the Corn Belt of the United States, would have become one of the richest food-producing regions of the world.[9]*

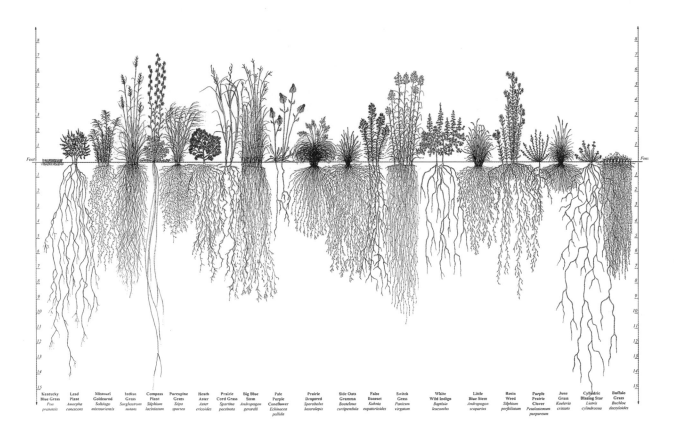

| Kentucky Blue Grass | Lead Plant | Missouri Goldenrod | Indian Grass | Compass Plant | Porcupine Grass | Heath Aster | Prairie Cord Grass | Big Blue Stem | Pale Purple Coneflower | Prairie Dropseed | Side Oats Gramma | False Boneset | Switch Grass | White Wild Indigo | Little Blue Stem | Rosin Weed | Purple Prairie Clover | June Grass | Cylindric Blazing Star | Buffalo Grass |
|---|---|---|---|---|---|---|---|---|---|---|---|---|---|---|---|---|---|---|---|---|
| *Poa pratensis* | *Amorpha canescens* | *Solidago missouriensis* | *Sorghastrum nutans* | *Silphium laciniatum* | *Stipa spartea* | *Aster ericoides* | *Spartina pectinata* | *Andropogon gerardii* | *Echinacea pallida* | *Sporobolus heterolepis* | *Bouteloua curtipendula* | *Kuhnia eupatorioides* | *Panicum virgatum* | *Baptisia leucantha* | *Andropogon scoparius* | *Silphium perfoliatum* | *Petalostemum purpureum* | *Koeleria cristata* | *Liatris cylindracea* | *Buchloe dactyloides* |

Fig. 9. (top) Deep roots survive fire and flood. The grasslands of the Midwest proved invulnerable to nature's most devastating disasters.

Fig. 10. (right) Rich deposits of windblown soil top the gifts of the glaciers. The great depth of loess dwarfs visiting geologists at work. The graphic additions indicate various levels of deposits: G = older Illinois Till; S = Sangamon Soil; Mr = silt; Wd = Wisconsinan Till; R = youngest loess.

The map (fig. 11) shows that a loess cliff at least twenty-five feet high borders the Cahokia Mounds region. The Indian farmers a thousand years ago planted their crops both on the floodplain of the Mississippi and around the smaller floodplains of the upland streams. This divided-risk strategy meant that if drought affected the uplands they could rely on the floodplain crops, or if severe flood affected the floodplain they could rely on

Fig. 11. A great depth of loess borders Cahokia's uplands. This loess map of Illinois shows the twenty-five feet of loess at the Collinsville Ridge. Graphic addition indicating Cahokia location by the author.

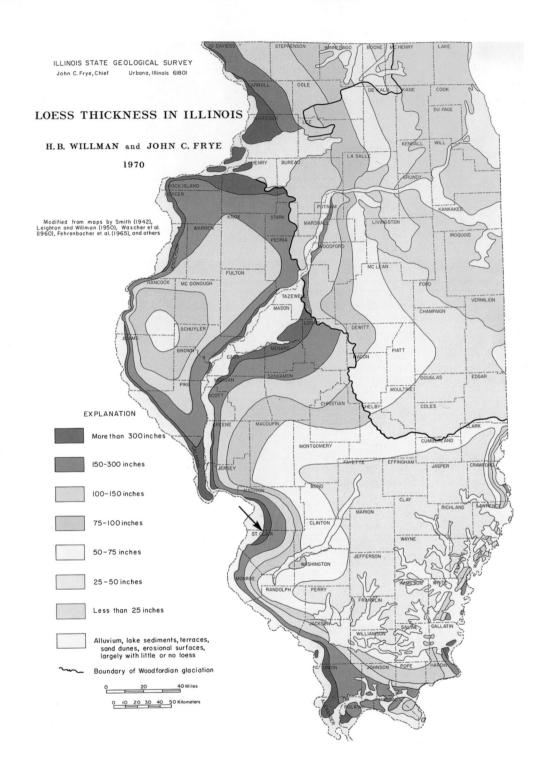

ILLINOIS STATE GEOLOGICAL SURVEY
John C. Frye, Chief    Urbana, Illinois 61801

# LOESS THICKNESS IN ILLINOIS

## H. B. WILLMAN and JOHN C. FRYE
### 1970

Modified from maps by Smith (1942), Leighton and Willman (1950), Wascher et al. (1960), Fehrenbacher et al. (1965), and others

EXPLANATION

More than 300 inches

150-300 inches

100-150 inches

75-100 inches

50-75 inches

25-50 inches

Less than 25 inches

Alluvium, lake sediments, terraces, sand dunes, erosional surfaces, largely with little or no loess

Boundary of Woodfordian glaciation

0    20    40 Miles

0  10  20  30  40  50 Kilometers

the uplands. The loess also nurtured the trees of the forest on the bluff edge and along the waterways, as well as the grasslands beyond, which in turn fed the animals that prospered in such abundance.

THE GREAT MELT

What was needed above all else for comfortable human habitation was warmer weather. When the thaw finally started it lasted for thousands of years, and it is still continuing in the polar regions. With the change in the weather the ice melted, and gravity guided the cold meltwaters into the low-lying channels that became Illinois's rivulets, creeks, streams, and rivers, creating the water system the state enjoys to this day. Along the banks of these waterways, where loess and water mingled, hardwood trees flourished. On the plains in between, the grasses gradually gained dominion, becoming amber seas of prairie capped by waving wildflowers. Since forests followed the stream edges that penetrated the prairie, the three strands became interwoven—water, trees, and grasses.

MINERAL ENDOWMENT

It is the mineral endowment left by the seas, whether washed down or windblown, that has always nourished the roots of Illinois's prairies, its corn and wheat and the soybeans of today. Grasses drink the rich mineral mix from the soil and convert it to golden kernels of grain, a legacy better than gold, for grain can be eaten by deer or cattle and converted into edible meat or pounded into digestible flour. Today's corn products even include fuel for automobiles.

We know from the archaeological evidence that one of the most important crops of the Cahokia Indian population was corn. Then and now, Illinois soil and climate favor the growth of this vital crop.

"Ten different chemicals are required for plant growth: carbon, hydrogen, oxygen, sulphur, iron, magnesium, calcium, nitrogen; phosphorus, and potassium. If any one of these elements is not available, the plant fails to develop. With all present in proper proportions, and under favorable climatic conditions, a large crop is assured . . . . Carbon, hydrogen, and oxygen come from air and water in unlimited amounts except in times of drought. These three elements constitute about 95% of the weight of the mature crop. The seven remaining elements, constituting but 5% of the crop, are obtained from the soil . . . . [But] if the supply of one of these elements is too limited, it must, as a consequence, limit the yield of the crop, even though all other factors essential to crop production are well provided . . . .

"Corn thrives best in well-drained, deep, warm, black loam with an abundance of organic matter. The most favorable climatic conditions for corn are an average summer temperature of about 75 degrees, with warm nights as well as warm days, and an average rainfall during the same period of 8 inches or more, well distributed through the three months. Illinois with its average summer temperatures of 70 to 77 and its average summer rainfall of about 11 inches for all parts of the state thus provides the ideal climatic conditions for this crop."

Douglas Clay Ridgley, *Geography of Illinois*, 152, 167–68

These complex interactions of geological forces set the stage for the thriving Illinois prairies, which in their turn provided a seemingly endless source of food for human beings and animals—a nearly ideal environment. The creeks and streams and rivers that interlaced the prairies provided abundant trees and water. Together food, water, and trees created a paradise for people—or so it has seemed to a succession of Indian, French, and American settlers.

Looking back, we could say that the success of the Cahokia Indian population in agriculture was a demonstration of the wealth of this land, a microcosm of what was to be possible a millennium later on a grand scale: the farmlands of the Midwest.

The Mississippians built their civilization in roughly the same geological conditions we find today. But this rich inheritance is also subject to changes, geological and man-made, for better or for worse. Geologic forces continue their unpredictable and inexorable movements. Erosion, dams, and pollution alter the nature of the soil.

Illinois's legacy of fertile soil, easily plowed, with a drainage system eminently suitable for agriculture, begins in the current Holocene Epoch, a mere 11,000 years of geological time. This period constitutes only .01 million years out of the 600 million years since the Precambrian Era. On a geological clock reducing this time span to one hour, the days of fire and flood and fearsome glaciers lasted over fifty-nine minutes of that hour. Our halcyon Holocene has lasted only a few seconds—less than a minute of favorable time.

### DYNAMIC GEOLOGY

All this could change in a literal few hours, for Illinois is also vulnerable to the sudden and violent action of earthquakes. Among other catastrophic changes, during an earthquake the fertile soil can suddenly absorb liquid from below, become fluid, and flow like a river. Forests can crash to the ground, geysers of sand, coal grit, and water spout from the earth, lakes become dry, and rivers run backward.

The very earthquake Schuberth describes in the accompanying box caused the mounds at Cahokia to tremble, terrifying the French Trappist monks who lived there, as we shall see in chapter 4.

A glance at an earthquake map of Illinois shows the centers of historical earthquakes with intensities of zone V or greater on the Modified Mercalli Intensity Scale (fig. 12). Southwestern Illinois is heavily dotted with epicenter marks. Three of these earthquakes occurred as recently as 1974, just a few miles southeast of Cahokia off the Cap au Gres Faulted Flexure. Tremors are periodically recorded in the St. Louis area. If there were an earthquake today similar in intensity to the New Madrid quakes of 1811–12, the lives of at least 12 million people could be endangered, from Little Rock, Arkansas, to Peoria, Illinois. Cities as distant as Chicago and Dallas could be affected, and property damage could run to more than $50 billion.

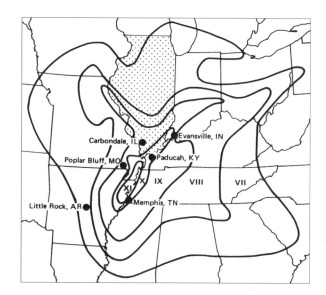

Fig. 12. Subject to imminent destruction. Illinois lies over fault zones subject to tremors greater than the San Francisco earthquake of 1906, as indicated by epicenters registering zone V or more on the Modified Mercalli Intensity Scale.

As geologist Christopher J. Schubert writes: "As I ponder the many ways our lands have been shaped and reshaped by the relentless forces of nature over the past 1.5 billion years, I am reminded of a catastrophic and cataclysmic event that struck the region only 175 years ago. That event radically changed the face of the land within a relatively small area. Had it occurred today, or should it happen again tomorrow, or within the next years, the tragic consequences could not begin to be measured.

"In the winter of 1811–12 three powerful earthquakes rocked the . . . region where Illinois, Missouri, Arkansas, Kentucky, and Tennessee are close together . . . . Large tracts of forests crashed to the ground and giant fissures opened up, some so broad that no horse could jump them. . . . At New Madrid, terrified residents leaped from their beds . . . and saw their cabins splintering around them. Eerie flashes of light like distant lightning streaked the sky, and the air was heavy with sulfurous fumes. Geysers of white quartz sand and black coal grit spouted from the ground, dotting the landscape of the bottomlands for miles. Hundreds of miles from New Madrid, Missouri [the epicenter], the early morning shocks were so powerful that windows rattled and chandeliers shook in Washington, D.C.; pendulum clocks were stopped in Charleston, South Carolina, church bells were set tolling in Richmond, Virginia; and residents in Pittsburgh, Pennsylvania, were awakened. Nearer, in Kentucky, naturalist John James Audubon remarked that 'the ground rose and fell in successive furrows like the ruffled waters of a lake. The earth waved like a field of corn before a breeze.'

" . . . The landscape changed beyond recognition. Fields and riverbanks were crisscrossed by a maze of furrows and deep fractures, and thousands of acres of prairie were converted into swamp. On the Mississippi, a lake bed was raised to become dryland, several lakes were created where none had been before. Reelfoot Lake in Tennessee was enlarged and deepened and Lake St. Francis, 40 miles long and one-half mile wide, was formed on the Arkansas-Missouri border. Islands disappeared, and in places the Mississippi's banks collapsed, temporarily damming the river. A vertical fault displacement of its bed caused the river to run backward for a time. New Madrid was leveled and the land under it slumped 15 feet . . . . The three New Madrid earthquakes were the most severe to have jolted the continental United States, far surpassing the famous San Francisco earthquake of 1906."

Christopher J. Schuberth, *A View of the Past*, 159–63

As Schuberth concludes: "On the Richter Scale, the New Madrid earthquakes would have registered magnitudes of 8.6, 8.4 and 8.7 respectively. No earthquakes larger then 8.9 have ever been recorded, a limitation not of the measuring scale but of the Earth itself . . . . For comparison, the first atomic bomb tested in the New Mexico desert in July 1945 released energy equivalent to a magnitude of 5."[10]

Schuberth is not alone in signaling possible danger for Illinois. In 1984 the Federal Emergency Management Agency granted $300,000 to the Central United States Earthquake Consortium to compile an emergency plan for the five corners area where Illinois, Missouri, Arkansas, Kentucky, and Tennessee are close together, plus Indiana, a zone called the Reelfoot Rift.

Cahokia lies not far from the Reelfoot Rift, in zone IX on the Modified Mercalli Intensity Scale, which shows the possible effects of an earthquake as severe as those of the 1811–12 events in the neighboring area of New Madrid.

*Man clings to the skin of a planet involved in the elemental forces of creation—ever-changing, never at rest. Earthquakes are an integral part of this change, no different than the processes of erosion, of volcanism, of the deposition of sediment in a lake, stream or ocean. There is nothing mystical or exceptional about them . . . .*

*For today and the future, people must learn to live with the inescapable certainty expressed best by historian Will Durant that "civilization exists by geological consent, subject to change without notice." . . . Such are the birth pangs of down-to-earth geology; Illinois is not exempt.[11]*

Gazing at the placid fields that cross Illinois today, it is hard to imagine that long ago the state was a molten mass of lava spewing from fierce, constantly erupting volcanoes. Not until they were extinguished and leveled at last by vast, utterly inundating seas did the volcanoes disappear. The seas that covered the whole Midwest came for millennia, again and again, before they finally withdrew. As the marine life that lived in these waters died, their bones and shells left us a rocky landscape, rich in minerals to nourish plant life and the building blocks of our future. After the titanic glaciers of the Ice Age ground the boulders down to loess and leveled the fields, and the winds deposited the loess over the earth, it seemed these titanic forces had left Illinois with all but two of the elements it takes to make a hearty environment: plenty of sunshine and the right amount of water. In this respect too Illinois has been geographically lucky.

## Geography Is Fortune: The American Bottom

Cahokia is in the center of an area so special that Euroamerican colonists gave it its own name: the American Bottom. The term bottom has a specific geographical meaning: "the ground or bed under the water of a lake or river; low-lying land, like a valley, or an alluvial hollow; the lowest point in a locality."[12] "American" was added to distinguish the area from the land on the other side of the Mississippi River just below the junction with the Missouri, which was called the Columbia Bottom, referring to its ownership by Spain.

Cahokia fits all the historical, geographical, political, and literal definitions. The low-lying land remains part of the Mississippi Valley, rich in the deposits of an alluvial hollow. But Cahokia also fits the broader or figurative definition of the term bottom, "that on which anything is built or rests." The land here was the foundation of the first agricultural civilization north of Mexico: it determined its fundamental character, created its quintessential reality. Some aspects of this character were immutable, remaining unchanged through centuries; some shifted with the winds of change like sand dunes evolving into juniper beachheads or pine forests.

From the window of an airplane one sees that this vast basin catches a fan of tributary waters that flow into the Mississippi between Alton, Illinois, on the north and Chester, Illinois, on the south, an eighty-mile stretch. From the Mississippi to the Collinsville Bluff just two miles east of Cahokia, this alluvial floodplain is nearly eleven miles wide.

The Mississippi curves broadly to the east here until it reaches Dupo, Illinois, where it curves back broadly to the west. On both sides of this backward S curve lies a blue watery world of rivulets, creeks, lakes, and puddles, intermittent sandbars, and small groves of trees. Farther from the shores the neat green-and-gold cultivated fields of Illinois farmers are scattered among the gray grids of typical midwestern cities.

## THE LAND OF FIVE RIVERS

A satellite map of Illinois (fig. 13) shows us the interweaving of rivers, fields, and cities that characterizes the site today.[13] The ruby-red ribbons in the map indicate the trees that line the Collinsville bluffs and the embankments of the dark sapphire lines of the creeks, lakes, ponds, rivers, and waterfalls. For Cahokia and its satellite Mississippian communities to the north, south, and west as well as for the current population in the American Bottom, five major rivers come together between Grafton and Chester: the Mississippi, the Illinois, the Missouri, the Kaskaskia, and the Meramec. Biologically, water means life, and both water and life are plentiful in this part of Illinois and Missouri.

Five rivers also means five floodplains, where the rich, mineral-laden silt of the surrounding hills and bluffs is carried by melting snow and rain down to the valleys and deposited wherever the waters flood and drain away.

Five rivers also mean five flyways, those long blue "maps" of the waterways that migrating birds use to navigate on their annual flights north and south. Guided by these navigational ribbons, they come to rest for the night in the seed-laden reeds and cattails that line the banks of streams, lakes, and rivers. For centuries every spring and fall waterfowl hunters here have turned homeward with bountiful catches.

Five rivers also mean five waterways for canoes, rafts, dugouts, steamships, and barges providing the links between prairie, forest, and floodplain, between

town and country—opportunities for adventure and the enriching exchange of goods and ideas.

When the Amerindian people we now call the Mississippians changed their way of life, gradually combining the ways of the hunter-gatherer with the more settled ways of farming, they picked a special place in the American Bottom as their home: an area surrounding the junction of Canteen Creek and Cahokia Creek. The choice was geographically brilliant. There was only one major risk.

The soil was both rich and easy to till, producing bountiful crops with minimal labor. Floodplains are ideal for this balance, with one obvious disadvantage: floods. The Mississippians hedged their bet on the floods with a kind of natural insurance policy: the *width* of the floodplain here. Settling far out, near the higher, more stable edge of the floodplain, they must have reasoned that a catastrophic flood of the mighty river would only rarely reach as far as their city and their crops and that in the years between the benefits far outweighed the risks. Time has proved them right. Although the disastrous flood of 1993 would have reached Cahokia if the levees at East St. Louis had not held, for most of its history the mounds area has been spared the devastation of Mississippi floods. Other benefits included annually plentiful, easily available water—ground conditions that modern people would regard as unacceptably damp and slimy.

Modern Americans try to *control* flooding, but the Native Americans learned to *adapt* to flooding, even to capitalize on it. In a floodplain like the American Bottom catastrophic flooding is relatively rare, but mud, ooze, and soggy conditions are common. The land the Amerindians inhabited was also considerably more watery than the land of today, surrounded as it is now by a network of levees and dams (figs. 14 and 15). Watery conditions permit using canoes to transport people, food, and fuel. Portages can shorten the water route by

Fig. 13. Interweaving of
forests, grasses, water,
and cities. This satellite
photograph shows con-
temporary water (blue),
vegetation (red), and ur-
banized (white) regions
of Illinois. Detail,
Cahokia area.

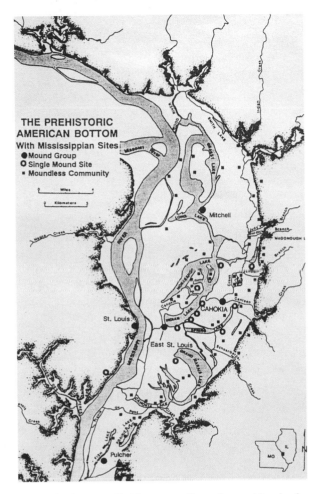

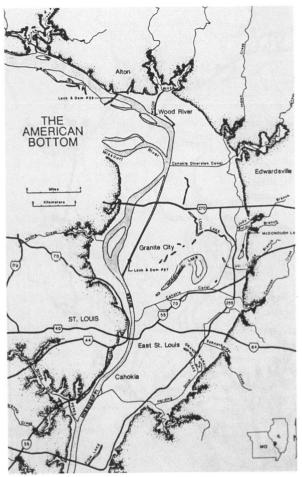

Fig. 14. Inland waterway ideal for canoes and boats. Streams, lakes, sloughs, and marshes show the possibility of easy movement by water in prehistoric times.

Fig. 15. The effects of levees, dikes, ditches, and other human interventions in our time are clearly visible in this map depicting modern Cahokia.

miles. Other advantages include easy backyard gardens and malleable clay for pottery. Mud in its various forms—gumbo clay, sandy loam, and tamped clay— was vital in the construction of the Amerindians' magnificent earth architecture, their great contribution to American cultural history.[14] Placing palatial temples, public buildings, and the homes of the elite on specially crafted mounds had the additional benefit of being a partial adaptation to watery conditions or

flooding. Scholars who say the Native Americans did not practice water management do not understand that the Mississippians did practice adaptive, though not controlling, water management.

Recorded history gives us some idea of what the Amerindians would have faced had they settled nearer the Mississippi River. Beginning in 1724, dramatic stories about floods fill the accounts of the American Bottom. Twenty catastrophic floods were documented by

1930, on average one every ten years. The modern geographer Ronald E. Yarbrough regarded the American Bottom as hostile to man, but largely because its later inhabitants ignored the risks of flooding.[15]

The bluffs to the east, at Collinsville (in places as high as ninety feet), that border and define the floodplain were another major advantage to the Amerindians: they were heavily forested—an inexhaustible (or so they thought) and handy source of timber for houses and other structures and fuel for warmth and for cooking. The delusion that the forest was inexhaustible may have contributed to the demise of the Mississippian civilization. But that is the subject of another chapter.

Yarbrough also tells us that the region around the Cahokia Mounds contains the largest area of lakes and permanent swamps on the American Bottom (fig. 16). This "ridge and swale" terrain[16] is mostly less than ten feet above the level of the Mississippi River, and Monks Mound actually lies on a natural levee of an abandoned channel of the Mississippi River known as the Edelhardt meander. The Grand Plaza to its south was created by leveling ridges and filling swales that were part of the point bar deposits of an earlier Mississippi River meander known as Spring Lake. Originally the whole area was a region of swamps, natural levees, sandbars, sloughs, and sluggish watercourses.

This watery landscape once gave Cahokia the atmosphere of a floating world. In spring the ponds and sloughs sparkled with the reflected light of blue skies and white clouds, and the channels running between the islets were bordered with stately cattails and wildflowers. And perhaps there were other aspects of the Mississippians' choice of a site.

Labyrinthine swamps offer good hiding places for hunters, good transportation links for canoes, and safe havens from attack. Abundant flowing water was also important in city planning, especially for a population without plumbing or a sewage system.

It is hard to imagine the original landscape of the Cahokia world, because today most of this ridge and swale region lies behind the enormous levees along the Mississippi River and the land is no longer so swamplike. "Modern engineers wanted to avert the flooding and internal ponding that were caused by upper

Fig. 16. A floating world atmosphere. The alluvial plain of the American Bottom is bordered by streams, lakes, sandbars, terraces, and ridges surrounding Cahokia.

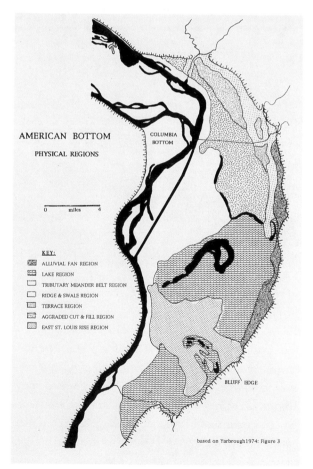

AMERICAN BOTTOM
PHYSICAL REGIONS

COLUMBIA BOTTOM

0    miles    4

KEY:
ALLUVIAL FAN REGION
LAKE REGION
TRIBUTARY MEANDER BELT REGION
RIDGE & SWALE REGION
TERRACE REGION
AGGRADED CUT & FILL REGION
EAST ST. LOUIS RISE REGION

BLUFF EDGE

based on Yarbrough 1974: Figure 3

Cahokia Creek to the north. A drainage system was started in the early 1800's by a channel dug through East St. Louis which cut off the 'Dead Creek Channel' into the Cahokia Slough. In 1915 the Cahokia Diversion Canal was added to carry the waters from the upland due west four miles to the river, bypassing the Cahokia Mounds site."[17] The lower portion that flows through the Cahokia site was also channelized at this time to help control drainage. And many former feeder channels were eventually blocked by railroad embankments, roads, and urban development. Before these man-made changes, Cahokia Creek was a large, copiously flowing stream. Modern flood control has now diminished it to a green, algae-clogged, sluggish channel in some places, a dry ravine in others.

## A TRANSPORTATION NEXUS

Originally the waterway system—creeks, sloughs, ponds, and rivers—also made Cahokia a transportation nexus.

Canteen Creek joined Cahokia Creek northeast of Monks Mound. One branch of Cahokia Creek entered the Mississippi just a few miles west at what is now East St. Louis, and the other branch entered at the village of Cahokia farther south. According to Charles Cooley, "population and wealth tend to collect wherever there is a break in transportation."[18] A "break in transportation" occurs when people have to change their mode of getting around—from canoe to footpath, for example. Metropolises burgeon at these geological junctions, and the area around Cahokia was no exception. As people had to change from canoe to barge, from covered wagon to ferry, from rail to steamboat, or from highway to airplane, the cities grew up. Cahokia established a pattern that has since been renewed in St. Louis and East St. Louis.

## THE CONSEQUENCES OF LATITUDE AND LONGITUDE

In cartographic terms Cahokia lies at 38° north latitude and 90° west longitude. The latitude ensures long days and steep sun's rays in summer with enough heat and light to grow staple food crops.[19] The midwestern plains lie in a wide belt between the Rocky Mountains to the west and the only moderately high Appalachians to the east. Nothing to the south obstructs the passage of wind. This central location ensures the right amount of rain because large moisture-bearing clouds (averaging about five hundred miles in diameter) that form in the low-pressure winds that gather over the Gulf of Mexico have virtually free passage to the plains, bringing abundant rainfall. Thanks to the sculpting and planing of the glaciers, the gentle slope of the land promotes an even distribution of the life-giving water.[20]

## CHANGEABLE WEATHER, UNCHANGING CLIMATE

Weather is changeable. Climate is unchanging in the short term because it deals with *averages* of the variables of weather—temperature, wind direction, storms, drought, or flood—based on observations extending over decades.[21]

For people who can think ahead, plant, plan, distribute food, and have enough communal organization to provide safe, adequate storage for times of drought or flood, it is obviously the climate, not the weather, that makes for long-term survival.[22] Illinois's equitable climate provides a happy combination of enough life-giving rain and enough sunny days to ensure plant growth. The balance is about fifty-fifty balance. Cahokia has 50 percent clear days annually, compared with 30 percent in Boston or northern California.[23] The frost-free growing season at Cahokia's latitude is about 190 days, ideal for corn and other crops.

The main difficulty with Cahokia's weather is the unpredictable summer rainfall. In spite of ample moisture-laden clouds from the Gulf of Mexico, shifts in the westerly wind from strong to weak can decrease rain 25 to 50 percent. On the other hand, too much rain or snow causes flooding in the spring, meaning delays in planting or the washout of an entire crop. Successful farming in the Mississippian period may have depended on dividing the risks by using both the bottomlands and the uplands—planting in both well-watered and well-drained soils to insure against the vagaries of nature.

Farming on this large scale improves the chances of survival by moving from individual to collective risk taking. In a year of flood, for example, farmers who tended the bottomlands would receive a fair share of the upland harvest and vice versa. Collective risk taking entails social control of the redistribution of the crops, an important factor in the establishment of social ranking in Cahokian civilization.[24]

## NATURAL FORESTS, GRASSLANDS, AND A RICH BIODIVERSITY

From the end of the Ice Age until as late as 1926, Illinois also has had a nearly a fifty-fifty balance is the percentage of forests compared with grasslands.[25] This part of the Midwest lies where the forests of the East meet the prairies of the West, a place where both can grow.

The long shaded portions on the vegetation map of Illinois (fig. 17) represent the woodlands, especially heavy in the south and along the waterways, that divide the prairies in the interstream spaces into vast reaches. For human occupation, this is the best of all possible

Fig. 17. Food, clothing, shelter, and fuel near at hand. Obtaining life's necessities is convenient when forests, grasslands, and waterways are close to each other, as this vegetation map of Illinois shows. Forests are in dark gray, prairies in white, rivers in black.

worlds: plenty of wood to house, protect, and warm, and plenty of food to nourish, near plenty of water.

As the waters were plentiful, so the forests lining them for miles on end were dense, prolific in cottonwoods and willows and such upland species as oak, hickory, and walnut. This water, prairie, and forest mixture encouraged biodiversity of fish and animal life. The leaves and twigs of trees, their nuts, berries, and roots, and the rich prairie grasses furnished an ample food supply for animals depending wholly on plants—deer and elk, for example. Beavers, otters, and muskrats were skillful in securing fish and other food from the water, which also offered favorable breeding grounds and nurseries for their young. The flesh-eating animals such as the wolf and bear found food among the smaller mammals, including birds and their eggs.

Archaeologists working in Mississippi Valley sites have found the bones of catfish, gar, sunfish, crappies, bullheads, dogfish, perch, snails, and freshwater mussels. Ducks, geese, swans, cormorants, gulls, loons, grebes, herons, snipes, and plovers were abundant. Land birds included pigeons, vultures, hawks, owls, cuckoos, kingfishers, woodpeckers, goatsuckers, swifts, hummingbirds, flycatchers, larks, crows, blackbirds, sparrows, tanagers, swallows, waxwings, shrikes, vireos, warblers, wrens, creepers, chickadees, kinglets, and thrushes. In addition there were fowl such as turkeys and prairie chickens. In this favorable environment numerous species of mammals also flourished, varying in size from mice to elk and including deer, beavers, otters, muskrats, rabbits, and other species.[26]

## THE IMPORTANCE OF PROXIMITY FOR HUMANS

With the arrival of the first human beings, the proximity of the trees, water, and grasses and their nearness to each other were crucial, for all food and materials had to be transported without benefit of the wheel or beasts of burden. Everything was carried by people—in baskets, on backs, on litters, or in dugout canoes.

## Summary

Ancient physical forces—astronomical, geological, and geographical—set a bountiful stage for human occupation in Cahokia. The American Bottom, in the heart of the Midwest along the central Mississippi Valley with its alluvial soil, near upland forests and prairies, in a land with dependable rain and sunshine, is indeed a special place within a special place. The importance of easy transportation and readily available food, fuel, and clothing is immeasurable if a civilization is to emerge from a people with a Stone Age technology. The relative ease of staying alive and healthy left the Mississippians plenty of time for arts and crafts—pottery, stone and wood carving, mat making, leatherwork, and, most impressively, the art of architecture.

An ecologist might look at Cahokia as the innermost in a series of nesting spheres, each one progressively more favorable for human habitation. To start with astronomy, what an infinite boon it is to be on the planet Earth. From there the nesting spheres get smaller and smaller, from the temperate zone to a southern position in a temperate zone—without parallel for plant and animal growth—to a smaller place where rainfall is abundant, to a niche within which life is enriched by easy-to-cultivate alluvial soil near canoe-navagible streams lined with trees. Cupped in the center of these nesting spheres is the smallest and the richest, the American Bottom, and at its heart was the ancient capital of Cahokia.

Since the dawn of the Pleistocene Epoch the land around Cahokia has been a mixture of forests, prairies, and streams. Later it was dotted by clusters of man-made dwellings, from the shelters of the Paleo-Indians to the thriving Cahokia Mounds metropolis of A.D. 1050 to modern East St. Louis. As time went on this mosaic shifted in places and in the proportions of the various parts. The great variety of places that different people created from the same elements, and the way they changed and shaped the landscape to fulfill different purposes and to express different meanings, is the theme of this book.

FIG. 18. BOUNTIFUL AND DIVERSE HUNTING
AND FISHING. THE EDGES OF THE WATERWAYS
PROVIDED NESTING PLACES FOR BIRDS,
BREEDING GROUNDS FOR FISH, AND ABUNDANT
RESOURCES FOR SKILLFUL HUNTERS.

# Human Beings Enter the Americas

Paleo-Indians, Archaic and Woodland Groups,
and Emergent Mississippians

Before the last stages of the Ice Age no human beings lived in the Western Hemisphere. Even if they could have traveled here from their origins in the Eastern Hemisphere, most of northern North America was uninhabitable, covered by mile-high glaciers. Lichen clinging to the surface of rocks that broke through crevices in the ice was one of the few available plant foods.

Why did the early Amerindians come all the way from northern Asia to this frozen landscape? Clues lie in the routes they followed. Some may have skirted the Pacific Rim in watercraft to hunt sea mammals, collect shellfish, catch fish, hunt inland animals, and gather other resources. Other migrants came overland, hunting caribou and other Pleistocene megafauna such as the mammoth, mastodon, and musk ox. These animals ate lichens and other plant foods, transforming them into huge bones and protein-rich muscles. But the wanderers did not rely solely on the large animals; they used plants and smaller animals as well, and they were protected from the elements in shelters made of skins and bones.[1] As bands of these Paleo-Indians picked their way across the frozen land of northern Asia, some eventually crossed the Bering land bridge (before it was covered by rising sea levels as the continental glaciers of the Ice Age melted), coming all the way from Siberia to Alaska. These prehistoric pioneers arrived possibly as early as 20,000 B.C. but at least by 10,000 B.C., and they were truly the first Americans.[2]

"[The mammoth] stood as high as thirteen feet at the shoulder, weighed between eight and nine tons, and could run perhaps twenty-five or thirty miles an hour. It was fifty per cent heavier than the African elephant, which is today a dangerous animal to hunt even with a high-calibre rifle. Like the elephant, a provoked mammoth probably slashed at and gored its assailant with its tusks; trampled, crushed, and battered him with its head; and, picking up what was left, flailed him about until the pieces flew apart in bloody gobbets.

"The Clovis hunters stalked mammoths with two particularly lethal weapons. The first, a thrusting spear, was for close-in work. The second may have been an atlatl—a spear launched with a throwing stick . . . . Both types of Clovis spears were tipped with a long, tapered projectile point flaked from stone [fig. 19]. The Clovis point was beautifully designed to kill a mammoth. Viciously sharp, and unlikely to break against the hide, it tore a big hole in the tissue and caused heavy blood loss. Everytime the mammoth took a step after being hit, the point would saw and slice the flesh. [It was not until thousands of years later that the bow and arrow was invented.]

"How the Clovis [people] hunted mammoths is disputed. They may have waited until a young animal strayed from its family group, hit it with a few atlatls, and followed it until it died. They also may have killed a full-grown mammoth by getting up beside it and shoving spear after spear through the rib cage into the vital organs. Either way, a mammoth took a lot of killing . . . .

"The Clovis [people] travelled hundreds of miles to find gorgeous, semi-precious stones suitable for their points: translucent agate, chert, smoky-quartz crystal, red jasper, obsidian. These stones were not just beautiful to look at; when knapped (chipped), they formed keen edges and glossy flakescars that were almost silky to the touch. To make pleasing flake patterns on the stones' points, the weapons producers used a technique that the French call *outré passé,* or overshot flaking. To carry out this exceedingly difficult procedure, the edge of the stone was struck in such a way that a long flake, shaped like a scimitar, travelled all the way across the face of the spearpoint. Sometimes the Clovis [worker] knapped the stone on the diagonal, for further decorative effect. When you hold a fine Clovis projectile point—maybe five inches long, leaflike, cool, deadly, balanced, luminous— you know that you are holding something more than a tool. It reaches beyond the utilitarian into the realm of aesthetics— each, like a piece of Shaker furniture, is an object made with skill, love, simplicity, and faith.

"About nine or ten thousand years ago, the Clovis [people] and their Paleo-American descendants disappeared—no one knows how or why—and the high art of stone-knapping disappeared with them. Nothing like it was achieved again for thousands of years. Even today, flint-knappers cannot re-create a Clovis point perfectly. Clovis points are rare, sexy, and extremely valuable."

Douglas Preston, "Woody's Dream," *New Yorker,* November 15, 1999, 80

## Paleo-Indian Life in the Mississippi Valley (9500?–8000 B.C.)

These bands of nomads were an ingenious, hearty, and hardy people. Anatomically they were "modern," *Homo sapiens* just like you and me, with muscles well adapted to walking and running. Sometime around 9500 B.C. the Clovis people, probably the first humans in North America, developed sophisticated tools and weapons for killing large Pleistocene mammals such as mastodons and mammoths, the largest land animals man has ever hunted on this continent, making them possibly the greatest hunters ever to walk here.

The giant beasts killed by hunters armed with Clovis points provided these early Native Americans with everything they needed to survive (fig. 20). Usually they butchered their quarry on the spot, eating some meat, drying the rest, and keeping the hides, tusks, and bones for clothing, shelter, and weapons and the fat for cooking and lamp oil. The dried meat from a single animal would support several people for weeks on end or even through the winter.[3]

These first Americans must also have been socially astute enough to organize themselves into small groups, to plan an ambush, or to start a stampede. As many generations of these nomads slowly worked their way south across Canada, a branch of vigorous survivors reached the Mississippi Valley about 9500 B.C. They were welcomed by the blessings of a gradually warming climate and a greater variety of plant and animal life.

In the uplands surrounding the confluence of the Missouri, Mississippi, and Illinois river valleys, a number of major Paleo-Indian sites have been discovered. Except for the Kimmswick site (Mastodon State Park), most are extensive open-air encampments. They provide

Fig. 19. (opposite) Viciously sharp, keen-edged. These beautiful Clovis points were designed to kill.

Fig. 20. Killing the giant mastodon. It took a team of well-organized, strong, and skillful hunters to kill the giant beasts that roamed the Midwest, but one success could feed and clothe many people for a whole season.

insights into the tool kits people were carrying across the land and the diversity of raw materials available, suggesting that these groups operated over large areas.

When the glaciers receded, the mastodons, woolly mammoths, and other giants of the Ice Age began to die off, and smaller animals such as deer, rabbits, beavers, and fowl of all kinds proliferated. Gradually people added these species and other new meats to their menu, embellished by the nuts and plant foods of the expanding deciduous forests. Since the animals remained in the nearby forests year round and plants were seasonally available, continuous long-distance movement was no longer necessary.

Gradually, by the end of the Paleo-Indian period and the beginning of Early Archaic times, making one successful adaptation after another, these early hunters and gatherers were able to be less nomadic and stay put for brief periods in seasonal camps, pitching tents or building temporary huts or camping under rock shelters.

## Archaic People Led a Comfortable Life (8000–600 B.C.)

During the Archaic period these resourceful people slowly made many adaptations to their changing environment, gradually improving their lives. By shrewd observation of nature and ingenious new technologies, they took advantage of the bountiful and diverse environments along the waterways of the Mississippi River system. The midwestern ecology provided them with life's necessities and many luxuries for the next five thousand years, as it has continued to provide for their successors, in different ways, until the present. Little by little they invented new tools or discovered better methods of catching fish, processing food, and making shelters. Tracing these changes, archaeologists have subdivided the Archaic tradition into Early Archaic, Middle Archaic, and Late Archaic periods.[4]

### EARLY ARCHAIC AMERINDIANS IN ILLINOIS (8000–6000 B.C.)

There is some direct evidence that Archaic Amerindians were near the junction of Cahokia and Canteen Creeks, but the best account of what life would have been like there is the evidence uncovered at a remarkable site nearby: Koster.

Since Koster is only fifty miles north of Cahokia, it shares the same climate and weather conditions, and it is also a riverine and bluff environment. Although the artifacts and features uncovered by Stuart Struever and his colleagues over the years were from a site on the floodplain but at the base of a bluff, whereas Cahokia is farther out on the floodplain, the resources of upland and lowland areas were within walking distance of both. Archaeologists at Koster have uncovered fourteen "horizons" or different settlement periods in this beautiful valley of the Illinois River, dating from 7500 B.C. to A.D. 1200.[5]

The hunters in this Archaic period frequently used a sophisticated weapon made up of two parts (fig. 21). The spear-thrower, or atlatl, consisted of a wooden shaft about eighteen inches long with a hook (often made of antler) at one end and a handgrip at the other. The long spear had a socketed base that engaged the

Fig. 21. A brilliant technological advance. The atlatl, a spear-throwing device, gave the hunter greater distance and thrust.

hook until it was thrown. The hunter gripped the atlatl and the spear together and hurled the spear, letting go of the spear shaft at the top of a wide arc but holding on to the spear-thrower. The atlatl effectively lengthened the hunter's arm, greatly increasing the force with which he could throw the spear.

Atlatls often had stone weights attached to them to counterbalance the forward thrust of the spear.[6] Later, especially in the Middle and Late Archaic periods, many of these weights, or bannerstones, were made of stones selected for their color and potential sheen and were beautifully carved and polished (figs. 22 and 23). Large stone points with stemmed or notched bases tipped the spears.

The first atlatls may have been brought from Asia by a few early migrants, but the atlatl did not become the dominant weapon on this continent until the Archaic period.

The atlatl dramatically improved hunting efficiency. Since it allowed greater distance between the hunter and the beast, it also made hunting safer. When a hunting accident could wipe out the sole provider for an extended family, the atlatl was a major advance over the spear alone.

The use of another stone tool—the adze—in this period is also powerfully suggestive of an adaptation to a forest environment. Adzes (fig. 24) are primary woodworking tools and were probably used to make dugout canoes. Although no canoes have been found near Cahokia, trade goods from faraway places have been uncovered, enough to justify the conclusion that Archaic people were involved in widespread intergroup ex-

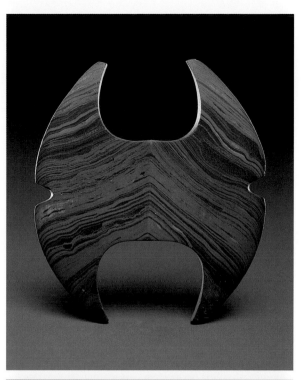

Fig. 22. (top, right) Double lunate bannerstone. This beautifully carved stone of banded slate from the Late Archaic period is a synthesis of form and function.

Fig. 23. (bottom, right) The glow of chalcedony. This Late Archaic work still radiates the spirit of the artist who carved it in the second millennium B.C.

Fig. 24. The adze: a useful woodworking tool. Adzes were probably used to scrape out the insides of previously charred tree trunks to make dugout canoes at Cahokia, promoting travel by water.

change in which people and goods may have traveled by water as well as by land.

To make a dugout canoe, you first char the inside of a large felled tree trunk by applying heaps of hot coals down the center of its length. When it has burned through to the right depth, you douse it with water, then scrape out the charred area with an adze or a mussel shell, repeating the process until the canoe is complete. All the advantages of life on a waterway followed the making of dugout canoes—travel, new foods, new markets, and new ideas.

Domestic techniques also improved gradually. Women arranged stones in the earth to make hearths for roasting meats, for example, and used grinding stones to process acorns and other nuts and seeds.

According to Struever, Early Archaic people in Illinois were able to go "shopping" for their basic needs, "only their list included hickory nuts, cereal-like seeds, white-tailed deer, and lots of fish. Of course, they did-

n't shop. They hunted and fished and gathered their basic foods, and their 'supermarket' consisted of the hillside slopes, forests, upland prairies, floodplains, rivers and lakes among which they lived."[7]

People were able to settle down as early as 6400 B.C. in Koster, much earlier than archaeologists had thought. Before Struever's work most scholars believed it was not until about 2500 B.C. that hamlet-sized communities lived nearly year-round in one place. Struever made a four-thousand-year correction in the record. The change to a more settled way of life was no doubt especially welcome to older people, women, and children.

*To our surprise, the Early Archaic people had learned how to exploit the wild-food resources in their environment so skillfully that they could go out and replenish their basic staples on a seasonal basis year in and year out with almost as much confidence as we drive to the supermarket for ours. As a result, they were able to live in great comfort and stability for thousands of years . . . . This evidence also shatters the stereotype that many Americans have about their prehistoric predecessors, that they were brutish people of limited intelligence who barely managed to scrounge enough food from the wilderness to survive.*[8]

## MIDDLE ARCHAIC SETTLEMENTS (6000–4000 B.C.)

Based on the archaeological findings, we can conclude that life in Middle Archaic Illinois was comfortable and easy. Nearly every fall hunters were able to stalk and bring down as many deer as they needed to feed a village population of over a hundred for months to come. Ducks, swans, geese, mussels, and fish were abundant in nearby lakes, and women were able to gather bas-

ketfuls of acorns, pecans, and walnuts. Fresh fruits were there for the plucking, including luscious persimmons that fell to the ground when perfectly ripe.

Middle Archaic times coincide with a climatic episode known as the Altithermal or Hypsithermal. Pollen diagrams studied by palynologists indicate a significant insurgence of grasses. This dramatic change in the vegetation represents the expansion of the prairies and is associated with a much warmer and drier climate. Settlements like those at the Koster site then clustered more tightly around the major river valleys, where resources were more readily available.

Fig. 25. A life of ease and abundance. The river valleys of Illinois were rich in natural materials. Fish were plentiful, the waving prairie grasses lured grazing wild animals, and nearby trees yielded bountiful fruits and nuts.

"It was a few hours before dawn in the little settlement, . . . and most of the villagers were still asleep, snug in their houses.

"There would have been about 100 to 150 people living in the Helton village then. [Helton is the name given to the people living in Koster in this period.] . . . While it was still dark, men began to emerge from the houses and to gather silently in little knots, preparatory to going off for their day's work . . . .

"Several groups of young men, about six to eight in a group, each from a different clan, set out for the uplands to hunt deer. The men, carrying atlatls and spears, ranged in age from about eighteen to forty, for deer-hunting required that a man be fleet and agile, in his prime.

"Several other small groups of men set out to hunt ducks and geese in the backwater lakes in the river floodplains. There were young boys and older men along as well as young men, since this task did not demand quite the degree of spryness that deer-hunting required.

"As they walked, some of the men chewed on pieces of jerky, dried deer meat. The women had prepared it by cutting the meat into strips and laying it out to dry in the air. Jerky (a version of which is carried by modern backpackers) makes excellent food for hunters or campers. It is light, easy to store, requires no water or cooking, and keeps for a long time. Although it is stiff as a board, it softens as you chew it . . . .

"All was silent for a few hours, and then, as the first hint of dawn appeared over the eastern part of the valley, other people began to stir. Stretching themselves, yawning, they came out of their homes and made their way to the creek right at the edge of the village for an early morning drink or to splash a bit of wake-up water on their faces. Some made their way to the area set aside, just outside the village limits, for their clan's toilet.

"A few women carried baskets, tightly woven of root fibers, to the creek, where they filled them with water and carried them back to their homes . . . .

"There was no formal breakfast time in the village. In fact, there were no set mealtimes as we know them. The Helton people would eat at anytime during the day when they were hungry . . . .

"Today we take it for granted that people eat meals at regular times each day. The concept of regular mealtimes probably did not arise among prehistoric people in Low-ilva [Streuver's acronym for lower Illinois Valley] until after they had been practicing agriculture for a while. In order to set regular mealtimes, the cook must know that food is available at predictable times and in predictable quantities. This is not possible when people are dependent totally on wild game and wild plants. The amounts of wild animals to be taken or crops of seeds, nuts or greens to be collected may fluctuate, depending on the seasonal patterns of various animal species, the weather conditions affecting growing seasons of plants, and the ecological balance of insects, viruses, bacteria and other factors that would affect either the animal or plant populations. Besides, hunters and gatherers may need to perform their tasks at totally different times of the day, according to when the resource is available or best taken.

"The Helton people, like most hunter-gatherers, made a very sensible adaptation to suit the unpredictability of their food supplies and the varying schedules of their work parties. They practiced perpetual pot cookery. The fire was kept going most of the time, and the housewife maintained a continually simmering pot of food. Actually it wasn't until about 500 B.C. that clay pottery was first introduced to the Illinois valley, so the `pot' would have consisted of either a leather pouch or a tightly woven basket, into which hot stones were placed, together with food and maybe some water . . . .

"The sun was now up, and the women went about their housekeeping tasks. Some pounded acorns to make flour [fig. 26], after having washed the nuts through running water several times to leach out the acid. To make the flour, they placed a handful of shelled nuts on a metate and pounded and ground them with a mano . . . . .

"When the men appeared, they were laughing and joking, and one quick glance revealed why. Slung over their shoulders were heavy strings of ducks, and an occasional goose or swan. Arrived home, they slung their catch to the ground near their houses and hastened to the fire to dry their wet clothing and warm up . . . .

"The fall had been a bountiful one for the Helton people. They were almost tired of all the ducks, geese, and delicious persimmons on which they had gorged themselves all season. There was no way for them to preserve any of these foods, so they ate their fill while they lasted. They had put away huge harvests of dried fish, jerked deer meat, nuts, and seeds. Because of the bounty of the harvest, the clan leaders, after conferring with the shaman, had agreed that there should be thanks offered to the spirits of the deer, the river and lakes, and the earth . . . .

"Finally the shaman emerged from his house. The people fell silent and made way for him as he slowly, solemnly made his way to the center of the open square. He was wearing a deer-skull headdress, capped with deer antlers, and a deer hide on his back, to simulate a real deer.

"The shaman stopped before the clan leaders, turned and faced them, and waited a few moments for absolute silence. Then he began to chant, offering prayers of thanks. He thanked, in turn, the spirits of the deer, the spirits of the rivers and lakes, and the spirit of the earth, for having showered their generosity on the Helton people.

"When his prayer was over, the shaman removed his headdress and joined the others. This was the signal for the festivities to begin.

"The feast was sumptuous. Besides the roast deer, ducks, and geese, there were roast squirrel, baked fish, and steamed mussels. The stew that night included fresh

Fig. 26. Grinding seeds and grain into flour between stones or in wooden mortars. Women spent long hours over these stones or mortars, since the ingredients of their daily bread had to be pounded by hand to make them edible.

meat, fish, meat from hazelnuts, redbud pods, and duck potatoes.

"There was a porridge made with two kinds of flour, one from acorns, the other from cattail shoots. There were also persimmons, pawpaws, hickory-nut broth, pecans, and walnut meats. And to wash it all down, there was hot tea made from sassafras roots . . . .

"Finally, when everyone had eaten his fill, the shaman stood up and resumed his deer headdress. He picked up a stick, which had been leaning against the wall of his house. A small pillow-shaped stone, called a banner-stone, was hafted at the end of a stick. It was made of orange quartz and beautifully shaped and polished; it symbolized his special role and high rank in the community.

"As he walked slowly to the center of the square, the villagers formed a ragged circle, leaving space in the middle for the dancers. The drummers banged down hard to start the music and simultaneously burst into song . . . .

"Faster and faster went the drums and the voices. The dancers leaped in joy, celebrating their successful hunt. Soon, the women, too, began to dance, but they moved more sedately. Little boys imitated the hunters, jumping up and down; the girls took short  mincing steps, emulating their mothers . . . .

"Near the fire, the old people, wrapped in deerskins to ward off the evening chill, dozed after their full meal."

Stuart Struever and Felicia Antonelli Holton, *Koster,* 260–73

Though the people had no fired clay pottery for cooking and storage and agriculture was in its infancy, some archaeologists believe the very richness of their ecosystem may have made it unnecessary to develop more advanced technologies. They simply did not need them, since they could readily harvest all they required from the wildlife surrounding the community.

Another discovery by archaeologists studying the Middle Archaic period that affirms settled village life is the use of cemeteries. Earlier nomadic people must have buried their dead wherever they were wandering at the moment, but when people settle down and erect permanent houses they also build cemeteries as "permanent homes" for deceased parents, other loved ones, and important community leaders.

Family, kinship, and community bonds are strengthened in the accompanying rituals. Although the Amerindian custom of mound building first began in the Middle Archaic period,[9] over the next five thousand years thousands upon thousands of man-made mounds become a dominant feature of the human-altered landscape of the eastern half of the United States (fig. 27).

Village life (as early as 5000 B.C., or Horizon 8 at Koster), with the security of helpful neighbors in time of need, also had all the amenities of a joyful social life, warm, permanent housing, the appreciation of art and craftsmanship, and being able to look forward to comfortable aging and finally to the solace of formal burial.

## LATE ARCHAIC (4000–1000 B.C.)

People continued to live in the valley of the lower Illinois River for millennia, and they left a rich repository of technology and ideas for those who came after them. But for the next major development in mound building we must look southward to the lower Mississippi River Valley in the Late Archaic period.

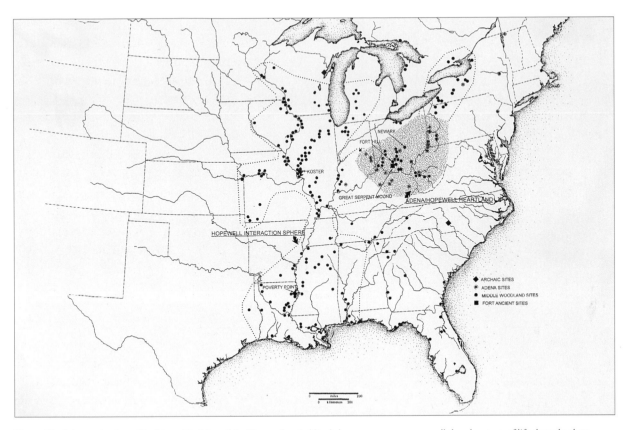

Fig. 27. Nestled near the rivers. The Mound Builders of the Hopewell period lived close to waterways to reap all the advantages of life along the shore.

One of the most extraordinary man-made landscapes in prehistory, Poverty Point, Louisiana, lies on a twenty-five-foot bluff overlooking the Mississippi floodplain. A colossal geometric complex, this stunning earthwork, now like Cahokia also a UNESCO World Heritage Site, can be best appreciated from the air (figs. 28 and 29).

*Six concentric semi-circular earthen ridges divided into segments average about 82 ft (25 m) wide and 9.8 ft (3 m) high. They are set about 131 ft (40 m) apart, each capped with midden and fill deposits in places over 3.2 ft (1 m) deep. . . . To the west lies an artificial mound more than 66 ft (20 m) high and more than 660 ft (200 m) long. A person standing on this mound can sight the vernal and autumnal equinoxes directly across the center of the earthworks to the east . . . where the sun rises on the first days of spring and fall.[10]*

Whatever the earthworks' original purpose, the imposing geometry of this spectacular mound complex and its orientation to the solar calendar endow Poverty Point with a sense of architectural perfection and cosmic significance that stirs the imagination to this day.

Fig. 28. Spectacular earthworks through imposing geometry. About 1000 B.C. a population of about 4,000 people erected this complex of six concentric earth ridges and a large bird-shaped mound at Poverty Point, Louisiana, and possibly oriented it all to a sun calendar.

*The Poverty Point habitation area covers about 494 acres (200 ha). Built between about 1000 and 700 B.C., Poverty Point took more than 1,236,007 cu. ft (35,000 cu. m) of basket-loaded soil to complete, an organized building effort that would not be undertaken again in North America for another millennium. One authority has calculated that 1350 adults laboring 70 days a year would have taken three years to erect the earthworks. Estimates of as many as 600 dwellings housing between 4000 and 5000 people* *may be somewhat optimistic, but even at a third that size, Poverty point is a unique and still little understood phenomenon.[II]*

Such a large population available for building enormous public works tells us there must also have been leadership capable of organizing and supervising this vast communal effort. Archaeologists have discovered more than one hundred sites nearby that are associated with the Poverty Point culture, and they are clustered into subgroups. Like the regionalism at Cahokia, the regionalism at Poverty Point suggests elaborate and far-flung ceremonial activity at this time.

As at distant Koster, the riverine sedentary life at Poverty Point, with its bountiful environment, had many benefits. Plenty of food was near at hand almost year-round, leaving the time and energy for other enriching occupations.

Although no one has estimated how time was spent in Archaic society, Richard Lee did an in-depth study of a contemporary hunter-gatherer group, the African

Fig. 29. Plan and reconstruction of Poverty Point showing relation to the surrounding terrain

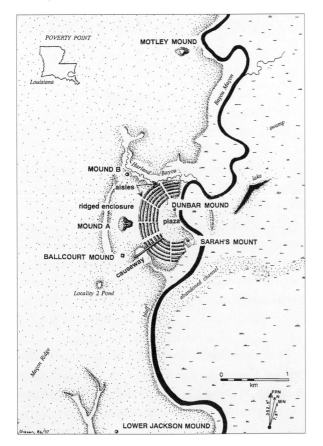

!Kung San people, who live in a much harsher environment. Among the !Kung San, children and older people work less than adults in their prime, who labor an average of two and a half eight-hour days, or twenty hours, each week.[12]

The Poverty Point people also planted squash and bottle gourds during the same period when people in Koster were cultivating pumpkins, bottle gourds, and other plants. If "plant cultivation" is the "*idea* of agriculture," it did not immediately grow into the large-scale *practice* of agriculture where people plant, weed, harvest, and store enough food for year-round subsistence. The very abundance of their wild resources may also have delayed the necessity of developing agriculture for two thousand more years, just as it did in Koster.[13]

Situated as they were on a waterway system connected to all of the vast Midwest to the north, the Poverty Point people imported a remarkable variety of exotic materials—argilite, slate, copper, galena, jasper, quartz, and steatite, to mention only a few of the materials found at the site, some of them from as far as 620 miles away.[14] These imports suggest that trade was widespread, encouraging barter, gift-giving, and the creation of ornaments for ceremonies, for people of higher status, and for grave goods. There are also stylistic similarities between weapon point styles at Poverty Point and contemporary American Bottom points. In addition, Burlington chert, later so important to Cahokians, was also imported to Poverty Point from quarries across the Mississippi in the northern Ozarks, just south of St. Louis (fig. 30).

## Early Woodland (600 B.C. in the American Bottom, 2000 B.C. in the Southeast)

If the idea of cultivating a few plants did not develop into agriculture on a large scale, another perhaps

Fig. 30. Bead of red jasper, shaped like a locust. Precious materials imported from faraway places were made into exquisite jewelry.

equally revolutionary idea did emerge at the end of the Late Archaic period and marks the beginning of the Woodland period: pottery.

Somewhere along the line a woman carrying water in a leaky old basket on a chilly fall day must have yearned for a waterproof vessel, or a cook longed for a storage jar that would keep out rodents or a pot that could be set directly on the fire, avoiding the scalds and burns incurred when putting hot stones into leather bags. Somewhere, someone must have observed that the clay used to line the hearths would hold liquid in puddles without letting it seep through. Or perhaps a fired pot was imported by canoe from another area. Whatever the sequence of events, the idea of fired pottery changed life for the better forever after. We know that pottery first appears in the Southeast about 500 B.C. and in the American Bottom about 600 B.C.

With pottery, better storage of food made it possible to feed larger populations through the cold months. It was a "container revolution" that Bruce D. Smith compared to the invention of tin cans in the twentieth century.[15] Larger populations then made

specialization of labor possible. Society became less egalitarian, with some differentiation based on individual characteristics. Art and artifacts to adorn people of higher status also appeared.

The most long-lasting of all the developments of the Late Archaic period was the beginning of a change in the attitude of human beings toward their environment: instead of just adapting their needs to what the earth offered, people began to reshape or modify the earth to meet their needs. Poverty Point is the first large-scale example of this in North America. The mound building activity was a brilliant beginning, but only a beginning.

## MYTHIC MONUMENTS: THE MOUNDS OF THE WOODLAND PEOPLE

Since time immemorial, all over the globe, the universal need of all people has been to come to terms with our mortality. What happens to us after we die? This is the all-compelling question, central to all the great religions. Close in importance to the religious beliefs that surround the various answers to this question at the heart of life are the burial practices that express the beliefs. Many of the domed or rounded mounds that swell above the surface of the earth in the Midwest cover the remains of the dead. (Sometimes the word conical is used, generally referring to round-based mounds that were actually dome-shaped.) We do not know the exact nature of the various prehistoric Amerindian beliefs, but landscape architecture to express those beliefs was clearly present in the Eastern Woodlands with the mythic transformations of the face of the earth.

With the onset of the Woodland tradition, Native Americans continued to build earthen mounds as an integral part of their burial ceremonies.[16] Sometimes the mounds covered only one person, sometimes several, and sometimes there were dozens of burials scattered throughout the site. Sometimes charming stone pipes (fig. 31), elaborate jewelry such as a fine hair comb (fig. 32) or mica cut in the form of an eagle's talon (fig. 33) might be interred with the honored dead.

Following closely upon practices for burial, the Middle Woodland people also erected mounds for a wide variety of other purposes. In a vast area generally west of the Allegheny Mountains, spreading south as far as Florida and west to Nebraska, they built tens of thousands of earth mounds, in different shapes and sizes and in different ensemble forms, sometimes enclosed within an earthen wall. One of the Early Woodland groups, the Adena (600–200 B.C.) in the middle Ohio Valley, is known for large conical mounds. A Middle Woodland group, the Hopewell (200 B.C.–A.D. 400), grew out of the Adena and developed mound building to an architecture of monumental proportions and expressive power.

Fig. 31. (top, left) The charm of an eager beaver. With eyes of river pearls, this beguiling stone pipe from the Middle Woodland period in Illinois continues to enchant, evoking the days when creatures of the water were the objects of tender reverence.

Fig. 32. (bottom, left) A trumpeter swan heralds eternity. This Hopewell burial gift, a comb made from a turtle carapace nearly twenty centuries ago, seems a fitting companion for a triumphant journey to the afterlife.

Fig. 33. (bottom, right) Shimmering eagle talon of mica. Mysteriously, a savagely elegant expression emerges from this fragile material. The exquisite carving, eleven inches high, was a burial tribute to a deeply honored person.

The heartland of the Hopewell centered in southern Ohio. While Hopewell culture is present in the American Bottom, including in and around Cahokia, it is best expressed in the lower and central Illinois Valley, and there are regional variants throughout the Midwest and South. The Hopewell are noted for their elaborate pottery and complex mortuary ceremonialism and mounds, as well as for their long-distance trade networks. The Ohio Hopewell built elaborate earthworks, constructing earthen ridges to form large geometric shapes such as octagons, squares, circles, and ellipses and to line the sides of their causeways. The lucid geometry of these monuments defined, enclosed, and set apart places that were clearly sacred.

Some mounds stood in solitary splendor; some were enclosed in an earthen embankment; others were clustered around a grand open space, their assorted sizes and shapes adding variety and mystery to the ensemble. Accompanying these majestic earth structures were often countless small mounds, some only a few feet high.[17] Yet in all their profusion, no two of these handmade landscapes or moundscapes were exactly alike. Each was composed in response to the surrounding natural features, to express a particular belief and to fulfill a particular purpose. We do not know what these beliefs were, but we still sense their symbolic power over two millennia after they were built.

At "Fort Hill" near Sinking Springs, Ohio, for example, the Hopewell built an earth mound complex surrounded by an embankment wall a mile and five-eighths long, with thirty-three gateways and enclosing about forty-eight acres, containing at least two ceremonial buildings and probably a village.[18]

At the Newark Works in Licking County, Ohio (fig. 34), for example, the earthworks covered approximately four square miles.[19] Separate groups within, each comprising a circle and a square, were connected by enclosed or earth-walled avenues. One of them, the Great Circle Earthwork, even served recently as a public fairground. About twelve hundred feet in diameter, the surrounding ancient earthen walls are eight to fourteen feet high, enclosing twenty-six acres. At the center of the circle is the Eagle Mound, a bird effigy. A long earthen avenue, now gone, once connected the Great Circle with a large square enclosure a quarter of a mile away.

A second avenue originally led westward to join another ensemble, the Circle and Octagon, which many consider the finest part of the Newark Works. Some scholars have observed that the structure aligns with points on the eastern and western horizons defined by the 18.6 year lunar cycle. It survives as the Octagon State Memorial, set in a municipal golf course.

Decades before the golf course, the place amazed an early observer, Ephraim G. Squier, who left us his marvelous drawings recording the mounds as they appeared in 1848, along with his commentary: "The builders possessed a standard of measurement and had some means of determining angles . . . .we find not only accurate squares and perfect circles, but also . . . octagons of great dimensions."[20]

Robert Silverberg, a modern authority, commented: "The low flat-topped mounds within the octagon serve now to test the skill of golfers, and the flags marking the eighteen holes mar the beauty and splendor of the scene only slightly. One walks across the flawless green grass of the golf course so stirred by the size and symmetry of the ancient site that one hardly feels like criticizing the use modern Newark has found for it."[21]

Sometimes mounds scattered in an asymmetrical pattern were enclosed within a perfectly symmetrical rectangular earthen enclosure wall, such as at Mound City (now called Hopewell Culture National Monument)

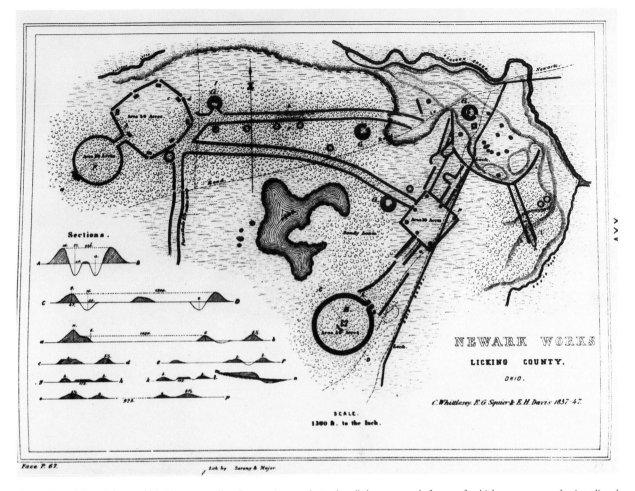

Fig. 34. An eagle in a circle, set within four square miles of geometric mounds. Earth-walled avenues nearly fourteen feet high once connected points aligned with the 18.6 year lunar cycle in this Hopewell complex in Newark, Ohio.

near Chillicothe, Ohio. Here twenty-four mounds lie within an enclosure covering thirteen acres and may be connected to other earthworks many miles away by a long "road" or pathway (fig. 35).[22]

Later on, beginning in the Later Woodland period, and chiefly in the Wisconsin-Iowa-Illinois border area, effigy mounds were shaped like huge birds, animals, and even gigantic human forms (fig. 36).

## THE GREAT SERPENT

The most famous of all the extant effigy mounds is the Great Serpent (fig. 37). Its huge body, just beginning to coil, lies on top of a bluff overlooking Brush Creek, near Peebles, Ohio. Its mouth is open, about to consume an egg-shaped mound. Nearly a quarter of a mile long (1,254 feet), most of its body is extended in seven

Fig. 35. (top) Hopewell Mound City. Set inside a perfectly symmetrical rectangular earthen wall, twenty-four mounds fill this thirteen-acre site in Chillicothe, Ohio.

Fig. 36. (bottom) Effigy mounds depict giant animals and a mythic man. Rows of bears in one area and a distinct human form in another emerge from this site in Dade County, Wisconsin.

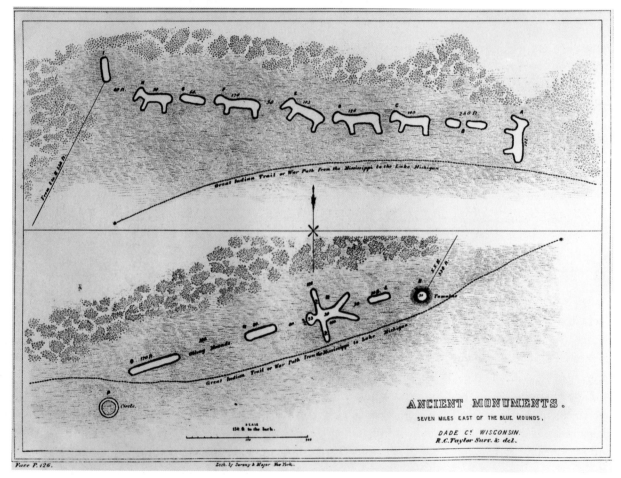

ANCIENT MONUMENTS.

SEVEN MILES EAST OF THE BLUE MOUNDS,

DADE C.ᵒ WISCONSIN.

R.C.Taylor Surv. & del.

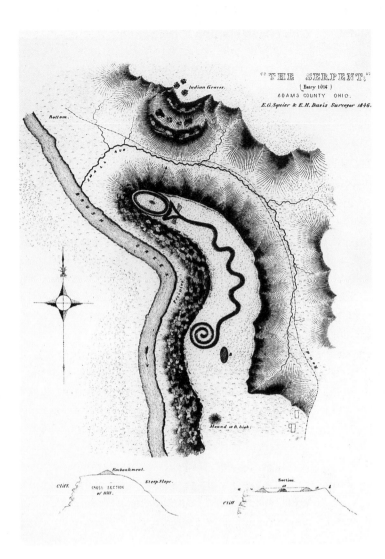

Fig. 37. A great serpent looking over Locust Grove, Ohio, or Halley's Comet? With its tail just beginning to coil, it seems the huge snake, over a thousand feet long, twenty feet wide, and nearly five feet high, is slithering on the ridge above Brush Creek in Peebles, Ohio. Or is it a comet? A new carbon dating of A.D. 1070 has led scholars to speculate that this monumental earthwork may actually reflect a sighting of Halley's Comet, which would have been visible to the Mound Builders in 1066.

deep curves, emulating the undulations of a snake. The body averages about twenty feet wide and four or five feet high. Because of the varying elevations and the way the snake slithers around the ridge of the bluff, a person walking toward its mouth disappears from the view of someone wrapped in the coils of its tail.[23] "Excavations have shown that the serpentine form had been carefully planned prior to construction, for flat stones and clay were laid on the original ground surface as a guide, and then earth piled on top."[24]

Recently carbon 14 dating has placed Serpent Mound in the Fort Ancient period, about A.D. 1100, contemporary with Cahokia.[25] Since the Hopewell culture has been found in both Illinois and Ohio, trade apparently strengthened the interaction between these two distinct societies.[26]

## Late Woodland (A.D. 400–800 in the American Bottom, up to A.D. 1000 elsewhere)

There is no known direct relation between the Hopewell culture and later Mississippian cultures, since an intervening tradition known as Late Woodland is present throughout most of the Eastern Woodlands. The Late Woodland people built mostly small, conical burial mounds with few elaborate mortuary artifacts and containing less elaborate ceramics than the Hopewell or Mississippian mounds. They expanded and intensified the dependence on agriculture, and by the end of this period corn had become an important food crop. Their villages were generally larger and more permanent than some preceding Middle Woodland villages. Perhaps the most important innovation during this period was the introduction of the bow and arrow, which probably appeared about A.D. 400. This is indicated by the sudden appearance of small stemmed and triangular arrow points, mistakenly called bird points by many collectors. The bow and arrow transformed hunting strategies.

No one is sure about the relation between these various cultures. Perhaps their interchange was a dynamic process, a language of landscape architecture that evolved over several centuries. The Mississippians may have built upon, added to, edited out, and changed the syntax of the earlier mound building cultures to suit their own cultural needs. If these mound complexes have something in common, we sense it is always the meaningful interplay between people, earth, water, and sky. Universally, humans act as the creators of connections between nature and culture.

## The Mississippian Emergence

The mighty Mound Builders who grew out of the Woodland culture were first called Mississippians around the turn of the nineteenth century by William Holmes, who applied the term to a cluster of ceramic types found primarily in the valleys of the Mississippi and its tributaries. Canoe traffic and trade on this unrivaled network of waterways was extensive, with connections to rivers emptying into the Great Lakes, the Atlantic Ocean, the Gulf Coast, and the tributaries of the Missouri River leading to the continental divide. The multiple Mississippian domains nearly covered a large portion of what is now the United States (fig. 38).

This riverine life spread in all directions along both banks of the myriad waterways, laying a new web of human settlements over eastern North America. In some places Mississippian hamlets remained small, in others they grew to villages or large towns. With their distinctive mound architecture, they were part of political units known as chiefdoms. People in these communities had frequent contact with each other, creating a remarkable regional network.

Loose, flexible, and even shifting centers of communal activity were part of Mississippian life. Gatherings of the clans may have focused on a southern town for the winter solstice, a northern one for the summer solstice, and other sites for special sacred ceremonies. The seasonal rituals or ceremonies attracting many visitors became, in effect, like markets, so population estimates for their communities are problematic. Cahokia may have had only 10,000 people at its height, perhaps 14,000, but when crowds came in from the surrounding region for festivals the population may have doubled or even tripled.

These Amerindians reaped the benefits of both a stable and a mobile life. Their year-round homes were

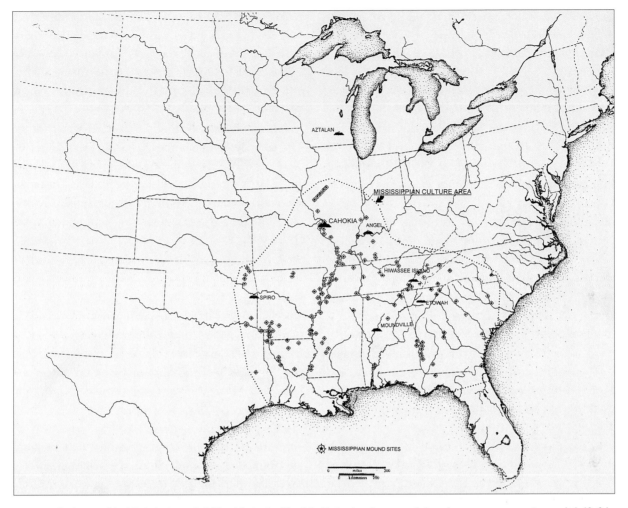

Fig. 38. Multiple sites of the Mississippian period. The rich riverine life of the Native Americans spread along the waterways, occupying nearly half of the future United States.

near their farmlands, where they planted and harvested enough corn to provide a steady food supply for a large population, and extensive trade networks brought them riches from faraway areas.

A change in agricultural methods illustrates their adaptive ingenuity. As one of my anonymous reviewers pointed out, earlier the Mississippians had used digging sticks to make holes in the earth to plant seeds:

*They planted in wooded areas without sod where they girdled the trees so the leaves would die. After several seasons weeds started to become a nuisance, so the planters moved to another area. Hoes were not necessary in such an environment because there were no weeds to hoe for several seasons, and there was no sod to cut through. Flint hoes became useful later when it was desirable to plant year after year in the same place and therefore necessary to keep the weeds down. Digging-stick planting with shifting fields was labor efficient but required much land. Hoe cultivation was land efficient but labor intensive.*

Hundreds of these flint hoes, made from Mill Creek chert from southern Illinois, polished to a high shine by use (fig. 39), now rest in museum display cases near the major Mississippian sites. Flint hoes can be resharpened, and the distinctive polished flakes removed in this process are common finds at Mississippian villages.

Traders brought the riches of half a continent to each other's doors—granite, basalt, diorite, flint clay, galena, fluorite, and quartz were exported from Missouri, Tennessee, and Kentucky, mica from the southern Appalachians, seashells and sharks' teeth from the Gulf of Mexico, and copper from the upper Great Lakes. Salt, tools, pottery, jewelry, and ceremonial goods were exchanged at the main mound centers throughout the territory. New ideas were imported and exported, and Mississippians also profited technologically and intellectually from their regional interaction.

Fig. 39. Fusion of form and function. Leather thongs glued around the notches once bound this hoe blade from about A.D. 1000 to a wooden handle.

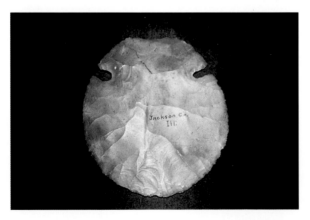

We do not know for certain, but some authorities suggest that many of the midwestern Mississippians may have been speakers of the Dheigan Siouan language (as were the later Kansa, Omaha, Osage, Ponca, and Quapaw/Arkansa), and southern Mississippians probably spoke many other languages.[27]

Their settlements dotted the eastern half of the United States. Some of the larger Mississippian towns were Aztalan, Wisconsin; Angel site near Evansville, Indiana; Moundville, Alabama; Etowah, Georgia; Spiro, Oklahoma; and Hiwasee Island, Tennessee. The largest by far was at Cahokia.

## DIFFERENCES IN DEGREE BECOME A DIFFERENCE IN KIND

The rich Woodland culture had given the Mississippians successful technologies for hunting, including the bow and arrow, plant cultivation, the hoe, and pottery. In their turn the Mississippians expanded this legacy—in both complexity and scale—so that the differences in degree became a difference in kind. When the hoe replaced the digging stick as the instrument for cultivating fields, large-scale agriculture became feasible. With the same tool, they dug trench foundations for the supports of their buildings, speeding up construction time, and also dug earth for their mounds. When potters added shell tempering to their clay, larger, thinner, and lighter containers provided better cooking and storage ware.

In the process of their growth, the Mississippians radically changed the face of the heartland of North America. Fields upon fields filled with rows of corn and other crops were dotted with houses, or villages that sometimes grew into towns. Everywhere they built grand public works, and as all their inventions reinforced each other, the new culture thrived.

Architecturally the Mississippian tradition was characterized by the organization of permanent towns around plazas containing or flanked by platform mounds that were the sites for council houses, temples, and the lodges of the chiefs. Often these towns were surrounded by palisades. Agriculture was practiced on a large scale, granaries were erected or food was stored in the ground, and grinding stones and wooden mortars and pestles for processing grain were in abundance. Architecture and agriculture on a grand scale, pottery, basketmaking, and a dozen other arts and crafts together made up the civilized life that flourished a millennium ago in the valleys of the Mississippi.

Most authorities also agree that the Mississippians established a wide variety of political systems, ranging from egalitarian societies in smaller communities to hierarchically organized chiefdoms, or theocracies, in larger ones. These were administered by priests and noblemen, an elite class just under the chief. Below were artisans and other specialists and leaders of kin groups, and the lowest-ranking individuals provided labor for their public works. Social ranks and political organization made this lively culture possible.[28]

In sum, the Mississippian Mound Builders, like the ancient Mesopotamians, the Egyptians, or the Chinese, created architecture on a monumental scale; they divided their society into different ranks, with specialized labor and a ruler-chief governing a large population; their economic system encouraged vast trade in a far-flung region; they controlled the growth and distribution of their food supply; their knowledge of the cosmos provided them the design of a sun calendar with predictions precise enough for dealing with the agricultural cycle.

## Summary

Some scholars say that since the Mississippians had no mathematics or written language their culture cannot be called a civilization. Yet they obviously had standard units of measure and a simple geometry. More important, the Mississippians and those who preceded them had an enduring language, a language that has been passed down to us over the centuries—the language of art or, more specifically, the language of the art of landscape architecture. It is up to us to decipher it. If we leave out an account of the Mississippians, we leave out a vital part of the story of human adaptation to a unique riverine environment in the southern part of the temperate zone on the North American continent. We leave out the remarkable emergence of interaction spheres, exchange networks, and the erection of monumental architecture right at the center of American history. At the center of this center, geographically and culturally, was the metropolis at Cahokia.

There are some similarities in the mounds from all over the globe in different climates and at different stages of human development. Earth mounds abound in Europe, the Middle East, Asia, and Africa. In these we can discern a common human motive: the struggle to come to terms with death through art, architecture, and ritual. There are also astonishing differences, and we can delight in the enormous variety to be found in human initiative and in the myriad meanings given to people's relationship to the givens of the natural world and to the supernatural worlds of their own spiritual beliefs. At Cahokia the Mississippians shaped a unique and spectacular world of their own as part of this common human heritage, as we shall see in the next chapter.

FIG. 40. A SETTING FOR MYTHIC RITUALS. MAJESTIC
MOUNDS AND FOUR PLAZAS MARK THE CARDINAL DIRECTIONS,
A REFLECTION OF THE COSMOS IN THE HEART OF THE
MIDWESTERN PRAIRIE.

**3**

▼

# Cahokia

## Cosmic Landscape Architecture

Over six thousand years of continuous, gradual cultural evolution . . . culminated in one of North America's most brilliant achievements—the Mississippian tradition.

BRIAN M. FAGAN

Seen from high above, the Cahokia landscape had mythic dimensions (fig. 41). Stretching for six square miles, more than one hundred mounds rose from the earth with monumental presence. At the center lay four vast plazas, honoring the cardinal directions, to the north, east, south, and west (fig. 42). At their crossing the great Monks Mound towered more than a hundred feet in the air. At other points woodhenges (large circular areas marked off by enormous red cedar posts) enclosed large circular plazas or ceremonial areas.

A whole city aligned with the cosmos! The idea reverberates with expressive power. The stars in the heavens shine radiantly; they are constant in both position and movement; they appear with reassuring regularity generation after generation. The North Star orients a hunter in the forest so he can find his way home. The moon lights his way in the darkness. The Pleiades promise a frost-free growing season. Our orbit around the sun brings four seasons, from spring to winter, echoing the life cycle of a person from youth to old age, with the promise of continuity in new generations.

Are there other symbolic messages hidden in the placement of the mounds and plazas in this eleventh-century city? How was its plan designed? What kind of social and political organization was necessary to erect public works of this magnitude? How was the labor force organized and motivated? What kinds of surveying and engineering methods ensured stability and endurance?

Fig. 41. Ceremonial cynosure and synedoche. The clear-cut geometry of the mounds and plazas, and their orientation to eternal cosmic events, identifies Cahokia as a sacred ceremonial center, a place of perfection and permanence drawing pilgrims from miles around to the microcosm of the great universe of the sun beyond. The heart of the great metropolis was the Grand Plaza at Cahokia, with Twin Mounds in the foreground and Monks Mound as the ceremonial climax to the north.

Even today, traces of the four main plazas demonstrate their orientation: Monks Mound is aligned with the cardinal directions; the North Plaza is bounded by four mounds on each of the cardinal sides; the principal mounds in the center are aligned with Monks Mound and with each other. Seven mounds are lined up north-south in line with the west edge of Monks Mound (fig. 43). Another eight align with the east edge. Nine mounds are on an east-west line across the site and line up with Monks Mound.[1]

As if designed by a landscape architect, each mound has sufficient space around it to set it off from the others, and the modular spacing between the major mounds serves to unify them (fig. 44). At the equinoxes two poles of the reconstructed Woodhenge align with the rising sun in the east. Solstice posts in the Woodhenge align at the beginning of summer and winter at sunrise and sunset. Several of the principal mounds are also on these alignments (fig. 45).

We do not know exactly what the religious beliefs of the Cahokians were, but when authorities with background knowledge allow themselves to speculate, the results are illuminating, especially about what might have happened during religious celebrations or on the other special occasions for which this elaborate sacred landscape was designed and built.

At the center of John Pfeiffer's imaginative account (see box) lay the four logs pointing to the cardinal directions. Experts have recently provided some convincing arguments that the story is largely accurate.

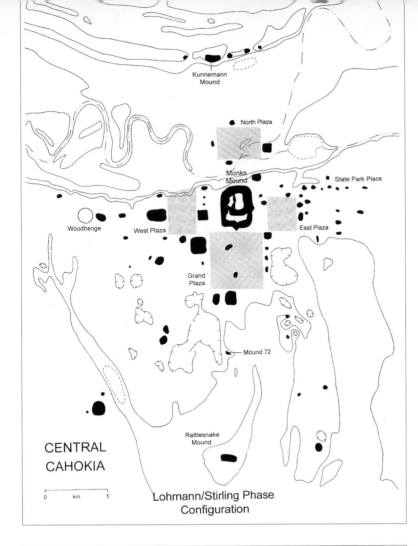

CENTRAL
CAHOKIA

Lohmann/Stirling Phase
Configuration

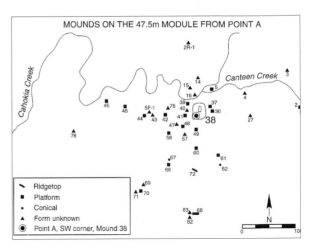

MOUNDS ON THE 47.5m MODULE FROM POINT A

Ridgetop
Platform
Conical
Form unknown
Point A, SW corner, Mound 38

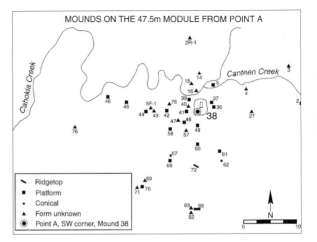

MOUNDS ON THE 47.5m MODULE FROM POINT A

Ridgetop
Platform
Conical
Form unknown
Point A, SW corner, Mound 38

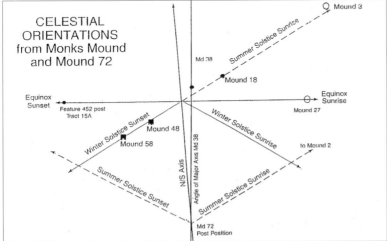

CELESTIAL
ORIENTATIONS
from Monks Mound
and Mound 72

Fig. 42. (top, left) Aligned with the stars. Mounds tuned to the cosmos, in a setting of spacious plazas. The shaded areas indicate the positive role played by the negative spaces as they foreground the mounds complex and give it meaning.

Fig. 43. (top, right) Mounds lined up. Seven mounds are clearly set out from north to south, and nine from east to west.

Fig. 44. (bottom, right) Unity through modular spacing. Mounds that lie on a 47.5 meter module from a point on Monks Mound seem set out by a landscape architect.

Fig. 45. (bottom, left) A solar calendar. At the solstices several mounds align with the rising sun in the east and the setting sun in the west; shown here are celestial orientations from Monks Mound and Mound 72.

### Festival Life in a Sacred Landscape

"A late prehistoric . . . sunrise—and a man dressed in a cape of shell beads and a high crown of feathers stands alone on top of a four-terraced earthen pyramid 10 stories tall. Staring at the dawn, the Great Sun, the paramount chief who bows to nothing human, emits three prolonged howling cries as he falls on his knees to greet the sun.

"There are answering cries from below. The Great Sun stands up, raises his hands and looks down the steep sides of the pyramid, past the sloping terraces to a huge open plaza about 40 acres in extent (nearly five times the size of St. Peter's Square in Vatican City), where thousands of people are watching and waiting [fig. 46].

housed in a temple antechamber at the summit, the only fire burning in the community.

"The warrior, among the people now, comes to the center of the plaza, where a great cross of four logs points in the cardinal directions. Bending down, he empties the contents of the bowl onto a pile of leaves and branches, and blows on the embers. A shout comes from the surrounding crowd as the rising flames leap from the cross. A miracle has occurred, a renewal, fresh fire from the heavens captured and brought down to earth through the auspices of the Great Sun.

"It is the beginning of the harvest festival, a combination of Thanksgiving and Mardi Gras. The corn is green [ripe], and for the next four days there will be dancing and

"Suddenly a murmur passes through the crowd. A tattooed warrior, face painted bright red, appears not far from the chief and begins a slow, solemn walk down ramps and stairways towards the plaza. He carries a bowl in his hands, bearing red-hot embers from the eternal fire

feasting, the taking of an emetic 'black drink' to induce ritual vomiting, purification by bathing in a nearby creek, tributes to the Great Sun and finally a rekindling of fires throughout the countryside."

John E. Pfeiffer, "Indian City on the Mississippi," 125–27

The evidence indicates that many Amerindian societies deliberately planned their communities after a cosmic model. Henri-Frédéric Amiel said in his nineteenth-century journal, "A landscape is a condition of the spirit." Scholar Paul Wheatley put it another way:

*Sacrality (which is synonymous with reality) is achieved through the imitation of a celestial archetype . . . . Although the whole world was the handiwork of the Gods its maximum potential sacredness was realizable only at a few points. Before territory could be inhabited, it had to be sacralized—that is cosmicized. Its consecration signified its reality and therefore sanctioned its habitation; but its establishment as an imitation of a celestial archetype required its delimitation and orientation as a sacred territory within a profane space.[2]*

With its plazas aligned on the cardinal directions and the mound of greatest height at the crossing of the plazas, it is clear that Cahokia is a landscape cosmogram. John E. Kelly advocates looking for an explanation by approaching the question from both ends of a chronological continuum. Did other Native American communities create any analogous sacred landscape before the Cahokians? After the Cahokians? The answer is yes to both questions. We know the Hopewell circle-and-octagon mounds were used for sacred ceremonies and for astronomical observations. We have seen the evidence of a solar calendar at Poverty Point about 1500 B.C. Another pre-Cahokia example is the McKeithen site at Weeden Island in northern Florida, occupied between A.D. 200 and 700. Here three mounds form the corners of an isosceles triangle, and a perpendicular from the center of the baseline to the apex points toward the rising sun at the summer solstice (fig. 47).

Fig. 46. (opposite) The great chief greets the rising sun. Standing in the angles of a four-terraced pyramid over a hundred feet high, Brother Sun raises his hand to signal the beginning of the equinox ceremonies.

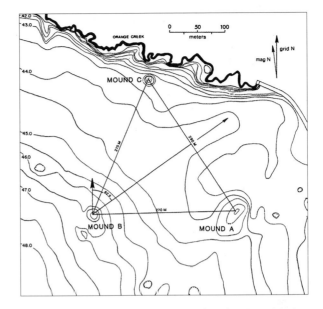

Fig. 47. Three mounds form an isosceles triangle. Other Native American groups also made mounds in geometric patterns and oriented them toward the rising sun, as shown by this example from the McKeithen site at Weeden Island, Florida.

After Cahokia, examples can be found in many Amerindian tribes, and we gain many insights through the ethnographic analogies that follow.[3]

## An Animated Landscape at Once Past, Present, and Future

Skywatching has always been a vital part of Native Americans' life, and it has influenced their religious beliefs, agricultural practices, social organization, and landscape architecture. As scholar William G. Gartner put it:

*Native American architecture is an amalgam of design rules and always encodes many messages . . . .Many ancient astronomers sought to equate the regular patterns of the heavens with cultural and natural phenomena here on*

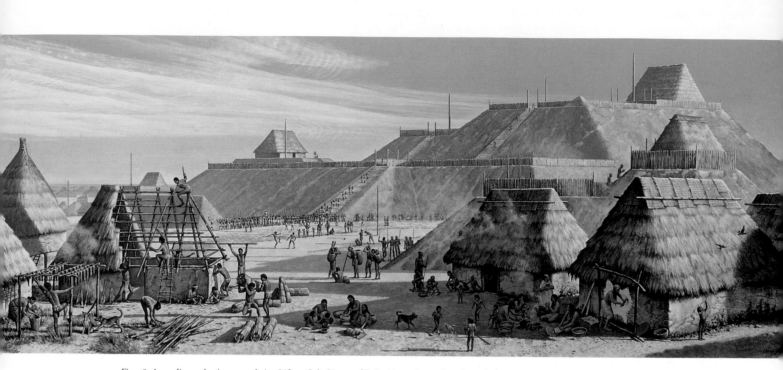

Fig. 48. An ordinary day in a sacred city. Life at Cahokia was filled with workers going about daily activities and the tasks of house building in the shadows of the tall mounds occupied by the elite.

*earth, thereby empirically validating an established world view . . . . The primary goal in many North American contexts was commemoration, often times a religious celebration of world creation and the once present and future animated landscape. Ancient sky watching was merely one empirical component for constructing a sacred geography.[4]*

This sacred geography, a material manifestation of a belief system, also could serve as a teaching device and a constant reminder to young and old of all classes of the society's religious views and social organization. As you walked out your front door every morning you saw a virtual replica of the orderly universe. On your way to work your path took you through this celestial microcosm. This three-dimensional cosmic diagram

was also like an organizational chart of your community's class structure. Your own place in it was literally traced by your moccasins. If you were a worker, on ordinary days you were outside the palisade wall; on festival days you gathered with other common people in the plaza (fig. 48). If you were a member of the elite, you greeted the day from your house on a medium-sized platform mound within the palisade. The chief dominated the world around him as far as he could see from the height of the largest platform mound.

Seeing some similarities in the emphasis on the cardinal directions in Cahokia and in contemporary Native American beliefs, Robert L. Hall suggests that Cahokia contained a "world center shrine" similar to those observed historically among the Zuni, the Hopi, the Tewa pueblo, the Osage, the Arapaho, and the

Cheyenne. Many of these Native American villages are perceived by their inhabitants as being the cosmos in microcosm, and their own village center is seen as the center of the world. Hall also draws on the field observations of Frank Hamilton Cushing, written over a century ago:

*The Zuni of today number scarcely 1,700 and, as is well known, they inhabit only a single large pueblo . . . . This pueblo, however, is divided not always clearly to the eye, but very clearly in the estimation of the people themselves, into seven parts, corresponding, not perhaps in arrangement topographically, but in sequence, to their subdivisions of the "worlds" or world-quarters of this world. Thus, one division of the town is supposed to be related to the north and to be centered in its kiva or estufa, which may or may not be, however, in its center; another division represents the west, another the south, and another the east, yet another the upper world and another the lower world, while a final division represents the middle or mother and synthetic combinations of them all in this world.⁵*

This four-part horizontal division of the world (into north, east, south, and west) plus a three-part vertical division (into lower world, this world, and upper world) was also reflected in the ritual behavior of the Zuni around their religious shrines.

## Ritual Behavior in a Sacred Land

*Arrived at the field, [the Zuni man] goes to a well-known spot near its center. Here he digs in the soft sandy soil by pushing his prod down with his foot, equally distant from the central place; the first to the North, the second to the West, the third to the South and the fourth to the East. By the left side of the north hole he digs another to represent*

*the Sky regions, and by the right side of the southern hole still another relating it to the Lower regions. In the central space he kneels facing the East, and drawing forth the plumed prayer-wand first marks by sprinkling prayer meal, a cross on the ground—to symbolize not only the four cardinal points, but also the stars which shall watch over his field by night-time. Then with prayer, he plants the plumed [prayer] stick at the intersection of the cross, sprinkles it with more corn meal . . . and withdraws."⁶*

John Kelly notes a similar physical manifestation at Cahokia with the "quadrilateral configuration of the plazas" plus the vertical dimension present in the Monks Mound, standing as the great mound does between the lower world and the upper world of the sky, with the ascending ramp like a cosmic stairway tying together earth, land, and sky.⁷

Humans all over the globe have wanted height in their symbolic religious places, and the Cahokians solved the problem of their flat topography by creating enormous earth mounds. Where there were no natural heights, they created architectural heights to fill their spiritual needs.

Height is also a metaphor for power, and the Cahokian elite were powerful people. Conveniently, and not coincidentally, height served the personal-communal need for a sacred place and also the social-political need for a statement of civil order and a method of civil control. Tall structures are imposing. They demand to be noticed, respected, sometimes feared. If they are taller than the structures of a rival tribe, city, culture, or nation, they are also emblems of victory, trophies symbolizing the possession of the best engineering, architecture, social, and military organization and the greatest wealth. Tall structures demonstrate vigor and success. They show the surrounding world that the inhabitants are big, bold, and in command.

*Interlude: The Humanist Perspective*

What is it about this landscape that transcends its surface forms? Why do I feel a powerful presence of deep meaning, coming from the past but making itself felt in the here and now? Something in this city of the mound builders crosses a thousand years and strikes a chord in me that resonates vibrantly.

As in a great cathedral or a great public square, it is the living beings who give presence and vitality to the surrounding forms. We perceive the intentions, for we receive the feelings, and in turn we feel alive and vital in their presence. We are the reciprocating part of the experience, the strings stretched taut over the sounding board of the forms. The experience does not happen without the amplification of the surrounding forms, and only certain forms vibrate on human frequencies, quickening us to life. The cosmic landscape at Cahokia is one among these treasured human creations.

The mounds defy conventional architectural analysis. Today they have no visible ornament. Each one is a solid that does not enclose space, as far as we now know, although collectively they define and mark large plazas. The structural system is simply compressed dirt. Yet the emotion the mounds evoke is profoundly architectural. Separately each mound is a work of earth architecture reduced to only one of architecture's attributes: mass. Yet the masses of the mounds, shaped in an ensemble, give proportion, scale, and scope to a human need to feel at once closer to the earth and at one with the universe. The landscape fulfills the desire as it arouses it. There follows the sense of deep satisfaction and completion that is somehow everything.

Mass, which gives scale and proportion to experience, also provides the dimension of height at Cahokia. Being up high is physically, mentally, kinesthetically, and aesthetically akin to the religious experience. Climbing a gradual slope tunes up the body: the blood pressure rises a little, the skin tingles, the heart beats a little faster, the senses become more acute. The visitor smells the freshness of the grasses, hears the songs of the meadowlarks.

This simultaneous awakening of all the senses and being open to the sensations of all *at the same time* causes a kind of psychic shift, a change from a linear, one at a time mode to a holistic awareness. One tunes in to the whole of experience all at once rather than to one part at a time.

This heightened awareness is accompanied by a loss of the sense of self and of personal time. It is closely related to the experience art and music lovers speak of in describing their utter absorption in paintings or concerts and the acute pleasure that accompanies this absorption. This "aesthetic experience" is quintessentially holistic; when it happens, it enhances religious emotion. This leap to the holistic state occurs most easily in a place of great height. In the change from linear to holistic, from the part to the whole, from the everyday to the aesthetic, there is a parallel sense that we have moved from the profane to the sacred. When it happens, being up high is a metaphor for immortality.

Ideally the city below is an exciting place to contemplate. Its many fires and plazas are where opportunities abound, where the stories of returning travelers find sympathetic listeners, where the imagination is fired. Seeing the city as an orderly whole—visible and material—symbolizes the continuation of civic values. It is a metaphor for civic vitality.

Having monuments or mounds from the past, places where objects may be passed from one generation to the next, where memories are preserved, brings a sense of inner peace to older generations, for they need to believe their legacies will continue. A temple mound is a visible symbol of the continuity of life—a metaphor for civic longevity.

The ruler—the religious leader or the chief of state—must above all others be protected from physical harm, from outside enemies and from criminals within, because in protecting his power the community keeps itself safe. A high fortress atop a high mound is a metaphor for invincibility.

By their almost superhuman earthmoving, by their arrangements of geometric mounds of varying shapes and heights disposed among spacious plazas of various sizes, by their climactic Monks Mound, the Cahokians altered the flat mud plain they inherited, glorifying and transfiguring their landscape into an exalted world.

## A Microcosm on Earth

The Midwest not only lacked natural heights, it was also devoid of limits, borders, or boundaries. Most often compared to an ocean of grass, the prairies too could be terrifyingly vast. Within the wild forests that bordered them the confusion could be equally disorienting. The microcosm on earth, the mound city, calmed by mirroring the cosmos as it clarified and ordered human experience, giving it a meaning it would otherwise not have.

No set place for humans was provided by Mother Nature. The work of the human hand in marking a portion of the terrifying vastness with an ordered place gave material form to the workings of the human mind, orienting the self and the community within the scheme of things. The mounds create a sense of *here,* as opposed to infinite *thereness.* Mounds, terraced pyramids, cones and ridge-tops, and plazas—all these geometric shapes are clearly hand-made. Nature is altered, assisted, made neat and orderly as well as fructified by the efforts of human architecture and husbandry.

### VERTICAL AND HORIZONTAL COSMOGRAPHY REFLECTED IN THE SACRED MOUND CITY

The human place in the cosmos is situated along two vectors, the horizontal and the vertical, and given scale as well as scope by the insertion of geometric shapes. Here in this broad land is our place in the horizontal sense. Here is the protected place; beyond is the place where we can travel, have adventures, and yet always return to an oriented place because the mounds do not move. The sun and the stars move, but the mounds always stay where they are.

If I am an ordinary Cahokian I find my vertical place in the social hierarchy in the lowest parts of the city. If I am a priest I am above all other creatures, approaching the celestial world.

Like the Mayans, the Cahokians probably believed the upper world represented order, the lower world disorder, and the middle world, or this world, a mixture of the two. Symbols of the upper world found in Cahokian artifacts are symbols of the sun's rays or of birds such as the falcon and the eagle. Snakes, frogs, and fish appear as emblems of the lower world. Deer, rabbits, and raccoons are of this world. Some animals thought to live in two worlds became special symbols, such as the beaver, the owl, and the cougar (fig. 49).

Among some peoples, such as the Cherokee, the water spider was heralded as the bringer of the sacred fire of the sun to earth (see box). These spiders appear on most of the Mississippian shell gorgets in the area around Cahokia (fig. 50).

The first fire burned in a hollow tree on an island in the Tennessee River. The animals gathered and planned to secure the fire, but all attempts failed. The spider then volunteered and was successful by weaving a web basket and placing a small ember inside. She then placed the basket on her back and swam back to shore. The Cherokees have had fire ever since.

Charles M. Hudson, *The Southeastern Indians*, 135–36

Many Native American ceremonies refer to myths of creation—the origin of people, fire, water, or other natural forces—all helping to make sense of life on earth. Their rituals may also serve as commemorative occasions, such as thanksgiving at harvestime, giving the participants a sense of connection with the past, the present, and the future. There are elements of their religious beliefs tied to directing natural processes such as rainfall, fertility of the soil, abundance of crops, or birth and death and other events in the life cycle. It is possible that even their sporting activities, such as chunkey (fig. 51) were influences by their myths.

## THE SACRED ORDER OF THE CITY PRESERVES THE SOCIAL ORDER

Scholars also believe that the physical order of cosmographic cities played a vital role in expressing the social order of the city and preserving its political order.

Fig. 49. Beaver at work! Animals were popular subjects for Mississippian potters. This charming ceramic bowl shows a swimming beaver chewing on a stick held in his paws, no doubt on his way to build his home.

Fig. 50. Water Spider brings fire to the people. This motif, inspired by a shell gorget, honors the heroine of a popular Native American myth about the first gift of fire, brought as an ember carried on the back of a water spider in a web of her own making.

Fig. 51. A game of chunkey. In this favorite sport at Cahokia, two contestants threw spears toward a carved concave stone as it rolled. When it stopped the closest spear won.

Many eastern and midwestern Native American tribes that we know from historical records divided not only the physical aspects of their villages but their social order according to the cosmological principles of their religion. Garrick A. Bailey gives one good example for the Osage:

*Just as the cosmos was divided between sky and earth, so the clans were divided into groups or moieties . . . .the nine clans of the Sky People symbolically represented all of the forces of the sky, whereas the fifteen Earth clans symbolically represented all of the forces of the earth . . . .Osage vil-*

*lages . . . were organized as mirror images of the cosmos. They were divided in half by an east-west street that symbolized the surface of the earth—the ho'-e-ga—and the path of the sun on its daily journey. Each clan had its own section of the village. Families of the Sky People were arranged by clan groupings in precise locations along the north side of the street. Similarly, families of the Earth People were arranged in clan order along the south side.[8]*

Archaeological discoveries in the late twentieth century indicated that some aspects of festival life in Cahokia dealt with what we would call the darker side of life. There are examples of human sacrifices of all kinds in other cultures, and apparently Cahokia was no exception. Although we do not know the nature of the ceremonies that accompanied such ritual behavior, Melvin L. Fowler's discovery of four headless and handless skeletons buried in Mound 72 suggests a foundation for this speculation.

## PUBLIC WORKS RITUALLY RENEWED TO PRESERVE CIVIC ORDER

Perhaps human sacrifice was also part of a system of social control of the labor force. The archaeological evidence clearly demonstrates that the mounds were built in stages and, like the plazas, palisades, woodhenges, and other public works at Cahokia, had to be regularly repaired and reconstructed. Although wood is a durable material if it is constantly wet or constantly dry, wood in damp earth is subject to the wet/dry conditions that promote rapid rot. Urban renewal was necessary almost continuously in Cahokia, and sometimes groups of buildings and even whole neighborhoods were swept away so as to reorder the earthly cosmos or clear land for new or rebuilt structures. Only strong social control and political power can make possible such large-scale changes in the civic fabric. In addition, public works of such magnitude required mobilizing and maintaining a large labor force.

## THE HUMAN COST OF PUBLIC WORKS

Estimates for the hours of labor needed just for the palisade and its regularly placed bastions are an illuminating example of the time required for large structures. Nearly twenty thousand logs are needed for the kind of stockade fence that surrounded central Cahokia. A person with a stone ax can fell two nine-inch-diameter trees in an hour, meaning that 10,000 work hours would be needed just to obtain the raw material.

Sizing, trimming, and debarking would require another one to two hours per tree. Transporting all the logs from the forest to the site takes more labor. Excavating the trenches for the foundation adds about 20,800 hours. The labor of erecting the posts, backfilling the trench around them with soil, tamping down the fill, collecting and preparing cordage and ropes to lash or interweave the supports with cross members, and other finishing operations such as mixing and applying daub plaster (which could make logs last longer) brings the total to nearly 180,000 work hours (fig. 52). Under ideal conditions (good weather, accessibility of timber, a sizable workforce, and ease of transportation) it would

Fig. 52. Stockade designs evolved. The size and shape of the bastions along the protective walls surrounding central Cahokia changed periodically as these wood and clay constructions were replaced.

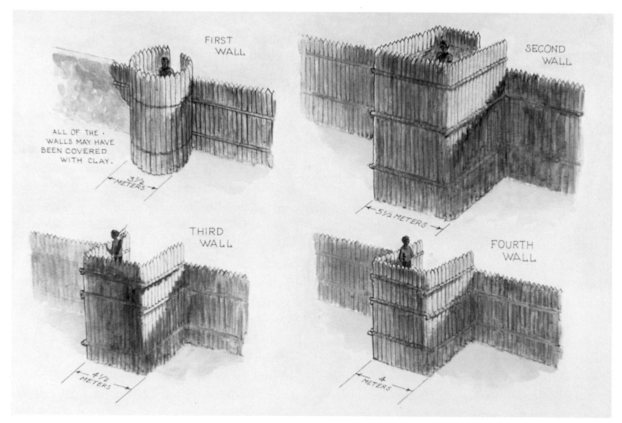

Fig. 53. Erecting a woodhenge. A solar calendar of the sun's movement helped determine when to hold ceremonies in preparation for planting, harvesting, and other events in the agricultural cycle and marked the all-important spring and fall equinox celebrations.

take two thousand men a week to build a palisade. But it probably took much longer.[9]

Some useful numbers also help us grasp the enormous effort that goes into making a structure the size of Monks Mound with human labor. This pharaonic enterprise required carrying 14,666,666 baskets, each filled with 1.5 cubic feet of dirt, weighing about fifty-five pounds each, for a total of 22 million cubic feet. For comparison, an average pickup truck holds 96 cubic feet, so it would take 229,166 pickup loads to bring the dirt to the site. If thirty people each carried eight baskets of earth a day, the job would take 167 years.[10] Various scholars have calculated time and labor estimates that differ widely, and we do know that the mounds usually were built not all at once but in a series of stages, sometimes over many years.

In addition to the four palisades, more than a hundred mounds, and five woodhenges, there were many other public buildings—granaries, the palace-temple of the chief, and the residences of other members of the elite. Erecting a woodhenge was complicated; it involved digging large bathtub-shaped foundation holes, aligning and measuring, and coordinating the work of pulling the posts upright (fig. 53). Large work crews were also assigned to level the plazas, filling in the swales and tamping the surface smooth.

It is clear that organizational control was a vital part of Cahokia society.[11] Archaeologist Timothy R. Pauketat supports the view that the Cahokia public works were more than symbols of religious beliefs in the powers of the cosmos: "Cahokian monuments it seems, to be monuments, required the regular mobilization of community labor, no doubt a means of perpetuating both elite control of community labor and the common perception that elite caretakers were necessary for the very existence of the community."[12]

Archaeologist Rinita Dalan continues the argument persuasively:

*Delayed returns associated with agriculture necessitate the establishment of a stable and cooperative labor pool . . . . The communal construction and use of mounds, plazas and other earthen features would have provided a means of creating and perpetuating social relations, and establishing and maintaining the labor force necessary for large-scale agricultural pursuits. The durability of this construction and its attendant message of group permanence would have assured a commitment to place and to the transformation, both social and ecological, of the landscape . . . .*

*Monks Mound and the Grand Plaza were clearly critical in the definition and creation of a large integrated community . . . simultaneously emphasizing the importance of the ruling hierarchy and the masses. The large, accessible plaza, which appears to have been capable of accommodating the resident population and more, provided a centralized location for ritual activities and served as a collective representation of the group. In contrast, the mounds represented an intricate system in which the relationships of different community and polity groups were ordered. The power of the chief was manifested in a mound that stood above all others. The power of the center was expressed in the profusion of its mounds.[13]*

In this way powerful chiefs and their affiliated ruling class could perpetuate their control and position.

By associating themselves with the power of the sky they provided celestial legitimacy for their status, and by erecting a monumental city around them they perpetuated the belief system and their own place at the top of the social, religious, and political hierarchy. In addition, the system ensured public safety.

In other words, the chief at Cahokia appropriated the celestial cosmology that ordered the religious beliefs of his people to strengthen the social hierarchy he headed. Melvin L. Fowler summed it up well:

*The creation of a sacred landscape is accomplished through the building of monumental constructions within, or near, a specific community. These sacred landscapes serve as the focal point of ceremonies in the ritual calendar in which "chiefs acted as gods on earth connected to cosmic forces."[14]*

*The astronomical connotations of woodhenges and other constructions at Cahokia belong to the vocabulary of consolidated political power during the decades preceding Cahokia's Emergent Mississippian era. Because authority in this community was always in contention, the community was stabilized through the use of symbols which legitimized the status of the elite. The construction of mounds, post circles, and plazas consumed labor on a massive scale. Through civic construction, Cahokia's elite created highly visible expressions of the power that mobilized that labor in the first place. These displayed the social structure of Cahokia with daily reminders that no one residing in the city, or visiting it, could ignore, for they defined the geographical, social and political landscape with architectural spectacle . . . .*

*The greater Cahokia site . . . relates the hierarchy of the social structure to the architecture of the cosmos. Through mythical ancestors and celestial divinities, the elite allied themselves with the power of the sky. Plazas located at the cardinal directions link the architecture of Cahokia to the architecture of the heavens, providing celestial legitimacy for social stratification and elite ranking. The plan of Cahokia is a portrait of Cahokia society.[15]*

*. . . A complex community like Cahokia establishes its territorial claims and prerogatives, then, by operating symbolically as a miniaturization of the cosmos, it conforms itself with the topographical features of the sacred landscape by making its layout a template of cosmic order. This usually means that celestial events, which reveal cosmic order, are in one way or another incorporated into the design. Cardinal orientation, seasonal solar alignment, and calendric ritual all may play a role.[16]*

We have seen the cosmological legacy the Mississippians inherited from their predecessors—for example, the solar calendar at Poverty Point—and we know there are historical analogues of their beliefs in the Amerindian tribes that came after them. The interpretation of Cahokia as a symbolic microcosm seems reasonable at this stage of our understanding.

## A Shared Vision

The creation of such a mammoth civic and sacred landscape was possible only because everyone at Cahokia shared the same belief and the same vision. The religious, social, political, agricultural, and even personal all found expression in a work of landscape architecture that gave people's existence structure, meaning, and a dimension of significance it would not otherwise have had. It has remained unrivaled in North America ever since.

### ORDINARY LIFE IN A SACRED LANDSCAPE ABOUT A.D. 1000

On an ordinary day in Cahokia, life for the average citizen moved at a slower pace than when there was a fes-

tival. As the lower rim of the sun cleared the horizon and there was enough light to work, people emerged from their houses and began the day's labor. Their place in the larger scheme was so familiar and accepted that the constant reminders along the path through the mounds and plazas scarcely needed notice. It all went without saying. A crew of kinfolk assembled to build a house for a newly married couple. Half of the men busied themselves digging a trench one to two feet deep all around their rectangular plan, about twelve by sixteen feet. The others built a frame of wooden poles to insert in each of the four trenches. When both jobs were done, the two crews joined together to erect the frames and fill the trench foundations with dirt. Then they lashed the corner poles together with cordage of some kind and began framing the roof (fig. 54). Although the illustration shows a slanting roof, which most research supports, Nelson Reed believes the roofs were bent-pole construction, which would have given a more domelike appearance.

Nearby another crew was finishing a larger house for a member of the elite. The workers picked up a supply of handwoven cattail or reed mats to cover both the interior and exterior walls of the house and large bunches of prairie grasses to thatch the roof. On rare occasions, for extra protection against the elements or for special buildings, they applied a stuccolike mixture of clay and grass (called daub) over the walls, which was interwoven with saplings (wattle), creating wattle-and-daub construction. The new house was snug and warm in the winter and insulated against the heat of the sun in summer.

All construction at Cahokia was done with variations on these same techniques, even public buildings such as council lodges, granaries, saunalike sweat lodges, menstrual huts, marketplace ramadas, and charnel houses for preparing and storing the bodies of the dead elite. (Most ordinary people at Cahokia were

Fig. 54. A versatile construction technique. Most buildings at Cahokia were variations on the pole-and-thatch method. Frames of wooden poles were set in trenches and lashed together; the trenches were filled and the roof framework was erected; then the sides were covered with cattail or reed mats and the roof with thatch.

buried in cemeteries.) Even the largest structure ever built, the home of the great chief at the top of Monks Mound, measuring 104 feet by 48 feet (5,000 square feet), was probably erected by this method. The posts of the stockades were also embedded in trench foundations.

On certain occasions of renewal, the Cahokians would ceremonially scoop out clay, sand, and gumbo (another type of clay) for various stages in the erection or reconstruction of mounds and plazas. As they carried the dirt in baskets on their backs from the borrow pits to the construction site, the ceremony of building

a mound was probably directed by a priest (or a priest-architect or priest-engineer) who oversaw the shaping of the earth into three forms—ridge-topped, rounded or conical, and platform mounds. At the same time, the priest watched carefully to ensure the proper alternation of different materials to ensure long-term endurance of the mounds: sand and silt for drainage, clay or gumbo for stability (fig. 55).

Platform mounds were often used as bases for buildings, elevating their occupants above everyday life and protecting these buildings made of organic materials from the dangers of water damage on the flood-

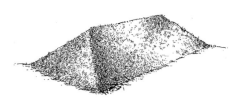

RIDGETOP

CONICAL

PLATFORM

Fig. 55. Unity and variety. More than 120 mounds were built at Cahokia, but there were only three shapes: ridge-top, rounded or conical, and platform. The repetition of geometric forms gives unity to the whole, while the different silhouettes give variety.

plain. Platform mounds range in height from a few tenths of a foot to over one hundred feet in Monks Mound, which covers more than fourteen acres—the largest platform mound in the Mississippian tradition and the largest prehistoric totally earth structure in the Western Hemisphere. Even if we include pyramids that used stone in their construction, Monks Mound is the third largest pyramid in the Western Hemisphere: only Mexico's Pyramid of the Sun at Teotihuacán and the pyramid at Cholula are larger.

Rounded or conical mounds sometimes rose as high as forty feet and ranged in diameter from twenty to two hundred feet. Few of these mounds have been explored, and our knowledge of them is limited. Many of these are in fact rectangular platform mounds.

Four of the ridge-topped mounds at Cahokia are especially intriguing. Three were placed at the periphery of the community and marked the end points of the diamond-shaped boundary and its axes, which Fowler interpreted as the city plan of Cahokia (fig. 56). Workers building these mounds no doubt knew they were destined for burials, as excavations of three of them have subsequently shown. One puzzle remains, however: their size varies greatly. Powell Mound, the largest ridge-topped mound at the site, on the western edge, was 310 feet long, 180 feet wide, and 40 feet high before its destruction (discussed in chapter 6). Several burials were uncovered during its demolition. Mound 72, the diminutive ridge-topped mound excavated by Fowler, was only six feet high, yet it contained nearly three hundred human skeletons, among them mass human sacrifices including the four headless and handless men mentioned earlier. It also held the skeleton of an early Cahokian chief (see chapter 7).[17] As they carried their baskets of dirt, the workers must have been well aware of the meaning of the mounds they were building.

When spring came, many of the residents at Cahokia put their hoes over their shoulders and set out for the fields. A large workforce was needed to plant the large crops necessary to feed the growing population. At planting time and later at harvestime every able-bodied person was helping to produce corn. But that work occupies only part of each season. Avoiding idleness and keeping such a large labor force produc-

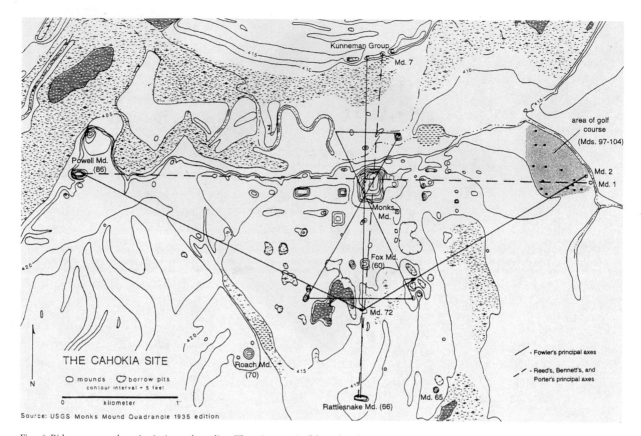

The Cahokia Site map labels:

Kunneman Group
Md. 7

area of golf course (Mds. 97-104)

Powell Md. (86)

Monks Md.

Md. 2
Md. 1

Fox Md. (60)

Md. 72

THE CAHOKIA SITE

○ mounds ◯ borrow pits
contour interval = 5 feet

Roach Md. (70)

Rattlesnake Md. (66)

Md. 65

- Fowler's principal axes
- Reed's, Bennett's, and Porter's principal axes

N

0          kilometer          1

Source: USGS Monks Mound Quadrangle 1935 edition

Fig. 56. Ridge-top mounds are intriguing and puzzling. Three (2, 66, 86) of the eight ridge-top mounds at Cahokia were at the edges of the site and gave archaeologist Melvin L. Fowler a clue to its city plan and to his great discoveries at Mound 72.

tively occupied were paramount in maintaining a stable society. House construction, mound building, plaza leveling, and other public works filled the workers' hours with meaningful labor the rest of the year.

What about other kinds of work for ordinary citizens? Hunting and gathering remained time-consuming tasks. In addition, making weapons, pipes, containers, mats, and other handcrafted items gave everyone plenty to do. After hunting, strong younger men would butcher their prey in the forest, or sometimes they would bring home a whole deer to flay, carve up, and prepare for use (fig. 57). Nearly all parts of the deer could be useful—skin, meat, bones, and sinews.

INGENUITY WITH NATURAL
MATERIALS

The Cahokians made needles of animal bones and ornaments from mica. They fashioned turtle shells into bowls, combs, and rattles; the talons, bones, and feathers of hawks and turkeys became tools, necklaces, capes, and headdresses. Snake rattles and bear claws appeared as status symbols. Freshwater pearls and copper were frequently used as adornments. Pigments such as red and yellow ocher, hematite, and galena were processed to make paints, and vegetable dyes were often used for clothing. The plentiful wood was fash-

Fig. 57. Waste not, want not. The Cahokians used nearly all parts of the deer.

ioned into tools, implement handles, canoes, war clubs, and later bows and arrow shafts. Tanning was a developed craft.

*Rawhide—the result of stretching, scraping clean, and drying a skin—made strong bindings, but was too stiff to be worn. In order to make garments, the Cahokians simmered rawhide in [deer] brain soup, and then massaged more of the greasy organ into the hide to further soften and protect it. They stretched and dried this tanned hide and rubbed it with smooth stones, finally smoking it over a smouldering fire to assure that it would remain supple even after getting wet.[18]*

No animal skin was wasted. Presumably

*possums, bears, rabbits, and raccoons were made into bags, blankets, robes, and other items of clothing . . . . [They used the antlers of deer] for arrow points, ceremonial headdresses, flintknapping tools, and pins for garments and the hair. They made scrapers, hammers, ornaments, fishhooks, needles, awls, and weaving tools from bones. Hooves became medicine, glue and rattles and sinew served as bindings.[19]*

Women traditionally spent much of their day in farming, food preparation, and other domestic tasks.

The tender sweet corn of summer was delicious grilled, boiled, or roasted. The ripe corn of autumn had to be dried, to be kept as kernels or ground into cornmeal and stored for the long winter months. Among the most versatile of foods, cornmeal could be made into bread and cakes or used as a thickening in stews, with meat, fish, pumpkin, squash, and sunflower seeds sometimes added. Other seeds, nuts, berries, tubers, and leaves were also gathered when available. Grinding grains and nuts occupied many hours, and time left over went into other household tasks such as making clothing or caring for children.

Some women became skilled potters, producing cookware and storage vessels of remarkable strength by adding bits of burned and crushed mussel shell or limestone or broken pottery (grog) as tempering agents, which reduced shrinkage and cracking as the clay dried before firing (fig. 58). The mixture was then kneaded and rolled into long ropes, which were coiled, modeled and smoothed into a wide variety of shapes—bowls, plates, beakers, pans, bottles, jars, and even figurines. After a long drying period, the "green" pots were fired in an open pit.

### TOOLS OF ALL MATERIALS

The Mississippian men used granite, basalt, diorite, quartzite, and other rocks to make axes and the chunkey stones used in their game. They were skilled flint knappers, fashioning arrow points, knives, drills, picks, hoes, maces, and many other tools out of chert, a flint-like stone available from quarries in southeastern Missouri and southern Illinois. Complete tools were also imported from workshops in southern Illinois.

The Mississippi basin and the lakes and streams of the American Bottom were full of freshwater clams or mussels. After eating the shellfish, the Cahokians made scrapers, spoons, and even small garden hoes out of the shells. Some were burned and crushed to be used in tempering clay. Some mollusks would yield freshwater pearls. Whelk shells with especially beautiful shapes were imported from the Gulf of Mexico and made into beads, pendants, and other ornaments for the elite, who probably controlled their redistribution even down to the lower classes.[20]

The prairies nearby provided grasses for thatch used in roofing all the Mississippians' enclosed structures (fig. 59). They also

*made fine baskets and fabrics from the inner bark of the cedar tree; woven floor mats from the flexible stems of bulrushes; and sewn mats that covered walls, roofs and doorways from cattail leaves. They spun animal fur and silky*

Fig. 58. Woman's work included making pots and other hand-coiled vessels.

Fig. 59. A Mississippian ramada beside two houses. Shaded, open-air structures made life pleasant in midwestern summers, and the snug construction of the houses was welcome during cool nights in all seasons, as these reconstructions at Angel mounds, Indiana, show.

*fibers from plants like milkweed and dogbane into thread which they used to fingerweave sashes and other fabrics. The inner bark of basswood, ash, cedar, willow, and hickory were twisted into cordage. Braided strips of rawhide made especially strong cord and bowstrings, and, because of the tendency of rawhide to shrink as it dries, it created a tight attachment between tools and handles.[21]*

The level of craftsmanship of the artifacts found at Cahokia points to artisans who made objects for use in ritual ceremonies. Since items made at Cahokia have been found all over the Mississippi basin, there was also a vigorous trade network. The exchange of goods often accompanies festival days or religious feasts, and we may imagine that at the fall equinox the plazas at Cahokia were filled with dense crowds (fig. 60).

Some of the goods exchanged were also made of wood, ubiquitous at Cahokia. "In addition to providing the raw materials for four stockades, five woodhenges, and thousands of buildings, trees were used in the manufacture of tools, weapons, handles, baskets, bowls, oils, dyes, foodstuffs, and canoes. Without wood for fuel, warm winters, cooked food, and fired pottery would have been impossible." Many kinds of trees were available, including oak, poplar, tulip, and cottonwood. Osage orange, ash, and hickory trees all had "the right combination of toughness and flexibility" for bows . . . .Straight willow, native cane and maple shoots worked best for arrow shafts, which were tipped with points made of antler, wood, or stone, and then feathered to assure straight flight."[22]

## Why Was Cahokia Abandoned?

No other issue in scholarly circles is thornier than the question of Cahokia's abandonment. Why did the Mississippians leave this splendid constellation of mounds, buildings, plazas, council houses, lodges, palisades, and woodhenges behind them? Why does the site show no signs of human habitation from about 1400 to about 1650, when Illini Indians moved into the

Fig. 60. Bantering, bargaining, and buying. Trade was vigorous on festival days, when dense crowds from the countryside came to Cahokia.

area? Did circumstances force the Mississippians to leave, or did they choose to take advantage of better resources in another place?

Until new evidence is uncovered, we might content ourselves with a simple answer: we do not know why Cahokia was abandoned. But being content with this would impoverish our understanding, because in the midst of the various speculations advanced by the experts lie valuable insights into the nature of Mississippian life.

### CLIMATIC CHANGES AND ENVIRONMENTAL STRESS?

A major change in midwestern climate about 1250 may have caused considerable stress in Cahokia. The overall temperature of the region cooled during this infamous Pacific Climate Episode. The traumatic weather some-times brought hard frost in late spring, killing fragile young corn plants, or in early autumn, icing over sensitive crops such as squash. The climate change sometimes also shortened the growing season, ruining the harvest or resulting in smaller yields. This change affected both the cultivated crops and the wild plants that nourished the local fauna, further depleting the protein supply. Apparently this period of climatic change was also worsened by devilishly shifting rainy seasons. As William R. Iseminger put it, "The evil twins Flood and Drought alternated their devastating work."

Some scholars suggest that smog may have become a tremendous problem because the increase in population at Cahokia's height brought thousands of campfires burning day and night.[23] Others dismiss this possibility because the open terrain was unlikely to contain the smoke.

## DEFORESTATION AND AN UNINTENDED SUICIDE?

William I. Woods, a scholar at Southern Illinois University at Edwardsville, suggests that

*the great detriment to Cahokia was the very population density that originally gave it a transforming energy. When thousands of people lived in a small area and relied heavily upon corn to survive they had to clear many nearby forests. Clearing had to increase even more to supply wood for houses, defensive stockades, and heating and cooking fuel. As they felled trees by the thousands, moving upstream on both creeks [Cahokia and Canteen], the deforested land began to erode. When it rained runoff increased siltation and clogged bottomland streams causing flooding even during the summer, ruining the corn crop. When their leaders could not cope with the increasing disasters, social collapse followed famine. Over exploitation of wood caused "an unintended suicide" of the great metropolis . . . .*

*Perhaps the population felt ill-served by their priests, abandoned by their Gods, and, when they survived and had the strength, sought protection and sustenance elsewhere.*[24]

## NUTRITIONAL STRESS?

Other experts have suggested nutritional explanations. Successful corn agriculture, the foundation of the Mississippian civilization, unfortunately also had hidden negative consequences. Corn, although high in carbohydrates, is low in protein. A heavy reliance on corn, without sufficient meat, causes malnutrition and all its attendant illnesses. There is evidence that some people suffered from dietary stress during lean winter months.[25] Physical anthropologists have found that the bones of the elite and commoners at some Mississippian sites often showed differences owing to different diets, with the elite having had the benefits of more animal protein.

## HEALTH AND SANITATION PROBLEMS?

So many people living in close proximity probably also fostered conditions that spread diseases.[26] A dense population, especially one whose sanitation system depends on moving creek water, is more prone to intestinal diseases. Disposing of human waste and other garbage and the pollution of the water supply must have plagued Cahokians as they do residents of densely populated modern cities. Many human remains also showed signs of crippling arthritis.[27]

Sociologically, the problems of "urban sink" or "urban stress" might also have besieged Cahokia, promoting riots and civil unrest.

CONFLICT?

Although there is no consensus on this point, some archaeologists have found evidence for warfare around Cahokia: burials with weapons, burned buildings, sacrificial victims, bodies found with embedded arrowheads or smashed skulls. The most convincing evidence is the erection of the four successive high defensive stockades or palisades at Cahokia, each with evenly spaced bastions for archers. Of course these could have been used for maintaining civil order, a form of special protection for the elite who lived within the stockade, but this in itself signals civil unrest owing to stress.

Some people speculate that because of their dense population Cahokians were forced to intrude on the lands of their neighbors, and that might have been the cause of warfare: "Mississippian farmers did not manage water, either through irrigation or field drainage. Instead of expanding into areas where water control would have been necessary, they had to compete for the best alluvial land. The evidence of warfare is strong for an area that might appear to modern farmers to have been rich in productive land. The stringent land requirements . . . led to competition for the best fields."[28] A Late Mississippian shell gorget suggests a martial society (fig. 61).

In any case, it seems clear that eventually the Cahokians began to develop new ways of coping with life's stresses and dispersed to more viable environ-

Fig. 61. Two Late Mississippian birdmen. Stressing the powerful character of falcons, the two birdmen shown on this engraved shell gorget may have symbolized spirit guardians or high-status Mississippian warriors.

ments.[29] According to this theory, overestimating the abundance of their unparalleled environment, the Cahokians ultimately overstepped the bounds that kept the people in balance with nature and with each other. When natural forces like colder climate and traumatic weather added unprecedented stresses and the threads of their tattered urban fabric fell apart, people deserted by the thousands. Without the vibrant energy of their center, the Cahokian civilization collapsed.

ALTERNATIVE EXPLANATION

Some recent scholars, among them one anonymous reviewer of this book, believe that

*it is a real put-down of the Indians that Cahokia's depopulation and abandonment should be viewed from a Eurocentric perspective as a decline or fall when it could just as easily and more accurately be portrayed not as a tragic finale but as an enormously successful adaptive strategy to take advantage of newly available resources—primarily a new variety of more pest- and drought-resistant corn with a shorter growing season plus an increase in the population of buffaloes west of the Mississippi (none were available in Illinois until about two centuries after Cahokia's abandonment).*

At the "Contested Grounds" symposium at the Chicago Historical Society in May 1999, historian Eliott West argued persuasively that a typical misconception about Indian lifestyle was that it was static, whereas in fact Native American history is a succession of brilliant and creative adaptations to changing circumstances and to the invention of new technologies such as the spear, the atlatl, and the bow and arrow.

The anonymous reviewer also argues:

*The first two cities in Illinois were Cahokia and Nauvoo, each in its day a sacred city on the Mississippi River. The abandonment of Nauvoo and the Great Trek westward to Utah are regarded by Mormon historians as adventurous preludes to greater things to come. Both Cahokia and Nauvoo have been the objects of archaeological investigations and on-site programs of interpretation. Why should the abandonment of Cahokia be represented as a collapse or death rather than as a well-considered trade-off for new options available to Indians of the time, successfully leading to ways of life familiar from later history? When white Americans voluntarily left their homes in the east and settled on isolated homesteads on the Plains, historians spoke of it as the unfolding of America's Manifest Destiny. Were the heels of Cahokia's Indian inhabitants so round that they could only topple backward when facing the winds of history?*

At present, historians must deal with lack of hard evidence about Cahokia's abandonment and entertain several conflicting explanations. Perhaps the reasons were multiple, some combination of the possibilities above that we cannot yet discern.

## Summary

Looking back at Cahokia at the height of its growth as a city, we can understand why the Mississippian people beheld their known universe with wonder, why they had the emblem of the circle and crossed double lines emblazoned on their sacred pottery, carved in their stoneware, and perhaps even tattooed on the shoulders of their warriors. By their own efforts, carrying millions of basketloads of earth on their backs, they created a cosmic city, a place so majestic that it would be deemed a World Heritage Site a thousand years later. The Native American past is at the heart of the changes that would occur in the future. In the centuries between, we know from historical evidence that this same site filled the imaginations of immigrants from the Old World with very different ideas.

Europeans observed their known universe with scientific instruments and recorded their explorations on maps, with exact measurements of latitude and longitude. Their geometry was based on a calculated grid where X marked the spot of frontier fortifications, fur-trading posts, or friendly missions. What happened at one moment in modern Europe (after about 1670) could change the landscape in the New World a short time later.

FIG. 62. FRENCH EXPLORERS, SOLDIERS, AND MISSIONARIES. NEW ARRIVALS MINGLE WITH THE NATIVE AMERICANS IN THE NEW FRENCH COLONY, AS DEPICTED IN THIS PAINTING, *HENRI DE TONTI, FOUNDER OF PEORIA, AT PIMETOUI, 1691–93.*

**4**
▽

# French Explorers, Trappers, Priests, and Monks

Globalization was already a reality in the seventeenth century. Events in Europe could alter the face of the New World with ever-increasing intensity, and Cahokia was no exception. Circumstances in the 1660s were right for expanding French territories, and Louis XIV wanted to increase his wealth. When a French Canadian visitor, Pierre Boucher, brought a glowing letter from the governor in Quebec speaking of the new territory as "a land of golden opportunities for agriculture, industry and commerce," Louis's zeal was aroused. Hoping for substantial revenues from his new colony, perhaps as great as those Spain was amassing from her New World possessions, Louis granted the visitor a three-hour audience.[1] This conversation partially determined the fate of a large portion of North America for the next two hundred years. Ultimately the French also changed the face of the Cahokia Mounds.

As the king became more favorably disposed toward the development of French possessions in the New World, his officers and bureaucrats in Canada began to gather information from voyageurs, fur traders, and friendly Indians about the wide world beyond Quebec (fig. 63). Galvanizing all the discussions was talk of the Father of Waters, a major waterway somewhere to the southwest. This mighty river, if it could be found, would be of immense strategic importance, helping to secure the new country militarily and providing the economic link that would bring the wealth of the rich country back to Quebec and on to France.

Fig. 63. Illinois at the heart of New France. French settlers followed the waterways south to Illinois, where they wrote glowing letters home lauding the countryside as a "terrestrial paradise," with "wheat as fine as that in France," "all kinds of fruit with very good flavor," and "in the prairies many animals."

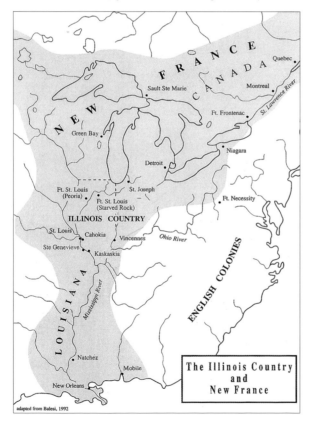

The Illinois Country
and
New France

adapted from Balesi, 1992

When the king in France nods in the affirmative, the ambassador in his turn nods, the provincial governor nods, and so on down the line. From that moment on, explorers found a more favorable atmosphere in official circles.

## The Marquette-Jolliet Voyage

When Louis Jolliet offered to lead an expedition in 1672 through the Great Lakes in search of the Mississippi River, his plans soon received official approval, although no government funds were available to help him. But the retiring provincial governor, Jean Talon, recommended to his successor, Louis de Buade, Count Frontenac, that Jolliet be granted a royal license with fur-trading rights. This did the trick. Jolliet was able to raise the money for outfitting his expedition from private investors, entrepreneurs seeking new wealth from the fur trade. When everything was in order Jolliet set out on the voyage that made history.

Luckily for the future of the colony (and for historians), Jolliet was no common adventurer. Educated by the Jesuits, he was a highly cultivated person. An accomplished musician, he was organist and harpsichordist for the cathedral of Quebec and professor of music at the seminary there as well as a fur trader with an understanding of cartography and a gift for Indian languages. His schooling had included study in France, where he took courses in hydrography. At the age of twenty-seven Jolliet was also remarkable for knowing his own limitations. He knew he lacked sufficient experience with the Indian tribes that lived farther south. To secure the services of a priest with more knowledge of the Great Lakes, Jolliet used his connections as a former pupil of the Jesuit college of Quebec to gain the support of the church. It worked. He obtained a letter from the superior of the Jesuits of New France ordering Father Jacques Marquette to join the expedition when it reached him at his mission, St. Ignace, on the Straits of Mackinac. Thus it was that a French priest joined a French Canadian fur trader and five other Frenchmen on a voyage to discover the Mississippi. Later joined by two Miami scouts, they at last left the Wisconsin River and entered the valley of the Mississippi by canoe in 1673, the first Europeans in recorded history to set foot on the river's upper banks. They had found the great continental waterway.

Ultimately Jolliet and Marquette ventured as far south as Arkansas. Perhaps they were disappointed that the river did not flow west into the Pacific Ocean after all, but emptied into the Gulf of Mexico. No doubt they also feared hostile encounters with Spaniards and unknown Indians farther downriver, but at any rate they turned back before reaching New Orleans. On their way down and again on their return voyage they might have been able to see the Cahokia Mounds, though there is no mention of them in their reports. But their cartography (figs. 64 and 65) figures prominently in the history of Cahokia.[2]

### THE POWER OF IMAGES: REASSURING MAPS

The explorers' maps must have stirred up the wanderlust and perhaps also the courage of another young Frenchman who had moved to Canada: René-Robert Cavelier de La Salle. With the success of Jolliet's explorations to back him up, La Salle also went to see Louis XIV in Paris in 1678. Louis nodded yes again, and this time he found some funds of his own to help finance the journey. A letter dated May 12 authorizes La Salle "to work at discovering the western parts of our country of New France." In the report he sent later to the French minister Jean-Baptiste Colbert, La Salle mentions the Cahokia Illini (the contemporary Indi-

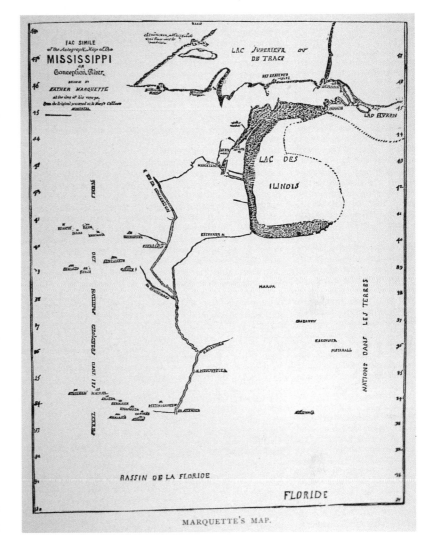

Fig. 64. Father Marquette's guide to the Mississippi. After the explorers Marquette and Jolliet discovered the Mississippi River in 1673, Marquette drew this sketchy map.

ans, not the Cahokians of the Mississippian period) for the first time in the annals of European discovery.[3] Perhaps just as important as La Salle's laying claim to the new territory was the contingent of French men from his expedition who stayed behind on the banks of the Mississippi.

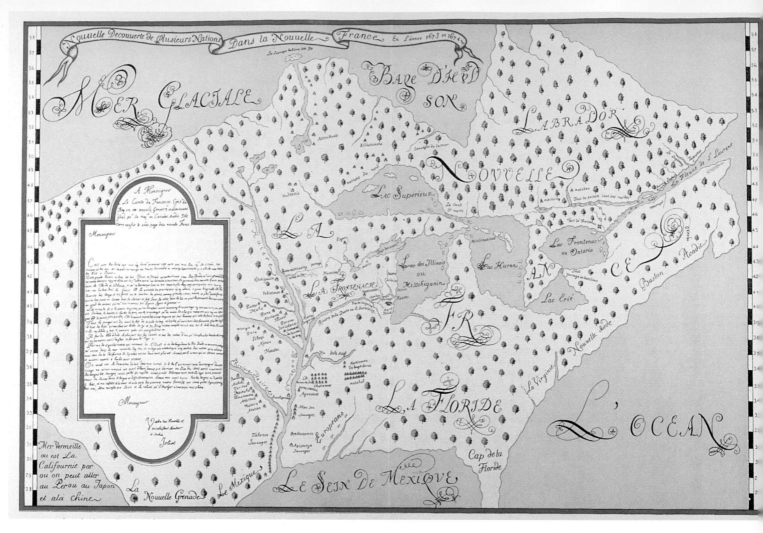

Fig. 65. Jolliet's understanding of the waterways of Illinois. A later map of 1674 shows the routes of passage in more detail. It named the essential rivers, such as the "Rivière de la Divine, ou L'Outrelaize," now the Illinois. Although broad in its conception, it contained the basic information needed for those traveling by canoe.

## La Salle's Men and Lasting Bonds with New France

When some members of his expedition who remained in New France married local Indian women, their new unions solidified the French-Indian relationship that was to be the human foundation of the future colony. The first of these men was Michel Accault, or Ako, who married the daughter of an Indian chief; another was Jacques La Violette. Several others later followed suit.[4] The wives and the numerous offspring of these men usually became Christians, further strengthening the presence of the Roman Catholic Church in Illinois life.

In 1699, the next to last year of the seventeenth century, the superiors of the French Seminary of Foreign Missions decided to establish a mission to the Tamaroa and the Cahokia Indians near an Indian settlement a few miles south of the Cahokia Mounds. At that time ninety families lived there. Thus the village of Cahokia was founded first as an Indian mission. Some French settlers did live across the river at Rive des Pères.

The French badly needed their Indian neighbors, not only to procure furs, but also to provide manpower and other services. Added to this was the local missionaries' zeal for saving the souls of the native population, prompting many letters to their superiors in Quebec. The more conversions, they reasoned, the greater the strength of the colony.

After their conversion the Indians were usually incorporated into local French society. It is true that unless they were married to French men, the newly converted were usually at the bottom of the social pyramid, just as peasants were in the old country. The Indians lived separately but gradually incorporated French ways, such as keeping chickens and growing wheat. Although living apart, the Indians were considered members of the French hierarchy, part of the larger whole. By contrast, the English on the East Coast moved the Indians out of their society, excluding them completely except for enlisting their help as warriors in military conflicts.

At the turn of the century the French and the Indians lived in relative harmony on the banks of the Mississippi. This peaceful period has been neglected by historians until recently. The different worlds of the Europeans and the Native Americans overlapped. Within the intersecting circles of their lives, which Richard White calls "the middle ground," people on both sides tried to accommodate those on the other side, and between them they creatively developed new social customs.

*The middle ground is the place in between: in between cultures, peoples, and in between empires and the nonstate world of villages. It is a place where many of the North American subjects and allies of empires lived. It is the area between the historical foreground of European invasion and occupation and the background of Indian defeat and retreat.*

*On the middle ground diverse peoples adjust their differences through what amounts to a process of creative, and often expedient, misunderstandings. People try to persuade others who are different from themselves by appealing to what they perceive to be the values and practices of those others. They often misinterpret and distort both the values and the practices of those they deal with, but from these misunderstandings arise new meanings and through them new practices—the shared meanings and practices of the middle ground.*

*This accommodation took place because for long periods of time in large parts of the colonial world whites could neither dictate to Indians nor ignore them. Whites needed Indians as allies, as partners in exchange, as sexual partners, as friendly neighbors.[5]*

A common Native American saying, for example, decreed that young unmarried women were "masters of their own bodies." This was usually taken to justify sexual experimentation, but in the late seventeenth century Jesuit teaching among the Illinois stressed the cult of the Virgin Mary, with its emphasis on chastity. The presence of a powerful female religious figure attracted a large congregation of young women and older girls, who then reinterpreted the old saying to justify sexual abstinence. A sudden rise in interracial marriages in the 1690s, because there were no French women, may be partially explained by this confluence of customs. The fur traders also needed to establish kinship connections with the Indians to remain in the territory after the French abandoned most of their western posts in the same period.[6]

For their part, the French adopted Native American gift-giving to strengthen alliances, smoking tobacco as a token of peace, carrying a calumet as a safe-conduct pass, wearing moccasins and leggings, and adopting Indian hunting techniques and wild food uses.

By the next generation, however, cracks began to appear in this mutually satisfying accommodation. As more French immigrants arrived, the tensions of living together (or side by side) mounted. The French resented the Indians' animals wandering over their fields and continued to build the tall palisades that were a part of their tradition (fig. 66). The Indians resented the whites' fences. When we remember that property rights were held almost sacred by Europeans, who had crossed an ocean and half a continent to own their own homes, we can better understand the six-foot wooden fences they erected around their house lots and their fencing in their common fields to protect these precious pieces of earth in the New World. But the Indians' belief was just the opposite. To the Indian population the communal nature of land was a sacred principle. To them hunting rights and communal access to the earth's bountiful grains, fruits, and nuts meant their very survival, the difference between life and death. Many years later the Indian chief Black Hawk despaired of trying to get the whites to understand that land cannot be bought or sold because the earth belongs to everyone. In the midst of all this conflict the missionaries at the Catholic church in the village of Cahokia celebrated mass and prayed for a peaceful resolution of the troubles that seemed to be erupting with ever greater frequency.

By the next generation the motives of the larger French community changed. Profitable trade and the conversion of the Indians to Christianity were no longer enough. Perhaps the French inhabitants tired of being in the minority, wearied of the pressures of having the odds against them all the time. They may even have looked enviously at their European counterparts in New England and New Spain, where things were easier. More French people in the population would

Fig. 66. French traditions on the prairie. The new settlers brought many Old World architectural forms with them to Illinois, including the "Norman kick" in the roofline over the front porch, enclosing palisades, and gabled windows in the attic story, shown here on the first hospital in the Illinois country.

FRENCH EXPLORERS, TRAPPERS, PRIESTS, AND MONKS

mean more French companionship and more French society, with its appreciation of leavened bread, a glass of wine, and fine tableware. In short, the people now wanted full colonization.

New fears soon heightened that desire. Word of the massacre of French settlers in the lower Mississippi region and the revolt of the Natchez Indians in 1729 increased the mounting distrust between the French and their Indian neighbors. When French soldiers killed many of the Fox Indians, the old enemies of the Cahokia, it must have crossed the minds of some Cahokia that the fate of their enemies might one day be their own. It certainly occurred to the Peoria, who brought more accounts of French atrocities with them when they fled south to the Cahokia to escape the terrors of the Fox war. The Peoria immigrants also swelled the Cahokia population, and even the rich agricultural lands were strained to feed them all on such short notice. Unrest seemed inevitable, and indeed it came soon.

In 1721 the French civil authorities had appropriated four square leagues of land around the mission in the village of Cahokia. Ten years later, just two years after the Natchez massacre, the village priest, Father Jean-Paul Mercier (1694–1753), bought some more land from the Cahokia and cut it up into linear farm tracts or "long lots" for new French immigrants.

## Open Hostilities Sever French-Indian Relationships

The settlers faced a dilemma. On one hand, matters hardly favored further settlement. Father Mercier wrote telling his superiors that the Indians had become "contemptuous and insolent" toward the French—that "they have the idea that once the French are strong enough they will expel them from their own lands." On the other hand, without more French people the

Fig. 67. Military protection at Fort de Chartres. As hostilities between the Native Americans and the French settlers increased, the new colonists sought protection within the walls of the fort south of Cahokia. The framework of the old Government House, in the right foreground, has been reconstructed.

whole occupation of the valley was imperiled.[7] Just two years later, in May 1733, a Frenchman was killed in a dispute with an Indian. Hostilities erupted. Filled with the dread of another massacre, the French inhabitants fled for their lives, traveling under cover of darkness more than thirty miles south to ask for protection at Fort de Chartres (fig. 67). Overnight the village of Cahokia was utterly deserted. One murder led to others, and matters escalated. From behind his thick stone walls, the besieged commandant, St. Ange, pleaded for reinforcements.

*Monsieur, you will permit me to tell you that this post needs a strong garrison and some very firm officers. The Illinois are the most restless nation that I have known. Each day they do everything in their power to cause new alarm. They are persuaded or want to appear so that we*

*want to destroy them in retaliation for the Frenchman
who was killed last year at Cahokia, and for the wrong
which they have done to the inhabitants by killing their
animals . . . .I have no drummer here and I need very
much one or two good sargeants. I have only one on whom
I can count and he is commanding the detachment which
I have placed at Cahokia.[8]*

Later that same year a new commandant, Pierre
Dartaguiette, came up the river from New Orleans
with two companies of soldiers to suppress the rebel-
lious Cahokia. His superiors in New Orleans wrote
home to France that Dartaguiette had made presents
to all the Indian villages except Cahokia and that "he
has forbidden this rebel nation to present itself to him
as long as they have not repaired the wrongs which
they have done. He has even decided in order to re-
press the insults of these savages and to bring them to
reason to build a fort in their post where he has put a
garrison of twenty men."[9]

Increasing hostilities finally prompted the local
French officials to draw up a plan to "remove" all the
Indians twelve leagues to the north, from the French
village of Cahokia to the site of the ancient Cahokia
Mounds. The local priests offered to build a new
church and parish house in the relocated village in exchange for being given the "abandoned" Indian lands
to repay them for the expense of erecting the new
buildings. Their request was granted. To further encourage the movement north, Father Mercier gave the
Cahokia Indians trade goods and promised to have
their new fields plowed.

## A New Beginning

The attraction for both the Indians and the white missionary priest accompanying them was the new site.

Fig. 68. The first Christian outpost on the great Mississippian mound. With
its wooden cross elevated against the skyline, this little French chapel marked
the arrival of a new religion in the old Native American territory.

The imposing presence of the ancient mounds and the
great terraced pyramid of the Native Americans who
came before them must have inspired the souls of the
Indians. The site rivaled the cathedrals of Europe and
must have inspired the missionary. The rich agricultural land in the surrounding country appealed to
everyone. Of all the places for miles around, the abandoned mound complex resonated with past splendor
and the possibility of future magnificence, even if all
that the refugees and their French confessor could
manage to erect at first was a small chapel eighteen feet
by thirty on a small mound that marked the southwest
corner of the first terrace (fig. 68). The cross on top was
visible for miles, and the view from the galleries
stretched to infinity. In the remaining two acres of this
terrace there was still enough room for a small cluster
of houses.

Optimistic about his beginning in the new French
mission, in a letter dated May 21, 1735, Father Mercier
asked the seminary in Quebec to send him "fine cloth,
a retable, a crucifix, six candlesticks, six bouquets of artificial flowers in pots, a cross to serve in processions

and burials, a little banner with a picture of the Holy Family painted on it, a statue of the Holy Virgin, and some packets of candles." Although it was only a small sanctuary, the little chapel was given more importance by its location on the first terrace of the great pyramid. The third and fourth terraces above and behind the building thus served as an imposing background, heightening its monumentality in a setting already the highest place as far as the eye could see. It was perhaps the first building to be erected on the mound since the Mississippians left several hundred years earlier.

Archaeologists have uncovered the wall trenches and post molds that constituted the foundation of this chapel (fig. 69), so we know the exact dimensions of the ground plan.[10] From our more thorough knowledge of other local French chapels of the period we can figure out what the elevation looked like and estimate that the chapel was about eleven feet high under the beams.

The walls were made by a combination of two traditional French construction techniques: *poteaux en terre* and *poteaux sur sole,* posts placed directly in the wall trenches and posts resting on sill beams. (Limestone foundations were not used in the Illinois country until the eighteenth or nineteenth century.) The mud fill between the posts was a mortarlike mixture of clay and straw. Topping it all off was a thatched roof made of tall prairie grasses from the nearby bottoms that "looked well and lasted longer than shingles."[11]

Fig. 69. Archaeologists uncover the ground plan. From the discoveries at Monks Mound we know the exact dimensions of the floor of the original French chapel.

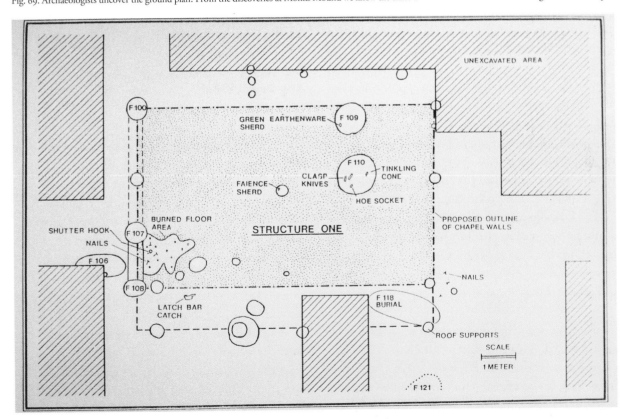

The chapel probably had two windows in its long sides and an entrance door on one short side on the west, to conform with centuries-old Christian practice of orienting the altar to the east, toward Jerusalem. Finally, two porches or galleries ran the full length of the long sides. The same roof covered the porches, which both provided shade and protected the sills from rain.

To the people who built and used the chapel, one of the most important considerations was defense. Sentinels keeping watch could see far in every direction. We know from the many domestic features and animal remains uncovered by William I. Woods in 1997–98 that people also lived and feasted on the first terrace. Both chapel and residents could be defended by firing down the steep slope on raiding parties attempting to storm the chapel and the adjacent settlement.

Aesthetics may also have played a part. To our eyes much of the charm of French colonial architecture is in the half-timbered walls and the taut line of the roof as it sweeps down over the galleries. Add to this the siting on the first terrace of a mound towering over one hundred feet and the seemingly infinite view from its precinct, and the spiritual responses the chapel inspired in the devout must have been profound. Perhaps at sunrise on the equinox reverberations of the old religion, like overtones in music, enhanced the emotions of newly converted Indians climbing the ramp to mass.

The little chapel and its missionary settlement endured for seventeen years, but toward the end of this time things began to fall apart. On March 28, 1752, the vicar general in Paris asked that another priest be sent to Cahokia.

*That mission has almost fallen, consisting of little more than a small French settlement . . . .all the Indian tribes being departed to go to the English . . . .On all sides it is surrounded by Indian tribes, and everyone that we lose is gained by the English. Religion is among the strongest mo-tives that tie the Indians to us . . . .I think, then, Monsieur, that there is no time to lose in reestablishing the mission little by little, sending this year at least one person; he could go to New Orleans and easily go up to Tamaroa [Cahokia] as the Jesuits go to their Illinois mission.*[12]

The little missionary colony did not receive a new priest, however, and in a few months most of the remaining Indian population died at the hands of the Fox. We know from an eyewitness account by an officer at Fort de Chartres that on June 6, 1752, a band of Sioux, Sauk, and Kickapoo, under the banner of the Fox, marched one thousand strong against the Cahokia and their Michigamea allies, "killing all they met." The attack was a deathblow to the settlement. The demise of the little French missionary chapel and its small colony of converts living on the great terraced pyramid was complete.

## The Death Knell

A small copper hand bell found by archaeologist Elizabeth Benchley may have sounded the death knell. The bell was uncovered near the right hand of a Cahokia Illini woman buried in a grave near the chapel. Although only eleven centimeters high, the little bell could easily be heard by neighbors on the first terrace. We know it was the custom of French priests in the Illinois country to delegate parts of ceremonies to their Indian converts. Perhaps it was this woman's duty to ring the bell to summon the community to services, or to call for the help that never came.

One of the many reasons help never came may have been that French power in the New World in general had begun to wane. Prelates in Paris, Quebec, and New Orleans and military men everywhere knew that France had already ceded part of Acadian

Canada to England in the 1748 treaty of Aix-la-Chapelle. Nearer at hand, colonists of every nationality knew that in such a vast new country control basically rested on relations with the Indians, where trade dominated.

Gradually British goods became better and cheaper than French goods, and Indian negotiators began to favor the British. More and more Indian tribes chose the English over the French. When the French and Indian War broke out in 1755 the fate of the French in Illinois was at stake. Eight years later it was all over. In the Treaty of Paris of 1763 the French ceded to England all of Louisiana east of the Mississippi except for New Orleans, which became Spanish. The territory west of the Mississippi also became Spanish.

On the other side of the great river from Cahokia, the town of St. Louis began to burgeon with Spanish-speaking merchants, soon joined by French immigrants who moved west across the river, preferring to live under Spanish rule in a Catholic country rather than submit to the Protestant English. With no civil authority either Indian or French, no ecclesiastical presence, and no community of people to tend it, the land around Cahokia Mounds languished. For a time the rich agricultural floodplains, the majestic mounds of the old Indian complex, and the dense forest bluffs were deserted, except perhaps for a few Indian stragglers and a lone Anglo-Saxon soldier on patrol. This peaceful but fallow condition lasted thirteen years.

On July 4, 1778, a bold new American, George Rogers Clark (fig. 70), and 175 of his men seized the British-occupied fort at Kaskaskia and claimed it and the surrounding territory for the new state of Virginia. Within sixteen years people in Cahokia (both at the village and at the Cahokia Mounds) had changed nationality three times—from French to British to Virginian American.

Fig. 70. George Rogers Clark frees the French and the Indians from British rule. After Clark took Kaskaskia from the British on July 4, 1778, he addressed the Native Americans, welcoming them to the new United States.

## Cantine Mounds

The spirit of the new country may have invigorated traders, even in such remote frontier outposts as western Illinois. Shortly after Clark's victory two aspiring businessmen, Isaac Levy and Jean-Baptiste La Croix, set up a store near the great terraced pyramid. Visible for miles around in canoe country, it was a logical place for a new American trading post or *cantine* (French for canteen).[13]

Business at Cantine Mounds, as the mound complex was called at that time, was apparently brisk enough to support three men for eight years, for we learn that La Croix, Levy, and Thomas Brady lived there until 1784. We don't know what the "establishment" looked like, for no description has been found and no archaeological evidence has been uncovered. In one document the Cantine is said to have been "the site of a former fort,"[14] which may have meant simply that it was surrounded by a stockade. Since the trading post was active during the Revolutionary War, this seems entirely plausible. Also, it was common practice for all French colonial "establishments" to be enclosed with palisades; the French system was still the local building tradition, and one of the owners had a French name.

The Cantine property changed hands a few times in the next decade, and one new owner, Jean B. Gonville (also called Rupulay), built a house there about 1783. We know nothing more about this house, but we do know that the Cantine itself was abandoned in 1784 because "the Indians grew too troublesome" and that Levy and his partners were obliged "to leave the same and come and live in the Village." The property was next sold to Nicolas Jarrot in 1799 for sixty-six dollars.[15] After that the price of the land declined. The next inhabitants bought it for only twenty-five dollars in the wake of another tumultuous event in European politics. This time it was not the affirmative nod of a French king's head but his decapitation that started things rolling.

## Trappist Monks

Only twenty years after the storming of the Bastille, the shock waves of events in France again transformed the built environment of the Cahokia Mounds. More Frenchmen arrived, but this time they came not as colonizers but as exiles. Soon after the French beheaded Louis XVI, they also took over the monasteries that had coexisted with the French monarchy for centuries. The new government forbade religious orders to live "in community" and confiscated their buildings and related property, enriching their own coffers at the expense of the abbeys and ridding themselves of clerics aligned with the old aristocratic regime.

The Trappists, a division of the Cistercian order, were not exempt. Forced to leave France, they moved to new locations—either to places where Catholicism was well established or to places where they hoped to find religious tolerance. One of the men chosen to lead a group of monks to a new location was Dom Urban Guillet. His dream of finding a place where he and his fellows could find peace led him on a journey of many years, to Switzerland, Hungary, Russia, Belgium, England, and Holland. Finally the party set sail from Amsterdam for the United States on March 24, 1802. Four months later they landed in Baltimore. There were thirty-four in all: seven priests, eighteen lay brothers, and nine students—a good-sized group for a new beginning in nearby Kentucky, a fertile country with a moderate climate.[16]

Six years later their new monastery was under way when a fire in October 1808 destroyed almost everything—their library, bedding, clothing, tools, and food. Only a few potatoes in their cellar, which had baked in the fire, kept them going. In the midst of the blaze their skilled clockmakers managed to save some clocks and most of their clockmaking tools. It was an odd legacy for a new beginning in the Midwest, where they decided to go.

One wonders why the monks did not simply rebuild their monastery where they were. We can only speculate. The answer may lie in the darker side of Guillet's psyche. The Trappists were an austere order, eating only two meals a day, one of bread and water and the other of vegetables. They kept severe vows of silence and slept on stone. Every day each monk was required to dig one spadeful of earth from his intended grave. They tonsured their hair to one thin circle, in imitation of the crown of thorns. Perhaps Guillet regarded the fire as a sign that he had chosen the wrong place. At any rate he decided to move west, to establish a new monastery in the middle of the midwestern prairies.

In his distress Guillet recalled a conversation with a man he had met on landing in Baltimore, one John Mullanphy. Mullanphy had offered Guillet 120 acres with two houses just north of St. Louis, rent free for a year. (St. Louis, part of the Louisiana Purchase of 1803, was now American, but its French heritage continued.) Shortly after the fire, Guillet and his group left for St. Louis. He must have hoped the new place would at least provide a haven while he looked around for a monastery site.

Guillet's ambitions, and the hierarchical nature of his French upbringing, led him to think of "going to the top," and he scheduled two other appointments on this trip: one with the governor of Missouri and the other with the governor of the Indiana Territory (which at that time included Illinois). His goal was to obtain "bounty land," a euphemism for former Indian territory. He might have spared himself the trip and just talked with local landowners, but as we have seen, Guillet was not one to spare himself, or to reach practical, close-to-home solutions with ordinary people.

## OUR LADY OF GOOD HELP MONASTERY

After Guillet's long and arduous journeys, a wealthy St. Louis entrepreneur, Nicolas Jarrot, offered him the four hundred acres he owned along Cahokia Creek, including the "Big Mound." The heart of the French priest must have stirred at the prospect of a monastery on its heights. Perhaps the monastery at Mont-Saint-Michel in his own country came to his mind, at the summit of a great promontory with a view for miles around. Guillet was also attracted "by the beautiful solitude and the excellence of the soil."[17] By fall 1809 the real estate transactions were complete, and new buildings were planned for what they still called Cantine Mounds. Most were sited on the top of a medium-sized mound, since Guillet was no doubt reserving the top of the Big Mound for their consummate building enterprise sometime in the future—a large monastic cathedral. Guillet named his new monastery Notre Dame de Bon Secours, Our Lady of Good Help. He was going to need all the help he could get.

In the beginning, however, hopes were high. Guillet ran an advertisement in the January 24, 1811, issue of the *Louisiana Gazette* to attract business and raise funds.

### NOTICE

*Several persons having shewed to the Monks of La Trappe a desire to purchase watches if they could sell them for trade, the said monks, in order to satisfy everybody, give notice to the public, that until the end of 1811, they will sell Watches, Clocks and other Silversmith's work and also fine Horses for the following articles in Trade, viz: Wheat, Corn, Linen, Beef, Pork, Cattle, Leather, Tallow, Blankets, &c.*
*Urban Guillet*
*Superior of the Monks:*
*Cantine Mounds, 9 miles above Cahokia*

*N.B. The above mentioned articles will be sold at a lower price to whoever shall pay cash.*

The idea of European-trained monks trying to sell watches, clocks, and silversmith's work to settlers on the Illinois prairie strains one's credulity. There were some wealthy people across the Mississippi in St. Louis, to be sure, but the market for these rarefied goods must have small. Such sophisticated instruments in such an unsophisticated place—the incongruity of the two worlds is striking. How would austere Trappist monks raised in Europe cope on the frontier?

One aspect of their French heritage did serve the monks well: their farming practices. The order introduced a good breed of cattle and even brought the first jackasses and jennies to Cahokia. The new cattle remained long after the monks left, although breeding the jackasses to mares to produce mules was not practiced there.[18] In addition, they planted vegetable gardens and fruit orchards on the upper terraces of the great pyramid, and perhaps even a vineyard.

Another part of their European upbringing, the use of coal, must have alerted the monks to the area's potential when they heard that smoke came out of the nearby bluffs for several days after lightning struck a tree there.[19] They would have been aware of the possibilities of a coal field for future development.

Pastoral responsibilities were also heavy. When the monks arrived at the Cahokia Mounds in 1809 the surrounding community had been without sufficient pastoral care for many years, so some of the monks who were also priests had to assume all the duties of baptizing, confirming, hearing confessions, marrying, saying mass, and giving last rites. People living across the river in Missouri as far north as St. Charles also needed attention. Father Donatien Olivier, at Prairie du Rocher, far to the south, was so old that he begged to be relieved of his duties and allowed to enter the monastery as a Trappist.

The life of a monk is different from the life of a parish priest. Each role appeals to a different temperament, and those who had taken their vows contemplating a life of prayer and solitude must have felt constraints on their natures in the endless duties of parish priests in such neglected areas, where they sometimes had to hear confessions until nine in the evening. Attention to building their own monastery had to be put aside. A visitor reported:

*The buildings which the Trappists at present occupy, are merely temporary: they consist of four or five cabins, on a mound about fifty yards [sic] high, and which is perhaps one hundred and fifty feet square. Their other buildings, cribs, stables, &c. ten or fifteen in number, are scattered about on the plain below. I was informed that they intended to build on the terrace of the large mound; this will produce a fine effect, it will be seen five or six miles across the plain, and from some points of view ten or twelve. They have about one hundred acres enclosed in three different fields, including the large mound, and several others . . . .the family of Trappists consists of about eighty persons [at that time].[20]*

## A SERIES OF DISASTERS

Before they finished digging their well, the monks were forced to drink the water of Cahokia Creek, which was fouled by dead fish. Illness began to plague the little group. To nurse the sick they built an emergency infirmary. Every month several more men were lost to malaria and other illnesses. By November 1810 five had died; in 1811 they lost four more, and by 1813, when illness struck again, there were "scarcely a sufficient number left to bury the dead." More than half the community had disappeared, and those who were still alive were pitifully weak.

Added to the woes of lethal illness was a bad harvest in 1811, yielding only one-third of the usual crop. Poor nutrition further debilitated those who were still alive.

The crop failure was followed by a flood, "higher than has ever been except for one exception."[21]

In mid-December of the same year yet another titanic calamity hit the small community: the worst earthquake ever recorded in the Midwest before or since—the infamous New Madrid quake described in chapter 1.

Catastrophic as it was at the beginning, the quake also seemed interminable. The earth under the monks' feet trembled almost daily for nearly two months. The demoralizing effects of this new disaster hit them hard. Guillet himself was "just within an inch of being killed by a falling chimney." Many of their buildings, so painstakingly built, were ruined. That same winter Guillet contracted a "cold" so severe the description strikes the modern ear as bronchial pneumonia. The illness left him coughing for four months, with "only seven days off," with spells striking him sometimes "as often as fourteen times an hour." Midwestern winters can severely test the endurance of even the hardiest soul: when earthquake devastates the land and when illness plagues the body and the spirit, total collapse may be near.[22]

By February 1813 Guillet could no longer go on. After four terrible years, he sold the four hundred acres he had painstakingly pieced together and left behind forever Cahokia and his dreams of building a monastery on the great pyramid. He and a few followers took a keelboat down the Mississippi, then up the Ohio. Eventually they made their way to Pittsburgh, where Guillet tried to found another monastery. This attempt was also futile, as was still another effort at a site near Philadelphia. Even the hardiest person must have felt weary and discouraged after so many failures. After Napoleon was defeated Guillet returned to France, where he and others helped found a new La Trappe at an old monastic site called Bellefontaine, near Cholet. He died three years later, on April 2, 1817.[23]

The changes wrought at the Cahokia mounds in the French period are now visible only in archaeological evidence, but the name Monks Mound for the terraced pyramid endures as the Trappists' legacy to the site.

## Surveying the Territory

European politics had another effect on the future of Cahokia at the turn of the eighteenth century. In the beginning of his era Napoleon too may have dreamed of wealth coming in from French Louisiana, for he commissioned a survey of the area from Georges-Henri-Victor Collot. Collot included the east side of the Mississippi, the borderland belonging to England, on his exploratory voyage for Napoleon in 1796, and the Indian mounds in the Cahokia area now known as the Lunsford-Pulcher site, near Dupo, Illinois, appear on his map (fig. 71). The full report included the western rivers of North America and an account of the contours of the waters, their principal cities, the character of the landscape, its vegetation and climate, and the people who lived there. The thirty-six plates include descriptive maps, drawings of landscape and architectural forms, and local inhabitants, including some Indian tribes.

Collot's descriptions may also have played a part in inducing prospective immigrants to come to the New World, for he spoke of the river valleys of the Midwest in glowing terms.

*This immense plain . . . is covered with forests, natural meadows, lakes, rivers, streams and falls of water . . . . The forests . . . bear no resemblance to those of the northern and eastern parts of America, the greater part of which forests are thick and humid, impervious to the beams of the sun, and through which the air scarcely circulates. Those, on the contrary, which cover the lands watered by*

Fig. 71. An elegant map accompanies glowing prose. In a survey for Napoleon in 1796, Georges-Henri-Victor Collot extolled the natural resources of the Midwest. The village of Cahokia is visible to the right. The "Indian Ancient Tombs" he indicated were the mounds of a Mississippian village, now called the Lunsford-Pulcher site. Collot's arrow points west instead of north.

*the Ohio, the Mississippi [etc.] . . . are composed of lofty trees, clear, without brushwood, open to the sun, and to the free circulation of the air. It is observed, also, that the height, the size, and the quality of the wood, are very superior to that which grows towards the north and east.*[24]

Historians of the "counterfactual" strain might well ask what might have happened if the French had not begun to consider Illinois a small and inconsequential colony. Why didn't the leaders in Paris see the rich agricultural possibilities of the territory? Illinois could have been a major power center for France. With a large force here, France could have dominated the upper Mississippi and the Great Lakes, and the relative strengths of France and Britain might have changed significantly, tilting the balance, perhaps altering the history of European imperialism.

Surprisingly, the French strain in Illinois is still perceptible in countless ways. The name Illinois is French for Illini. Towns and streets with French names abound, and the long lots of French towns can still be seen in a satellite photograph. Some local churches said mass in French until recently. When people with Polish ancestry moved to Bourbonnais, Illinois, they were told by a church committee that they were welcome in the parish "even though they weren't French."

In Prairie du Rocher thousands of visitors come to an annual "rendezvous" to celebrate their French heritage. At Fort de Chartres and other sites local people dressed in period clothing reenact historical events such as the mustering of Ste. Anne's Militia (fig. 72) and greet arrivals at Fort de Chartres (fig. 73), even sporting replicas of period medals on their uniforms (fig. 74).

Fig. 72. (top, left) Ste. Anne's Militia marches again. Reenactors at Fort de Chartres celebrate their heritage at annual Rendezvous events.

Fig. 73. (bottom, left) Reenactors Margaret Kimball Brown and Marvin Hilligoss greet visitors at Fort de Chartres during Rendezvous.

Fig. 74. (top, right) Carefully reproduced French medals. Marvin Hilligoss proudly raises his sword to his chest during a reenactors' dress parade.

## Summary

The monumentality of the great pyramid, the plazas (or foreground clearings), and the subordinate mounds built by the Mississippian Indians transformed this landscape into an awe-inspiring sight that resonated with the dreams of idealists and visionaries for centuries after it was built. At times the chords it struck in the souls of those who saw it were religious, at times commercial or opportunistic. Off and on over the next two hundred years it would inspire artists and scholars, including a German prince, to document and investigate its hidden secrets. For a brief period in the twentieth century it served as a rallying point for the dark forces of violence and prejudice. Ultimately this same monumentality became both sign and cynosure of the history of preservation in the area, as we shall see.

FIG. 75. GENTLEMEN SCHOLARS, BLACK LABORERS, JARS, SKELETONS, AND ARTIFACTS. ANIMATED BY THEIR DESIRE TO UNCOVER THE PAST, AMATEURS WERE THE FIRST PEOPLE TO DIG MOUNDS. SHOWN HERE IS A DETAIL OF *PANORAMA OF THE MONUMENTAL GRANDEUR OF THE MISSISSIPPI VALLEY*, BY JOHN J. EAGAN, ABOUT 1850.

**5**
▼

# Nineteenth-Century Turmoil

Situated as it was in the center of the country, nineteenth-century Cahokia was a microcosm reflecting the changes in the wider world of the United States. In the aftermath of the epic undeclared war of the whites against the Indians, soldiers and warriors on both sides moved inexorably westward, one with the force of irresistible conquest, the other in tragic withdrawal. Many groups of Europeans and their descendants followed in the wake of the conflict.

The first wave of European Americans coming to the Mississippi Valley had been explorers, lone-wolf trappers, missionaries, soldiers, and French settlers. In the ensuing decades new immigrants, scientists, artists, and writers arrived in the area around Cahokia. Why did they come in such numbers? What lured them there? Why, for example, would an artist born in Switzerland travel to the midwestern frontier in 1833 and draw the Cahokia Mounds?

The pace of change quickened as time advanced. No sooner had the immigrants settled in than a new army of industrialists and railroad men invaded their neatly plowed fields, laying a thick web of dark tracks across the land. When the century was over they had altered the land more than any people since the Mississippians. In the midst of all this social change, how did American archaeology develop from a hobby for gentlemen scholars to a rigorous discipline?

## Altering the Face of the Land

All Europeans arriving in the New World shared a common mind-set of land practices derived from the Romans. In the classical Old World way of looking at things, land is possessed by mapping it, dividing it, squaring it off, laying claim to it, and developing it. Accordingly the new immigrants gradually imposed an even patchwork of straight roads and rectilinear farms on the seamless sea of the Indians' prairie hunting grounds.

As early as 1785 geometry was made law. The federal Land Ordinance Act funded the surveying of the United States outside the original colonies into townships of six square miles. This macro-grid, still clearly visible from an airplane window in the roads laid down along township lines, was further divided into smaller and smaller grids. Blocks consisting of thirty-six sections of one square mile (640 acres) each were broken down and sold separately to individual owners, except for lots specifically reserved for schools or government buildings.[1] In their turn farmers divided their new property into fields, marked by plowed furrows in spring and straight rows of corn or rectangles of wheat in summer. At the same time, the small towns that grew up within this patchwork quilt added micro-grids of streets, echoing the larger pattern.

After the bloody battles evicting the Native Americans, the conquerors transformed their new country into what seemed to them a more rational, human-controlled order, neat and clear.

But the idea of control soon proved illusory. Shifts in alliances in Europe now had repercussions in the American heartland. One seismic political shift abroad was enormously to the advantage of the United States.

## European Power Politics Affect Cahokia Again

In the first three years of the nineteenth century the people across the Mississippi from Cahokia changed nationality three times. In 1800 the Louisiana Territory was Spanish. Back home in Spain the troops of Charles IV were no match for the rapidly advancing army of Napoleon, one million strong, and the king knew it. Choosing accommodation rather than defeat, Charles agreed, among other things, to restore the Louisiana territory to France.[2] And Louisiana might have remained French had it not been for an army of mosquitoes farther south that Napoleon could not accommodate or defeat. An African slave rebellion in Haiti and the fear of further rebellions were also factors in Napoleon's decision.

In 1801 there were 25,000 French soldiers in the Caribbean, on the alert to put down a rebellion in the colony of St. Domingue. They were also standing ready to move on to New Orleans and the Mississippi Valley to strengthen the French stronghold in North America when an outbreak of mosquito-borne yellow fever decimated their ranks and killed their commander. Two years later, with pressures in France mounting rapidly, Napoleon's desire to dominate Europe took priority over his desire to dominate the New World. Instead of sending his battalions to defend Louisiana, he thought of selling Louisiana to raise money for the invasion of Britain.

## The Louisiana Purchase

In Paris at the time, Thomas Jefferson cleverly leaped at the opportunity. He hinted at an American rapprochement with Britain and a possible declaration of war against France. To avoid the double-barreled threat, Napoleon sold Louisiana to the United States on May 2, 1803, for $15 million. The land constituted three-fourths of the country's future continental territory.[3]

One of Jefferson's first acts after acquiring Louisiana was to commission Meriwether Lewis and William Clark to explore the new territory. Although Lewis and Clark took no scientists or artists on their crossing of the continent, their maps were guides for other expeditions close on their heels, and Clark gave advice, help, and assistance to those who sought him out when he returned to live in St. Louis as commissioner of Indian Affairs.

## A Transportation Nexus

Cahokia lay across the Mississippi from the new territory, and the removal of the political barrier meant that Cahokia and the surrounding land were now at the center of a developing transportation nexus. Throngs of new settlers came across the Midwest down the Illinois and Ohio Rivers or on overland routes such as the National Road (formerly U.S. 40 and now Collinsville Road) that went directly through the Cahokia Mounds. These travelers needed supplies, food, and clothing or new modes of travel as they converged on St. Louis. Some settled nearby, and the agricultural products from the new farms were exchanged for goods from the industrial manufactories of the East. In those days East met West at the Mississippi, one of the United States's major economic exchange routes. By the end of the nineteenth century the view from the top of Monks Mound at Cahokia encompassed the ruts of countless covered wagons overlaid with a black net of railroad tracks. A steam locomotive ran right by

Rattlesnake Mound in the 1860s, and an electric interurban train ran past the base of Monks Mound in the 1890s. Other railroads crossed the site at the periphery.

## The Birth of Mississippi Archaeology

One enterprising young man who wanted to be part of all the action was Henry Marie Brackenridge (1786–1871).[4] Boyhood on the Mississippi seems to instill a permanent passion in some men, and Brackenridge lived on the river near St. Genevieve, Missouri, from age seven to ten. After earning a law degree in the East, by the time he turned twenty-four young Henry was back to start exploring the West. As he later wrote,

*The voyage was undertaken in the spirit of adventure, which characterized so many of our countrymen, and with little or no expectation of profit or advantage. The accounts received from different persons had greatly excited my curiosity. The conversation of Manuel Lisa, a man of an ardent and enterprising character, and one of the most celebrated of those who traverse the Indian country, had inflamed my mind of attempting something of a similar nature. I set off with the intention of making a summer excursion, as a simple hunter, unprovided with the means of making mathematical observations but little acquainted with any of the branches of natural history and without once imagining that I should ever publish the results.[5]*

Manuel Lisa was one of twelve founding members of the Missouri Fur Company. In its early years the company had hired 250 men, boatmen and hunters, to exploit the rich animal resources of the Missouri River and its tributaries. Beaver skins, so popular in Europe, continued to be in demand, and the junctions of the Jefferson, Madison, Gallatin, and Missouri Rivers were nearly choked with beaver dams. The "harvests" had yielded riches beyond their dreams in the early years, but troubles with the Indians the previous two years had reduced their income from an expected "three hundred packs [of furs] to hardly thirty the first year, and the second none at all." The company was in desperate financial straits by 1810 and its founders were almost ready to give up, but they decided to make one more effort. It was this small expedition that Brackenridge joined.

Before leaving for his long journey to explore the Missouri River, he had heard about the monks and crossed the Mississippi to visit Cahokia. Motivated by its growing reputation and his desire to be part of the ethnographic and topological discoveries of his times, Brackenridge, although an amateur, was a careful observer.

*Pursuing my walk along the bank of the Cahokia [Creek] . . . I reached the foot of the principal mound. I was struck with a degree of astonishment, not unlike that which is experienced in contemplating the Egyptian pyramids. What a stupendous pile of earth! To heap up such a mass must have required years, and the labors of thousands. . . . Were it not for the regularity and design which it manifests, the circumstances of its being on alluvial ground, and the other mounds scattered around it, we could scarcely believe it the work of human hands . . . . It is evident this could never have been the work of thinly scattered tribes.6*

Brackenridge's inspired words, first published in 1811, were soon read by energetic and curious young scientists who could not rest until they had seen these marvels with their own eyes. We cannot overestimate the impetus Brackenridge gave to subsequent explorers and scholars in the burgeoning antiquarian community. The views of the site and the insights, philosophical hypotheses, and religious speculations that followed upon his detailed, accurate, and erudite observations were cast in glowing prose. Brackenridge also underscored the connections between Cahokia and other archaeological sites.

*We find mounds in every part of the globe; in the north of Europe and in Great Britain, they are numerous, and much resemble ours, but less considerable. The pyramids of Egypt . . . of Mexico . . . have their origin hid in the night of oblivion . . . traces [of mounds] were found even in Arcadia . . . . the Greeks even erected pyramids over their graves . . . . A French writer has fancifully observed that civilization arises,* de la fermentation d'une nombreuse peuplade, *and that it would be as idle to expect this result without a numerous population as to think of making wine by the fermentation of a single grape. It is not without reason, that the Creator gave his command to increase and multiply, since many of the intellectual faculties would not otherwise be completely unfolded.7*

Brackenridge's ardor inspired many others to follow in his footsteps. Some scholars believe he must be credited with the birth of Mississippian archaeology, and there is some merit to this opinion.

*But the human race has everywhere experienced terrible revolutions. Pestilence, war, and the convulsions of the globe, have annihilated the proudest works, and rendered vain the noblest efforts. Ask not the sage, by whom, and when, were erected those lingering ruins, the "frail memorials" of ages which have long since been swallowed up in the ocean of time; ask not the wild Arab, where may be found the owner of the superb palace, within whose broken walls he casts his tent; ask not the poor fisherman, as he spreads his nets, or the ploughman, who whistles over the ground, where is Carthage, where is Troy, of whose splendor, historians and poets have so much boasted! Alas! "they have vanished from the things that be," and have left but the melancholy lesson, of the instability of the most stupendous labors, and the vanity of immortality on earth!*[8]

## The First Scientific Expedition

Just eight years after Brackenridge, a very different expedition was mounted by Maj. Stephen H. Long. It was commissioned in 1819 by the secretary of war, John C. Calhoun, with specific orders:

*The object of the expedition is to acquire as thorough and accurate knowledge as may be practicable of a portion of our country which is daily becoming more interesting, but which is as yet imperfectly known. With this view you will permit nothing worthy of notice to escape your attention. You will ascertain the latitude and longitude of remarkable points with all possible precision. You will if practicable ascertain some points in the 49th parallel of latitude which separates our possessions from those of Great Britain [at the Canadian border] . . . to prevent collision between our traders and theirs . . . . The instructions of Mr. Jefferson to Cpt. Lewis [of Lewis and Clark], which are printed in his travels, will afford you many valuable suggestions, of which as far as is applicable you will avail yourself.*[9]

Outfitted with state of the art scientific equipment and accompanied by a geologist and a botanist, Long's expedition set out with two sextants, a circle of reflection, an artificial horizon of mercury, an achromatic telescope, a box chronometer, a pocket chronometer, an instrument for observing degrees (drop) of magnetic needle, an azimuth compass, a surveyor's com-

pass, a fifty-foot chain, measuring tapes, a theodolite, three barometers, several thermometers, and many other instruments such as microscopes.

The final report contains meteorological records, latitude and longitude positions, vocabularies of seven major Indian languages, accounts of Indian customs, dress, and architecture, details of courteous reception ceremonies, and lengthy scientific descriptions.

Among Long's contributions were detailed measurements of twenty-seven Mississippian mounds just north of what was then St. Louis (fig. 76) and detailed descriptions of those at Cahokia: "In the prairies of Illinois, opposite St. Louis, are numbers of large mounds. We counted 75 in the course of a walk of about 5 miles . . . including that of La Trappe [Monks Mound] but [it was] so overgrown with bushes and weeds, interlaced with briers and vines, we were unable to obtain an accurate account of its dimensions."[10]

Here Cahokia studies may have fallen victim to the political line drawn down the Mississippi River. Technically the site fell outside the purview of the expedition; otherwise the team might have attempted to clear the ground or made other efforts to get more accurate measurements.

Long's description of one unusual mound north of St. Louis, called the Falling Gardens, is a good example of the accuracy of the work, and one wonders what the team might have done at Cahokia had it been within their assigned territory. What is helpful to Mississippian studies is that the mounds they did record at St. Louis had been in a suburb (or what Melvin Fowler termed a "second-level community") of the old metropolis at Cahokia. Much of what they recorded was later torn down, and Long's descriptions are all the evidence we have left. In addition, the charm of the mounds comes through even in the scientific prose: "It is called the 'Falling Gardens' and consists of 3 stages all of equal length, and of the same parallel organic

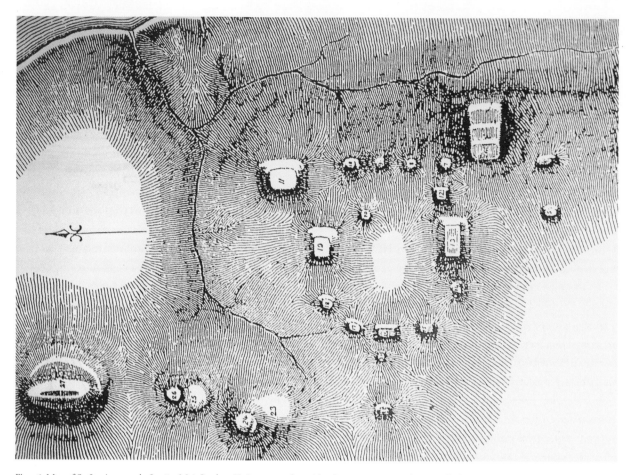

Fig. 76. Map of St. Louis mounds. In 1819 Maj. Stephen H. Long, together with other surveyors, a geologist, and a botanist, measured and described part of the newly acquired territory of the United States. Mississippian mounds in St. Louis, a "suburb" of the ancient Native American city of Cahokia, were investigated, and Cahokia itself, although on the east side of the Mississippi, was mentioned in the report. Titian Ramsay Peale, an artist who accompanied the expedition, made this sketch from Long's data.

form; the superior stage, like the five succeeding mounds, is bounded on the east by the edge of the second bank of the river; the second and third stages are in succession on the declivity of the bank, each being horizontal, and are connected with each other and with the first, by an abruptly oblique descent." The measurements followed the description.

· *Longitudinal base 114′[base means a line passed over the top of the mound from the termination of the base at each side]*
· *top 88′*
· *Transverse base of first stage 30′*
· *height of do 5′[do means ditto]*
· *Declivity to the second stage 34′*

- *Transverse surface of do 51'*
- *Declivity to the third stage 30'*
- *Transverse surface of do 87'*
- *Declivity to the natural slope 19'[11]*

Long's accounts reflect the scientific attitude of the 1820s that was supplanting the sketchier maps and narrative accounts of the fur traders.

## European Culture Affects Cahokia

European culture of the nineteenth century also touched Cahokia frequently and deeply. Europeans were fascinated by America and all things American, from the country's natural history to its folklore. Scientists imagined that clues to new discoveries and answers to stubborn questions were awaiting them across the Atlantic. In America it was still possible to see nature in its pristine form, since the new land teemed with unknown species.

In the spirit of the Enlightenment the opportunities for investigation excited the imaginations of scholars in every field—from botany and zoology to archaeology and ethnography. Long, arduous, and expensive scientific journeys were undertaken, specimens gathered, and findings recorded, classified, and deposited in the new museums that sprang up in all the major cities of the civilized world. The most momentous of all these enterprises, of course, was Darwin's voyage on the *Beagle* (1831–36). But there were also smaller expeditions that visited Cahokia. By the 1830s transatlantic cross-currents had carried tantalizing accounts of the new discoveries to yet another kind of inquiring mind—the European intellectual.

Galvanized by new studies in ethnology, botany, and zoology, the young Prince Maximilian von Wied (1782–1867) absorbed all the information he could gather during his university days at Göttingen. Conversations with his professors heightened his interest in human cultures around the world; training in description and classification of specimens sharpened his eyes and his desire to visit the New World. In his zeal to learn everything about America, he read all the books he could get his hands on in the superb library at Göttingen—including Brackenridge's and Long's accounts.

The call of the American West fired his imagination, and he dreamed of organizing an expedition to study, collect specimens, and write about his adventures. With the money available to one of his aristocratic background, the dream became a reality and on July 4, 1832, the "Writer Prince" launched a two-year expedition. Knowing the importance of accurate drawing, for recording and for illustrating any publications, the prince secured the services of a trained artist, Karl Bodmer (1809–93). Born in Switzerland, Bodmer had been solidly schooled in the classical European art tradition in Zurich and Paris.[12]

The two made a remarkable duo. Sharing a love of outdoor life, Indian culture, and adventure in the unknown, they also treasured this unique opportunity to report on a vanishing world. In the end their joint effort, written by Prince Maximilian and illustrated by Bodmer, was published first in German, as *Reise in das innere Nord-America in den Jahren 1832 bis 1834*, and later in French and English translations. Bodmer's accurate and beautiful illustrations brightened the pages of all three editions. Among the other drawings he made on this journey were two of Cahokia (figs. 77 and 78), one of Monks Mound from the east, and another of the Twin Mounds.[13]

No previous expedition had had both a writer and an illustrator, and the effect on the reading and viewing public is inestimable. The pull of the images alone must have been irresistible to land-deprived, land-hungry people in countries where tenant farming was the

Fig. 77. (top) A German prince and a Swiss artist visit Cahokia. The drawings Karl Bodmer made of Cahokia sometime in 1832–34, when he was a member of Maximilian von Wied's expedition, depict an almost bucolic view of the site. *View of Monk's Mound,* the first known illustration of Monks Mound, shows the farmhouse and outbuildings of Amos Hill's farm on the third terrace.

Fig. 78. (bottom) Karl Bodmer's *View of Twin Mounds.* Cattle graze in the foreground of Bodmer's landscape approach to the site.

rule rather than the exception. To own a piece of fertile land in America was to possess a piece of paradise. The 1830s and 1840s began the time of intensive German immigration to the United States. The Irish and scores of other nationalities would soon follow.

## The Indian Removal Act of 1830

Underlying all these converging forces of exploration, possession, and immigration lay a desperate yet futile opposing force. The Indians were not as willing to sell their native land to the Americans as the French had been to sell their largest colony. As we saw in the previous chapter, the Native American believed that the earth belongs to everyone and therefore no one can own it. The superior armies of the whites forced them to make concession after concession, in defeat after defeat, in treaty after treaty. In 1804, the year after the Louisiana Purchase, five Indian chiefs came to St. Louis to free one of their tribesmen who had been charged with murder. Entertained with rounds of free-flowing alcohol, they deeded away a large portion of their land to the United States in exchange for perpetual hunting rights (a promise broken shortly thereafter) and annuities of a thousand dollars each. Other treaties followed in 1816, 1822, and 1825.

During the presidency of Andrew Jackson the United States adopted a policy of "removing" all the Indian groups living on land east of the Mississippi. Later observers have characterized what followed as ethnic cleansing or genocide. At the time some European Americans on the frontier thought it necessary to "clear" the land not only of unwanted trees but of hostile Indians. By this time no frontiersman believed any longer in the possibility of a truce between Indians and whites, much less the cooperation once enjoyed by French voyageurs. They were declared enemies.

Part of the Manifest Destiny ideology of the period was that occupying the West was seen as the "white Americans' prerogative," indeed their responsibility. It followed that whites should annex Texas and occupy and possess all the land westward to the Pacific, even if it meant going to war against Mexico. As the art historian Robert Hughes put it, "If the Indians fought back they weren't just resisting invaders, they were up against history itself; and to see yourself as a force of history is to be freed of pity and guilt."[14] The policy spelled unmitigated defeat and tragedy for some

70,000 Cherokee, Choctaw, Creek, and Seminole Indians. The whole myth of empire, progress, and westwardness seems to have been endorsed by an Anglican bishop, George Berkeley (1685–1753), who wrote:

*Westward the course of empire takes its way;*
*The first four acts already past,*
*A fifth shall close the drama with the day;*
*Time's noblest offspring is the last.*

White people saw settling the West as an inevitable movement of progress and themselves as "Time's noblest offspring." For the Indian population it was an exodus on a biblical scale.[15]

After the defeat of the Sauk chief Black Hawk in 1833 a peace powwow was held in Chicago in which the Potawatomi and their allies ceded all their land in Illinois and moved west of the Mississippi, removing the last of the Indians from the state and from ancestral lands around Cahokia.[16] Some of the departing tribes were depicted by artist-ethnographer George Catlin, who painted a visual record documenting the customs of the retreating, increasingly decimated native population (fig. 79).

Although there were some groups aimed at reforming our Indian policy, most of them believed in assimilating Native Americans by converting them to Christianity, teaching them the methods of yeoman farmers, and educating them "to American ways" in government-sponsored schools.

As Frederick E. Hoxie has pointed out, it was not until the twentieth century that significant groups of articulate Native Americans, such as the National Congress of American Indians, organized to call for the protection of tribal culture and assert their right to have the dominant voice in national policymaking for their own economic development and legal protection.[17]

Fig. 79. A visual record. Fearing Native Americans might be on the verge of vanishing, artists like George Catlin ventured west in the nineteenth century to record the appearance of chiefs, warriors, women, and children, as in his *Old Bear, a Medicine Man.*

## Journalists and Travel Writers
## Discover Cahokia

When reports of a safe frontier combined with the glowing accounts of Brackenridge, the charming stories of Prince Maximilian, and the beguiling pictures of Karl Bodmer reached the general public, a wave of intrepid young journalists began to travel to the Mississippi.

As early as 1835 Charles Joseph Latrobe, who called himself the "Rambler," published his speculations on Cahokia. Awestruck by the mounds but bound by the political correctness of his times, he could not assert that they had been constructed by ancestors of the same "savages" being "removed" across the Mississippi. "The magnitude of the works will ever remain a marvel. They [the builders] were more civilized, more powerful, more enlightened than the Indian races of our day."[18]

Latrobe's opinion was part of a widespread belief that the "Mound Builders" were a magnificent lost race. One earlier writer thought the mounds must have been built by Danish Vikings who afterward migrated to Mexico and founded the Toltec civilization. As Robert Silverberg has pointed out in *The Mound Builders,* since the cities of the Aztecs and the Incas were in many respects as advanced as contemporary cities in Europe, many people believed the builders must have come from the Old World. Speculations abounded. The mounds were built by the Phoenicians, the people of the lost continent of Atlantis, the Ten Lost Tribes of Israel.

Writers of fiction joined in the mythmaking. In 1864 Daniel Pierce Thompson's story "Centeola: The Maid of the Mounds" recounted a terrifying cliffhanger. A maiden and her lover, about to meet a terrible fate, were saved by an earthquake. Although they were spared from death, the earthquake destroyed their civilization of Mound Builders. Today archaeologists and anthropologists agree that the Mound Builders and modern American Indians did indeed both belong to the same racial stock, but the scientific proof and acceptance did not really come until the 1890s. In the meantime, the journalists continued to profit from the romance of the Amerindian past.

Later two more "Ramblers," J. C. Wild and Louis Foulk Thomas, teamed up in 1841 to write an illustrated book on the Mississippi Valley. Wild, an artist of considerable skill, depicted beautiful scenes all along the Mississippi. He rendered not only Monks Mound (fig. 80) but views of many small towns as well as other enticing vistas.[19] These enticements would lure more newcomers, people who affected the Cahokia landscape by their passing through or by the infrastructures erected to help them pass through or to settle nearby.

Picture books, or "view books," with commentaries, made possible by the lithographic printing process, were extremely popular in the nineteenth century. You could travel all over the world in your armchair, even make a grand tour in your own living room. Each new edition of a series was eagerly awaited. Wild's *The Valley of the Mississippi Illustrated* was published in monthly editions containing four views, with an average of four pages of text to each view describing the scenery. At the end of the year a volume of two hundred pages, with fifty views, could be bound into a book. Each monthly installment cost one dollar.

The accompanying text by Lewis Foulk Thomas waxed enthusiastic about the beautiful Mississippi Valley depicted in Wild's scenes.

*Her extensive prairies of rich alluvial, gemmed with countless varieties of the most beautiful flowers, and ample enough for pasturage to many millions of cattle—her boundless forests, luxuriant with almost every species of timber—her myriad streams, affording incalculable water-power—her mighty rivers—her marble quarries—her exhaustless beds of coal—her mines of copper—her*

Fig. 80. Illustrated books lure settlers to the Midwest. In 1841 J. C. Wild's depictions of the Mississippi Valley, such as his *Monk's Mound, St. Clair County,* gave a romantic aura to the environs of Cahokia.

mountains of iron and leagues of lead, are teeming sources, from whence her inhabitants, for century after century, will draw the most abundant wealth.

On the banks of her rivers, cities spring up as if by magic, and Commerce pays for her produce in the luxuries of every clime. Tens of thousands of immigrants settle annually upon her fertile soil, to reap its blessings, and above her waving woods the church-spire points, and the glittering cross gleams with the light and hope of Heaven. She has reared proud temples, dedicated to Religion, the Arts, Sciences, and Laws, and she is the prolific mother and bountiful nurse of many noble sons, distinguished in every honorable field of ambition.

As we gaze upon her rich savannahs, her lofty forests and her majestic rivers, and think of her rapid growth as a portion of this powerful Republic, and of its future greatness, and the immense influence she must wield over its destinies, the imagination wearies, and we are lost in the contemplation . . . [of] the richest alluvial ever cut by a plow.[20]

One of the four foldout views in the last edition, a "Panorama of St. Louis," contains a view of the Big Mound across the river.[21]

Together these pictures and ecstatic words fueled the dreams and energies of swarms of settlers and immigrants. There were even hints of adventure. A close look at the pictures suggests danger lurking behind the trees (fig. 81). An Indian aims an arrow at settlers in front of a log cabin. Since things were relatively safe on the Mississippi by 1842, this intimation of violence may have been included on the cover as a note of romantic adventure to help sell the publication. Inside the book were peaceful views of charming little towns such as Alton, Illinois (fig. 82). Although mixed with a bit of romance, the pictures that dominate Wild's work are of idealized midwestern communities surrounded by a pastoral world of farms.

## Idyllic Nineteenth-Century Midwestern Life

The prose of the period shows that the perception of the quality of life in the environs of Cahokia has changed markedly.

*The view was taken from one of the smaller mounds and shows the principal group in perhaps the best aspect in which it could be seen . . . . The greater one, or Monks Mound, is in the form of a parallelogram, and is estimated to be one hundred and twenty-five feet high. Its top is flat and presents an area of about two acres, laid out in a garden, planted with fruit and shade trees, and containing the residence of the proprietor.[22]*

Even the ancient Indian mounds, so recently viewed as awe-inspiring and majestic, have become domesticated by the immigrant farmer.

*From the top of the mound the view is of exceeding beauty. The wide prairie stretches for miles its carpeting of green, gemmed with the most beautiful flowers, and dotted, at intervals, with clusters of trees, that look in the distance, like emeralds embossed in a rich embroidery, while there, where formerly the wild Buffalo ranged and the war-yell of the savage ascended, now herds of domestic cattle are grazing, and "Peace is tinkling on the shepherd's bell /And singing with the reapers."*

A new settlement near the site of the old Cantine trading post is now visible.

*To the west, at a distance of six miles, are seen the steeples and spires of St. Louis, to the north a dense forest, with Cahokia creek, like a huge silver serpent, winding in and out of it, and here and there a glimpse of the cottages in the settlement of Cantine, is caught, with the blue smoke, ascending straightly to the clear sky . . . . Six or seven miles*

THE VALLEY OF THE MISSISSIPPI
ILLUSTRATED
IN A SERIES OF VIEWS.

Edited by Lewis Foulk Thomas.
Painted and Lithographed
by
J. C. WILD,
Accompanied with Historical Descriptions.
Published Monthly in Numbers, each Number containing four Views, at $1 per number

St. Louis. Mo.
1841.
Published by the Artist. Printed by Chambers and Knapp.

Entered according to act of Congress by J.C.Wild in the Year 1841 in the Office of the Clerk of the District Court of Mo.

Fig. 81. (top) Danger lurking behind the trees. Scenes of adventure peppered the otherwise rather tranquil views J. C. Wild drew of the Mississippi Valley. This stereotyped view of relations between the new and the old inhabitants of Illinois was typical of the mid-nineteenth century.

Fig. 82. (bottom) Peaceful town life along the Mississippi. This charming view of Alton shows one of the many new settlements dotting the river valleys of the Midwest.

*across the prairie, to the south a large lake gleams in the sunshine, with the big pelicans flapping their lazy wings over it, and the white houses of "French village" studding its margin; back of these and extending semicircularly to the east, rise the bluffs, in some places perpendicularly, with their bare sides of rock and clay, and their summits crowned with majestic oaks, forming an impregnable wall, guarded by its forest sentinels in their rich autumnal livery of green and gold.[23]*

Both the landscape and the perception of Cahokia have changed. At midcentury it is idyllic or pastoral. Bodmer (1833) and Wild (1841) both depict tall trees well established on the top of Monks Mound and several other mounds nearby. In Wild's view the contours of Monks Mound are already nearly obscured by trees.

The perception of these trees in the twentieth century is very different. Far from finding them picturesque or pastoral, archaeologists and preservationists see them as menacing. Not only do they obscure the contours of the mounds, their root systems can destroy precious archaeological evidence. People who have visited the ancient Hopewell sites at Fort Ancient in Ohio can attest that the mounds there are so obscured by trees that their presence is discernible only to experts with maps, and the disturbance of the soil causes incalculable damage to the archaeological record.

### T. Ames Hill and the Early Pioneers

The "residence of the proprietor" Wild refers to belonged to T. Ames (sometimes called Amos) Hill. Hill was among the small group of remarkable men and women who settled Illinois. In 1926 the geographer J. Paul Goode gave a speech about these early settlers titled "The Character of Our People Is a Very Great Resource."

*It was only when our fathers came, bringing with them the economic and social culture inherited for forty centuries of European civilization, that the great transformation came to the Central Plain. In a very significant way they have shaped the material and social development of the region. They were pioneers, and sons and daughters of several generations of pioneers. And who are pioneers? They are a chosen people—young men and women of physical and intellectual courage and ambition; strong, resourceful, hard-working, temperate, self-respecting men and women. They have had the courage to pick up and leave the comforts of the old home and to brave the dangers and discomforts of the wilderness, to make new homes and fortunes for themselves and their families. The "Great Trek" of the eighteen hundred thirties, forties, and fifties was one of the most remarkable exhibitions of human-swarming which history has to record. The major part of that human stream was from the northern Atlantic seaboard, or from the Appalachian valleys and eastern forests, the product of a continual process of selection through several generations of pioneering ancestors. They set the standards and became the leaders, giving us a priceless heritage of culture and ideals.[24]*

One member of that "human stream" was Abraham Lincoln, who came to Illinois in March 1830 with his father and stepmother.

Succeeding waves of pioneer settlers came to Illinois, beginning with the French. In the early nineteenth century a new wave entered from New England and also from other parts of Europe, and Hill was among them. After John Deere invented the steel plow in 1837, yet another wave of immigrants flowed into

Illinois. This time they were farmers with capital to invest and with large holdings of livestock.

In the same year, to increase the appeal of settling the state, the Illinois legislature passed an "internal improvement bill" for more roads, bridges, and railroad land grants. Economic incentives increased when the federal Government Land Grant Act of 1850 gave rights-of-way to railroads and empowered them to sell sections of land for six miles on each side. (Profits from the even-numbered sections went to the railroads and those from the odd-numbered sections, at double the price, to the government.) It worked. The immigrant population increased exponentially.

A poster printed by the Illinois Central Railroad Company extolled the value of the land for farming (fig. 83).

*Illinois is known as the Garden State, and the extraordinary fertility of the soil is justly entitled to the name . . . almost the whole state is a natural meadow, lying in high, beautifully rolling or gently undulating prairies, with a soil of surpassing and inexhaustible fertility, all ready for the plough, without a rock, stump or even a stone to interrupt its action. With far less labor [italics in the original] a farm purchased here at the low rates ruling at present will yield more than one third [than in the east or middle states] . . . . The soil is a dark, rich vegetable mold varying from 2 to 8' in depth, capable of producing anything in the greatest profusion which will grow in these latitudes . . . and absolutely inexhaustible in its fertility . . . . The state is well watered . . . . Interest is 2% per annum, cost $5 to $25 per acre.[25]*

Resonating with the chords of their own dreams, the vivid advertisements amplified the hopes of the second wave of settlers. They wrote home that they had indeed found abundant streams to give them water,

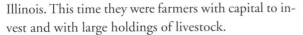

### IN THE GARDEN STATE OF THE WEST.

THE ILLINOIS CENTRAL RAILROAD CO., HAVE FOR SALE

## 1,200,000 ACRES OF RICH FARMING LANDS,

In Tracts of Forty Acres and upward on Long Credit and at Low Prices.

HOMES FOR THE INDUSTRIOUS
(Advertising cut widely used by the Illinois Central Railroad in 1860 and 1861)

Fig. 83. The richest and most fertile prairies dotted with magnificent oak groves. Advising that the lands west of the Mississippi were "destitute of Railroads," the Illinois Central tried to entice pioneers to settle in Illinois with views such as this *Homes for the Industrious*.

trees for building materials and fuel, groves full of game, and the rich soils that had been promised.

A Chicago newspaper soon reported, "Almost all vessels from the lower lakes are full of passengers . . . and our streets are thronged with wagons loaded with household furniture and the implements necessary to farming."[26]

To the west the land was a hive of activity—trees were felled, fields plowed and planted, houses built, and split-rail fences erected. Idealized views were circulated by the railroads (fig. 84). Not only in Illinois but in all the states bordering the Mississippi, settlement was so rapid that in 1818 Illinois became a state. Missouri filled up so quickly that it entered the Union in 1821; Arkansas joined in 1835, Iowa in 1846.[27]

After Hill died, the farmland around Cahokia was purchased by Daniel Page, who ran a sawmill by the creek. He sold it in 1860 to Thomas Ramey, who kept the site for many decades, a story to be continued in the next chapter. Perhaps Ramey had been lured west

by reading Frederick Gerhard's *Illinois as It Is*. In a chapter titled "Hints to Immigrants," Gerhard wrote: "A pair of good horses, a wagon, a cow, a couple of pigs, several domestic fowl, two ploughs (one for breaking the prairie, and the other for tillage), together with a few other tools and implements, are all that is necessary for a beginning."[28] Ramey erected a complex of farm buildings and tilled the soil right up to the border of the mound. His barn, fences, well and wellhead, carriages, house, and tilled fields reflect the growing prosperity of the second wave of immigrants to settle in Illinois (fig. 85).

## Archaeology at Cahokia: Early Days

It was during this second wave of immigration that the first professional-archaeologist-to-be came to Cahokia.[29] Charles Rau (1826–87), born in Germany, had attended the University of Heidelberg, where he studied mineralogy and chemistry. One of thousands of Germans to come to the Midwest in 1848, he settled in Belleville, Illinois, at age twenty-two and taught German to support his lifelong study of Indian artifacts. One day on a walk along Cahokia Creek Rau came upon a startling sight.

*At the point just mentioned [the left bank of Cahokia Creek] the bank of the creek is somewhat high and steep, leaving only a small space for a path along the water. When I passed therefore the first time, I noticed, scattered over the slope or protruding from the ground, a great many pieces of pottery of much larger size than I had ever seen before, some being of the size of a man's hand, and others considerably larger; and, upon examination, I found that they consisted of a grayish clay mixed with pounded shells. A great number of old shells of the* unio, *a bivalve which inhabits the creek, were lying about, and*

Fig. 84. Pastoral idyll in a new world. Accompanying flyers advertising lots for sale were images of prosperous farms like this *Prairie Scene in Illinois*.

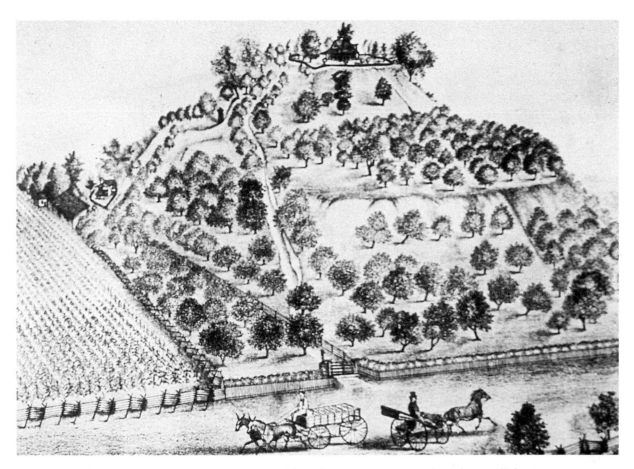

Fig. 85. View of a farmhouse atop Monks Mound: terraces of trees and fields of corn. An anonymous artist depicted Amos Hill's farm in 1873.

*their position induced me to believe that they had been brought there by human agency rather than by the overflowing of the creek. My curiosity being excited, I continued my investigation, and discovered at the upper part of the bank an old fosse, or digging, of some length and depth, and overgrown with stramonium or jimson weed; and upon entering this excavation, I saw near its bottom a layer of clay, identical in appearnce with that which composed the fragments of pottery. The excavation had unmistakably been dug for the purpose of obtaining the clay, and I became so convinced beyond doubt that the fabrication of earthen vessels had been carried on by the abo-*

*rigines at this very spot. All the requisites for manufacturing vessels were on hand; the layer of clay furnished the chief ingredient, and the creek not only supplied the water for moistening the clay, but harbored also the mollusks whose valves were used in tempering it. Wood abounded in the neighborhood. All these facts being ascertained, it was easy to account for the occurrence of the large fragments. Whenever pottery is made, some of the articles will crack during the process of burning . . . . The sherds found at this place may, therefore, with safety be considered as the remnants of vessels that were spoiled while in the fire, and thrown aside as objects unfit for use.[30]*

Rau had found an old Indian potters' site. The work that followed from this discovery occupied him for years. His careful drawings (fig. 86) and detailed analysis bespeak a scientifically trained professional of his era.

Rau's published articles in the *Annual Report of the Board of Regents of the Smithsonian Institution* (1864, 1867, 1872) demonstrate a professional approach to fieldwork, collection, description, and interpretation of the stone hoes, flint implements, and ceramic sherds he discovered. His footnotes also reveal that he was familiar with the pertinent literature over a broad range in several languages.[31]

During this early period, while moundless land was readily available nearby, farmers followed the path of least resistance and simply went around the mounds with their plows. From their standpoint, mounds were difficult and costly to raze, and abundant flat land was available cheaply nearby. Later, when urban areas moved ever outward, developers found it cost effective to raze the big piles of earth standing in their way and use the dirt to fill low areas and build dikes, levees, and embankments, notably at Big Mound in St. Louis and Cemetery Mound in East St. Louis. Mounds in a rural setting like Cahokia were farther from the eyes of real estate developers or industrial tycoons—at least for the moment.

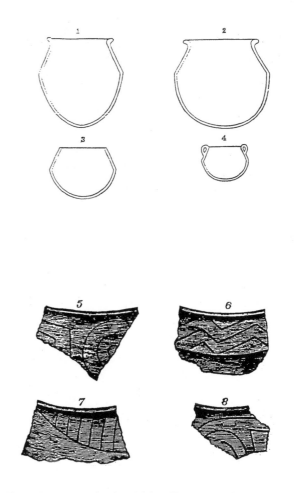

Fig. 86. An amateur archaeologist's labor of love turns professional. Charles Rau's careful drawings of the Native American artifacts he found near his home in Belleville, Illinois, and his published articles in the 1860s place him in the ranks of the earliest scholars of the area.

## Urban Expansion and Industrialization

At midcentury the major national transportation network was still the waterways. But as the nineteenth century moved on, ever more intensive land utilization threatened the very existence of the Cahokia Mounds. The swampy landscape around Cahokia had to be radically altered for the changing uses of the land. Soggy land had to be drained for farming, and new ditches and canals began to appear throughout Cahokia and the surrounding area.

At midcentury, just as it seemed the land had been altered sufficiently for drainage and was being fully exploited, a new network began to encroach: the black tracks of the iron horses of the railroads. Reaching out especially to the Midwest to carry grain in one direction and passengers and goods in the other, the railroad networks grew denser each succeeding year, especially after the Civil War. The commercial centers already established on the old waterways were natural focal points, and as the railroads paralleled the waterways, the old cities soon became crowded and congested.

As the railroads converged on St. Louis, Greater Cahokia was directly on the route. Many railroads laid their tracks along the very trails the Cahokia Indians had traced with their moccasins centuries before. As John Francis Snyder reported, one of these trails leading from Lebanon to Cahokia was so deep it was found as late as 1818. The mounds lining the paths of the new railroad lines not only were in the way, they were also irresistible sources of free dirt fill for causeways over the swampy land.

Urban growth was also responsible for the loss of twenty-six mounds in the late 1860s, including Big Mound in downtown St. Louis. In 1876 the great mound and several others at the Mitchell site were removed to make a smooth grade for three railroads, leveling part of an ancient Cahokia suburb near Long Lake. Many bodies and stone implements were exposed during construction, so there could have been no doubt that the mounds were ancient burial sites.[32]

One contributing factor in the loss of mounds was that some scientists, among them Amos Worthen, geologist of the Illinois Geological Survey from 1858 to 1875, still believed the mounds were natural phenomena—geological formations or erosional remains—and not man-made. It was perhaps convenient that such a distinguished scholar held this view, because it was no doubt very popular with railroad tycoons. But it helped hasten the destruction of the mounds. (Dr. A. R. Crook, director of the Illinois State Museum and a geologist, stated as late as 1921 that the mounds were remnants of glacial and alluvial deposits, a position that made life difficult for early twentieth-century archaeologists, as we shall see in the next chapter.) Ob-

servers called to Big Mound in St. Louis, however, noted burials of twenty to thirty bodies, all with feet to the west, covered from thighs to head with disc shells or *Marginella* beads (never both together). Each burial was accompanied by four to six quarts of small shells, with an average of 2,400 shells to the quart. The discovery should have put an end to the "natural phenomenon" theory, but it persisted, in fact, into the twentieth century—an example of useful, as well as wishful, thinking.[33]

At the time, however, the only people to raise their voices in alarm were archaeologists and a few scattered amateurs. The general public was indifferent, and the Native America population was not yet organized. The razings continued as the lines of the Litchfield and Madison, the Illinois Central, the Alton and Southern, and the Illinois Terminal Electric crossed Cahokia and its former suburbs. More incursions on the old Cahokia site to the south included the Baltimore and Ohio and the Pennsylvania Railroad tracks (figs. 87 and 88).

Fig. 87. Breathing fire and belching smoke. A locomotive of the 1860s roars across a bridge south of Monks Mound.

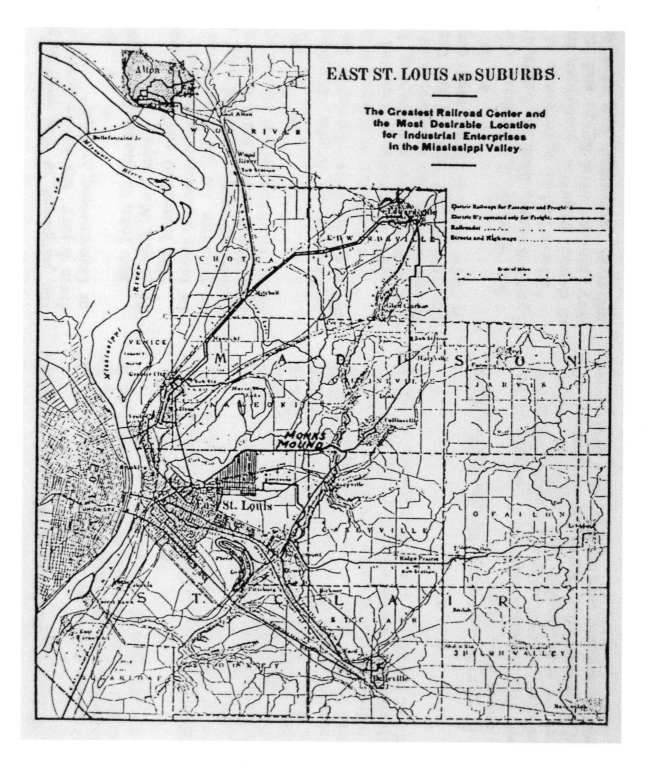

EAST ST. LOUIS AND SUBURBS.

The Greatest Railroad Center and
the Most Desirable Location
for Industrial Enterprises
in the Mississippi Valley.

Three spurs of the Illinois Terminal Electric also cut across to the north, one skirting the shores of Horseshoe Lake. The tracks of the Cleveland, Cincinnati, Chicago, and Saint Louis and those of the Wabash Railroad crossed the northwestern corner of Greater Cahokia. Another spur of the Alton and Southern crossed to the southwest. If the Cahokia Indians chose their homeland partly for its location at the nexus of a canoe transportation system, succeeding generations have endorsed their wisdom in thousands of tons of iron laid down during the railway age that followed the Civil War and in thousands of tons of concrete poured in the highway age that followed World War II.

At that time there were no American universities with departments of prehistoric North American archaeology. Archaeology professors devoted themselves mostly to ancient Greece, Rome, or sites on other continents and ignored their own country. The study of the mounds was left in the hands of dedicated amateurs from other scientific disciplines such as medicine, engineering, and dentistry.

And in the midst of all the incursions of the railway age on the landscape, a young doctor with an insatiable appetite for knowledge walked his own path in the territory.

## John Francis Snyder Demonstrates Archaeological Professionalism

John Francis Snyder was the son of a pioneer farmer from the first wave in Illinois. He was born in 1830 in Prairie du Pont, St. Clair County, where he lived on Square Mound Farm, later known as the Pulcher

Fig. 88. (opposite) Iron horses leave their tracks across ancient Indian territory. Heading for St. Louis, several railroads built embankments and laid tracks over the old Cahokia site.

Mound group. Snyder eventually earned degrees in both medicine and law, but the driving passion of his life was archaeology.[34] He devoted much of his time to a study of the mounds, producing carefully measured and oriented mapped descriptions that often included historical research material—the mark of a scientific professional.

Snyder was keen about publishing his findings, another attribute of professionalism, and his reports appeared first in the Smithsonian Institution's *Annual Report* for 1876 and thereafter in the *Archaeologist* and the *Journal of the Illinois State Historical Society.* Eventually he published more than thirty articles, all marked by a characteristic thoughtfulness.

Snyder's careful drawings of the artifacts he had assembled in his extensive collection were evidence of training in scientific observation he might have received in premedical studies in a biology laboratory (fig. 89).[35] On the other hand, he was also capable of depicting large landscape scenes (fig. 90).

*In trying to ascertain the composition of Monks Mound I examined the contents of a tunnel dug by Thomas T. Ramey 90 feet in length in the direction of its center, on the northside, about 30 feet above the base. In that exploration a small cube of lead ore was discovered, but no charcoal or ashes; not a flint, pot sherd or bone was found to indicate that the solid bluff clay excavated had ever been previously disturbed. But in that clay taken out of the tunnel I afterwards detected and secured several specimens of the small semi-fossil fluviatile shells, often occurring in the drift deposits of the bluffs, namely,* psysa heterostropha, limnea humilis, helix convaca, succinea obliqua, helix striatella *and others. In the same drift deposits fragments of galena are not uncommon. Close observers of the great mound have noticed that the south terrace and the lower part of the pyramid (made of clay) have retained comparatively well the integrity of their*

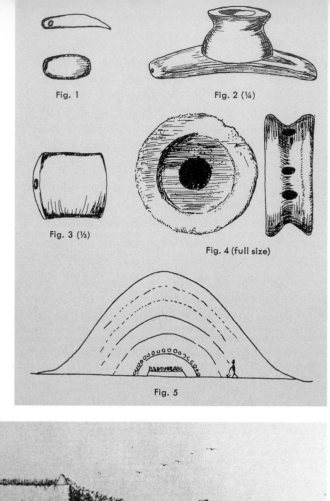

Fig. 1

Fig. 2 (¼)

Fig. 3 (⅓)

Fig. 4 (full size)

Fig. 5

Fig. 89. (top) Scientific observation of local Native American artifacts. John Francis Snyder, a doctor and lawyer, enjoyed a lifelong passion for archaeology. His careful drawings illustrated his many articles.

Fig. 90.(bottom) Birthplace of John Francis Snyder near Square Mound. Five miles south of Cahokia, near a temple mound, was the farm where Snyder spent the first three years of his life.

*original design; but the upper parts—particularly about the north-western angle of the summit—are deeply seamed and gashed by action of rain and frost. They have further noticed that the yawning channels of erosion seen there were cut through sandy soil and black silt. From this it is conjectured that the builders, becoming weary of carrying clay from a distance, concluded to complete the mound more speedily with such surface soil, sand or loam they could more conveniently scoop up near by.[36]*

Archaeological professionalism includes accurate and thorough measurement, clear description, objective interpretation, recognition of the necessity for publication, and also a rigorous ethical commitment with regard to future studies. Snyder demonstrated all these qualities. He was also an avid collector. In 1893 some of his specimens were placed on exhibit at the World's Columbian Exhibition (the Chicago World's Fair).

*In this interesting department we find a large case of the utensils and tools of stone, bone and shell, with specimens of pottery and woven fabrics and skulls of the cliff-dwellers from the cliffs of the Mesas [sic] Verde . . . .In different cases are displayed perhaps five thousand flint implements of all and every kind . . . .Other cases contain many curious vessels and vases of pottery ware taken from the mounds; stone pipes of varied designs, some very rude and some very brightly polished; armlets, beads and other ornaments . . . and implements of native copper hammered into shape with stones.[37]*

Later Snyder's country museum in Virginia, Illinois— a small building by his home where he exhibited his colection—attracted statewide notice.

In January 1897 Snyder's ability as a writer led him to assume the editorship of a monthly archaeological magazine titled the *American Antiquarian*. The low price of the publication was designed to attract the "working, thinking, investigating" portion of the middle-income group, although, the editor stated, he intended to place the magazine "on the level of the leading science publications of our country." Two years later, unfortunately (and through no fault of the doctor's), the magazine was bankrupt.[38] Added to Snyder's list of accomplishments must also be his stature as an early preservationist.

Snyder worked tirelessly to stimulate state-sponsored professional research into Illinois's prehistory. He was also one of the first to take part in the campaign to make Monks Mound into a state park. He helped organize a group called the Monks of Cahokia[39] and wrote a pamphlet titled "The Prehistoric Mounds of Illinois" to further this effort. Deploring the ravages of curio seekers and commercial enterprises exploiting Indian artifacts, Snyder thought that the remedy for piecemeal looting was state-sponsored scientific research. At the first meeting of the Illinois State Historical Society, January 6, 1900, Snyder (a founding member) presented his views in a paper titled "The Field for Archaeological Research in Illinois."

Fearing for the future of archaeology in his native state, and foreseeing that valuable prehistoric Indian mounds, as yet hardly explored, would be plowed under as railroads and highways spread across the state, Snyder argued in passionate terms for the preservation of Illinois antiquities and the granting of state aid to ensure their adequate investigation. He was indignant because Illinois universities subsidized archaeological expeditions to foreign lands while prehistoric Indian sites in the state lay virtually ignored.[40]

He had also planted the seed of the idea of state-supported research. Later the state finally sponsored archaeological work in Illinois.

## John J. R. Patrick Hires an Engineer to Measure Monks Mound

Like Dr. Snyder, John J. R. Patrick, a dentist who lived nearby in Belleville, Illinois, was an enthusiastic amateur antiquarian. Shortly after the Civil War he began his serious study of the mounds in the Cahokia Creek district. To ensure the accuracy of the work, Patrick employed C. H. Shannon, then chief engineer of the Wabash Railroad, to measure Monks Mound.

*By the method of triangulations familiar to civil engineers Mr. Shannon found the greatest height of the mound to be a fraction over 97 feet. Measured with an engineer's chain, and making due allowance for the indistinct line of junction of the mound's lower edge with the common surface of the plain, he ascertained the extreme length of its base to be 1010 feet and its width 710 feet. The area it covers—by his calculation—is 13.85 acres; the rectangular plateau of its summit comprises 1.45 acres and the earthen material of the mound approximates very closely 1,076,000 cubic yards.[41]*

The schematic drawing (fig. 91) was an act of abstraction, an effort at seeing the original geometry underlying the mound, for the mound's real appearance more closely resembled a drawing William McAdams had published at the same time (fig. 92).

*To form an adequate conception of the immensity of this earthwork, by comparison, it may be stated that the most gigantic achievement of aboriginal labor in the United States (next to the Cahokia mound) is Old Fort Ancient, in Warren county, Ohio, whose four miles of huge embankment and included mounds contain—as estimated by Orif Niiregead—738,000 cubic yards of displaced earth. The basal area, 760 feet square, of the pyramid of*

Fig. 91. An abstracted view of Monks Mound. Using a map made by a railway engineer he had hired, Dr. John J. R. Patrick, a dentist who was an archaeologist by avocation, drew this schematic view of Monks Mound. It is useful today in helping people visualize how the four distinctive terraces once appeared.

*Cheops, in Egypt, one of the "seven wonders of the world" is just 13 acres.[42]*

Patrick's map, not dated but probably drawn in 1865–76, remained the best if not the only plan of the whole of the Cahokia site until 1967, for most subsequent maps were based on it. To this day it is still an invaluable source of information about the state of the site in the late nineteenth century.

At the end of the 1880s writer Stephen Peet took up the cause. Paying attention both to singular finds of importance, and to the discoveries of Dr. Snyder and others, Peet was also a historian with a broader view, a man with an eye to compiling the literature that had come in bits and pieces before his time. This inestimable service to the cause is best illustrated by his article "The Great Cahokia Mound" in the *American Antiquarian* in January 1891. As editor of the journal, Peet

Fig. 92. A closeup view of Monks Mound in 1882. Ten years after he drew this picture, William McAdams prepared an exhibit for the World's Columbian Exposition, the Chicago World's Fair of 1893 that dazzled thousands of visitors.

Fig. 93. Masked man with a bird's beak, earspools, and feathers. The sky world of the bird, the earth world of men, and the underworld of the snake are all symbolically embodied in this one "Birdman Tablet." The snakeskin pattern is crosshatched on the back. Found on Monks Mound in 1971, this image is now the logo of the Cahokia Mounds.

also published nine other articles pertaining to Cahokia during 1889–1903.

*The conditions of life in the different parts of the Mississippi Valley seem to have varied according to the climate, soil, and scenery, but they are so concentrated into a narrow compass that one may, by the aid of steam and the railroad train, pass in one day from the midst of the wild savage hunters of the north into the very midst of the works of the semi-civilized agricultural people of the south, and may find the whole panorama of the prehistoric races unrolled and the whole condition of society in prehistoric times rapidly brought before the eyes.[43]*

Of Cahokia specifically Peet wrote:

*There is, perhaps, no spot in the Mississippi Valley which has been oftener visited by distinguished persons and no monument which has oftener gone into history . . . .a very beautiful pair of earth-works stands immediately south of the great pyramid, each one presenting its sides covered with varied foliage, the golden autumnal tints being set-off against the silvery radiance of the little artificial lake which lay in the background.[44]*

Calculated to appeal to the romantic artist and to the tourist seeking the sublime beauties of the plains, Peet's prose excited prospective travelers, tourists, and archaeologists in other fields. Peet also put the Cahokia earthworks in the context of other mounds in Louisiana, Mississippi, Georgia, and Alabama.

## The Razing of Big Mound: The First Steps toward Preservation

In the 1860s the razing of Big Mound in St. Louis caused widespread concern not just in archaeological circles but in the minds of the educated public as well. Photographs of the cavalier damage done enraged laypeople and professionals alike (figs. 94 and 95). Ironically, the publicity surrounding the removal of a mound for road construction and road fill may have

Fig. 94. The publicity surrounding the razing of Big Mound in St. Louis, shown here in the 1850s, became part of the collective memory of all educated people in the area.

Fig. 95. By 1869 the wanton razing of Big Mound was nearly complete. Recalling this loss served as a catalyst for the preservation movement in the next century.

been a rallying point for future preservationists, who could hark back to the wanton destruction with dire predictions for the future of Illinois archaeology.

What brought knowledge of the great Mississippian civilization to an international audience, however, was not newspaper articles about the loss of the Big Mound, which mostly were published locally or in magazines like *Harper's Monthly* for the educated elite, but the World's Columbian Exposition of 1893, the Chicago World's Fair.

### William McAdams Tells the World: No Other Stone Age People Went Further Than the Mound Builders of Illinois

The White City, as the fair was nicknamed, attracted visitors from all over the globe. World's fairs were the showcases of art and scholarship in those days before online exhibitions, and archaeologist William McAdams prepared a stunning show, "The Stone Age in Illinois," for the Geology and Archaeology section of the Illinois Building. With professorial authority, the respected scholar, who had already published several articles, declared:

*The mounds on the Cahokia creek are the work of a great nation, for here in the midst of a level plain rises a pyramid over a hundred feet in height and covering sixteen acres of ground. And this mighty pyramid—for it is pyramidal in shape—is surrounded by nearly a hundred others of great size, and made only with a prodigious amount of labor . . . .*

*Finally, these mound builders became a great nation with an established religion and an organized government. They lived in large communities on the rich bottom lands . . . with colonies about them for a hundred miles or more . . . . These people became so numerous and strong and so well organized that they were able to erect enormous temples . . . on which to have their ceremonies or religious observances.[45]*

All of McAdams's evidence came from the material culture and from the scientific accounts of his predecessors. The McAdams display cases at the fair were filled with hundreds of artifacts to back up his claim that *no other known Stone Age people went further than the Mound Builders of Illinois.*

Citing several examples to prove his point, McAdams demonstrated that a wide variety of stones had been used for a wide variety of purposes—hunting, agricultural, ceremonial, recreational, domestic, ornamental, and aesthetic. The exquisite craftsmanship of a fifteen-pound granite ax found in Madison County, for example, made it the "finest grooved axe" he had seen in thirty years of fieldwork.[46] A celt of quartzite he regarded as "exquisitely wrought" with "great labor."

Other examples of ceremonial objects he described as "beautiful relics . . . for the most part finely and symmetrically shaped and well polished. They were too small to have been weapons and were doubtless made with great labor and almost inconceivable patience, for some sort of ceremonial purpose."[47] No primitive people could have produced such objects. Only a society organized into specialized groups would need them; only a division of labor into classes that included craftsmen would be capable of such refinement.

*The incentive to manufacture these objects is, of course, unknown to us, but it must have been a most powerful one. Possibly [the celts] were carried to designate some peculiar position the wearer held in the tribe or nation. They may have had a religious significance . . . . At any rate these peculiar ceremonial stones stand today as the highest examples of stone carving, or rather of stone working of the ancient inhabitants of this region or of the continent.[48]*

The carved stone pipes in the exhibit also entranced the visitors. As McAdams wrote of a resting frog of red flint clay (fig. 96) found on the bluff east of the great mound in Cahokia, "the legs and feet are well delineated, the eyes projecting and full, and the general appearance of the object quite spirited . . . .the right hand holds a sort of mace or knobbed instrument, evidently some sort of symbol indicative of position or other meaning."[49]

After an exhaustive account of the stone objects, McAdams examined items made of copper, bone, shells, and pottery. Each class of artifacts further substantiated the conclusion he had drawn from the stone objects, or "lithic evidence": the Stone Age people of Cahokia were a great nation.

Most people even today do not understand the sophistication of some Stone Age technologies, especially in the Western Hemisphere, where the Stone Age was

Fig. 96. A spirited frog sings and rattles. William McAdams exhibited this carved stone pipe of flint clay at the Chicago World's Fair of 1893 as part of his claim that "no other Stone Age people went farther than the mound builders of Illinois."

not cut short by metallurgy as it was in the Eastern Hemisphere. Although in the Western Hemisphere some Native Americans in the Lake Superior region started using copper about 3000 B.C., they did not smelt metals. By the time of the Mississippians, Appalachian copper was in use. All of this is a warning that certain assumptions about the social, economic, and political dynamics of Stone Age societies in the Western Hemisphere can not be made based on what we know of Stone Age societies in the Eastern Hemisphere. Long-distance expeditions for scarce resources and competition for these resources, for example, did exist among many Stone Age peoples, not just among later groups.

McAdams had built on the accounts of others—Brackenridge, Wild, Rau, Patrick—but it was his re-

port that reached an international audience. His claim that no other Stone Age people on the globe had reached such heights gave a new luster, and a new meaning, to Cahokian studies, which for the first time acquired a worldwide reputation with the general public.

In the late nineteenth century world's fairs were not just the commercial and tourist attractions they became in the twentieth century but were major scientific events as well. They provided a forum for international meetings of scientists and religious and social leaders and offered displays of the arts. International conventions, or congresses as they were called, were held in the fair cities and offered matchless opportunities to exchange ideas and information. At the Electricity Building at the Chicago fair, for example, the new arc lights, incandescent lights, and colored floodlights first demonstrated that light could be used as an architectural medium. Ecumenism and women's suffrage were debated in the auditoriums of participating institutions in downtown Chicago during the months the fair was open.

Drawing on the cachet of the Chicago fair, and in anticipation of the fair to come in St. Louis in 1904, magazines like *Harper's Monthly* shined a new light on Cahokia.

An article by Harlan Ingersoll Smith titled "The Great American Pyramid" is a good example. The author, an anthropologist from the American Museum of Natural History, extolled the Cahokia site and made a plea for its preservation.

*Unguarded from the elements, unprotected from the plough, the great Cahokia mound, which rises, in terraces, from a base eleven hundred and eighty by seven hundred and fifty feet, to a height of one hundred and two feet, covers an area greater than that occupied by the Great Pyramid of Egypt . . . .constructed by probably the most powerful and highly civilized of the aborigines of the United States . . . the Cahokia mound is by far the most imposing, as it is, indeed, of all the aboriginal mounds.*

*The entire archaeological exhibit of the State of Illinois at the World's Fair of 1893 is said to have been made up of pottery and weapons found in a single excavation not far from one of the sixty smaller mounds lying nearby and subordinate to the mass of the Cahokia . . . . The interest in all things American which is already aroused, and will be continuously increased as the date of the St. Louis Fair draws near, could be no better utilized than by taking the right steps to preserve the Cahokia mound in a public park, free from taxation, under the auspices of the State or of the national government.[50]*

The author then goes on to tell of laws protecting the Great Serpent Mound in Ohio and of beginning efforts in Michigan, Colorado, and the territory of New Mexico. There is no doubt that archaeology and preservation went hand in hand at the turn of the century and that archaeologists like Snyder and Smith were our first preservationists. Smith went on:

*The preservation for future generations of the site . . . the safeguarding against the waste of time, and the desecration by ignorance of this colossal memorial of that civilization of which we have such scant knowledge; the exploration by skilled hands of the interior of this American pyramid; the discovery of its import and the deciphering of its records and relics—surely all this would be a fitting task for the American people, and especially for the people of the State of Illinois when about to celebrate at St. Louis, close by the Cahokia site, and later events which perhaps are no more intimately bound up in our common history . . . . No pyramidal monument of any size approaching this has yet been scientifically explored. Of them all the Cahokia mound is the chief of the type . . . . Prompt action is necessary to prevent the ploughing down of the sides and*

*the heedless digging away of the structure and contents of the Great American Pyramid.[51]*

## Summary

At the dawn of the nineteenth century Cahokia was still as it had been for hundreds of years. French and Spanish were spoken more than English, and the landscape looked very much the same as at the height of the Mississippian civilization a millennium before. But European power politics and even European cultural aspirations affected the area with growing frequency and increasing force. At the same time, and with epic devastation, the armies of the United States "removed" the Native American population from the land. Shortly thereafter, the forces of the Industrial Revolution and the urban expansion that followed wreaked drastic changes on the landscape.

In the midst of these historic forces a handful of scholars, artists, writers, and scientists began their quiet work on the Cahokia Mounds. Aside from curio hunters, interest at first was confined to gentlemen scholars. Educated men, often from professions such as medicine and dentistry, were captivated by the mystery of the Mound Builders and made significant discoveries, which were then expanded by more careful studies in the second half of the century. With the advent of world's fairs, beginning with the great exhibition in London in 1851, collectors of Amerindian artifacts began to display their findings in glass cases for the world to see. But it was the spectacular success of the World's Columbian Exposition of 1893 in Chicago that affected Cahokia's future the most. At its close Cahokia's reputation as an important prehistoric site was secure. Reputation alone, however, was not enough to resist pressures of a different kind looming in the century to come.

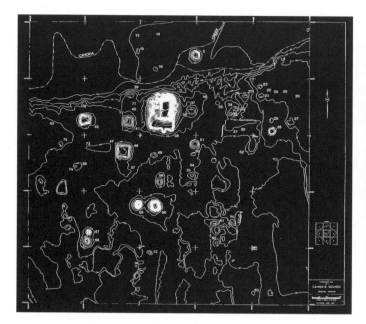

FIG. 97. MAP OF CENTRAL CAHOKIA IN AMERINDIAN TIMES
WITH MOUNDS AND PRINCIPAL CREEKS (LEFT). THE SAME
TERRAIN IN 1966 WITH STREETS, HIGHWAYS, RAILROAD
TRACKS, A DRIVE-IN MOVIE, AIRSTRIP, STORES,
HOUSES, AND OTHER MODERN ADDITIONS (RIGHT).

# Early Twentieth-Century Cahokia

Setting the Stage

Although the transformation of the Cahokian landscape was greater in the nineteenth century than in any other period since Mississippian times, the land uses of the early twentieth century were more varied. In the early part of the century the mounds were nearly lost to the forces of greed, ignorance, and negative attitudes toward Native Americans and their traditions. With the passing of years, technological and cultural developments changed both the meaning and the appearance of the mounds. Their very survival hung in the balance.

One major cultural event, the Louisiana Purchase Exposition—the St. Louis World's Fair of 1904—set in motion repercussions that affected Cahokia for decades. And on one night in 1923, in a frightening symbolic gesture, the Ku Klux Klan burned a fiery cross on top of Monks Mound with unsuspected consequences. During the same decade, daring flier-photographers revealed unforeseen archaeological possibilities east and south of the great pyramid.

We know from United States Geological Survey (USGS) maps and other sources that part of the old Mississippian grounds became the site of a drive-in movie theater in the 1950s; other metamorphoses included a racetrack, nightclubs, a golf course, and even an airport, although it is hard to imagine why anyone would build an airport in the swamp east of Mound 95, where flooding was a frequent problem. We shall see later that only a unique and short-lived cultural expectation accounts for this anomaly. The maps prompt other questions: How could sixty houses sprout at the foot of Monks Mound in about fifteen years and disappear (with few exceptions) about forty years later? How did archaeologists manage to work amid all these changes, and what did they accomplish?

## St. Louis Greets the World and Cahokia Receives Thousands of Guests

In 1904 "Meet me in St. Louis" meant meet me at the crossroads of the world, the St. Louis World's Fair. Like the Chicago World's Fair of 1893, the St. Louis fair was much more than a place of commerce and amusement. The pavilions of the various states and nations exhibited the latest inventions, promoted new manufacturing devices and models of industry, and displayed illustrious examples of contemporary sculpture and painting. People from exotic places such as Indonesia or the Philippines were also "imported" and put on display as examples of "primitive societies." Visitors came from all over the globe as the host city showed off its hotels, restaurants, and local attractions. Plans for the fair had galvanized St. Louis for months. One of the key attractions was an excursion to Cahokia.

The Great East Side Electric Railway System (fig. 98) was painted and polished for "swift-speeding" trips over the Mississippi to East St. Louis and Monks Mound or, as a brochure of the times boasted, to the "Mecca, or Grand Central Shrine of the Mound Builders' Empire." Trolley parties on two special "palace cars" called *The Mounds* and *The Bluffs* were organized for special excursions or family outings on Sundays even before the fair opened and lasted after it closed.

You could charter a whole private car for the day, complete with "wilton carpets, velvet portieres, windows draped with Morie Damask [*sic*]," and each car was supplied with "portable tables, which can be placed at any window." The conductors and motormen wore special uniforms, and each car seated sixty passengers. Rates for a chartered car over the entire system, from East St. Louis to Belleville, and thence to Edwardsville via Caseyville and Collinsville and return via Monks Mound, was fifty dollars, less than a dollar per person. Stopovers en route were provided "at

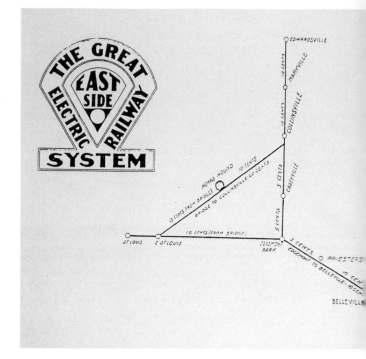

Fig. 98. Meet me in St. Louis and ride the trolley to Cahokia. Electric interurban trains took visitors to the St. Louis World's Fair of 1904 across the Mississippi to see the "Mecca of the Mounds Builders' Empire." *The Great East Side Electric Railway System* shows a logo, map, and private trolley car party.

pleasure," and "extra floral or other decorations" could be added at moderate cost.[1]

For Cahokia this sudden metamorphosis into a world tourist attraction was a double-edged sword, as was widespread dissemination in *Harper's Monthly* of the rave reviews of scholars such as Harlan Ingersoll Smith, head of the Anthropology Department at the American Museum of Natural History. In the long term, knowledge of the mounds contributed to the preservation of the site. In the short term, however, its effect was alarming. According to photographs taken before and after the fair, visitors literally picked the site to pieces, completely denuding the surrounding trees by taking leaves for souvenirs.

Why would people do this? The answer is a clue to the central theme of this book: the changing meanings of the great pyramid and the new values accruing to the site over time. While it is true that the cumulative effect of the little acts of leaf picking was wholesale vandalism, what was the larger meaning of these acts?

## New Values Accrue to the Site

Over the centuries the sight of the great pyramid has always moved people deeply, but their responses have varied in different periods of history. At the time of the St. Louis fair, Americans were becoming interested in the American Indians' way of looking at the land, in their spiritual attitude toward nature. Since many were living in increasingly crowded cities, the need to feel closer to the earth was also growing. Their new urban world, they felt, was "anti-nature" or at least "apart from nature," but they believed the Indians' world was intertwined with nature because the "Great Spirit" embodied all living things. By taking home a leaf of a tree from the same soil the Indians held sacred, visitors could partake of something of the Indians' spirit, of a view of life they yearned for.

The sight of the great pyramid had also filled visitors of all periods with thoughts of the courage and determination of the human spirit in adversity, and tourists from the fair were no exception. How could an ancient people, without beasts of burden or the wheel, have built such a magnificent monument? Awe, admiration, and fellow feeling also played a part in the early twentieth-century visitors' experience. Together the yearning and the new kind of appreciation fostered a public atmosphere in which a preservation movement could grow.

There were no souvenir shops at the mounds, and pressing flowers and leaves in books was a common Victorian practice, a way of preserving memories or treasured thoughts.[2] Fortunately, some of the visitors also recorded their thoughts in published words.

*During a sojourn in that fairyland of modern marvels, the Louisiana Purchase Exposition, held at St. Louis . . . it was the privilege of this writer in company with a party including several students of American archaeology to make an inspection of the world-famed Cahokia Mound . . . . We climbed the jagged flank to the summit and stood upon the elevation that lifted us above the surrounding plain . . . . Roundabout on every hand, like contrasting features of a face vanished and forgotten and a people now world predominant, were interspersed the weather-beaten and depleted mounds and the prosperous farm homes. . . . Here certainly was one of the great centers, if not the chief center, in the western continent of this mysterious people. . . . Here in greatest number were found their largest monuments, which bear testimony to their patience and industry and long sojourn.[3]*

*This mound stands like a solemn monarch; lonely in its grandeur, but imposing in its presence. Though many trains go rumbling across the valley and through the great bridge which spans the river, yet this monster stands as a mute witness of a people which has passed away. It is a silent statue, a sphinx, which still keeps within its depths the mystery which no one has yet fathomed . . . .*

*Was it some mighty tomb erected to be the fitting mausoleum of a great conqueror or chief—some terrible Attila, or invincible Alaric, a Caesar or Napoleon of savage days? Small wonder that the scene presented from that Cahokia summit awakened one's curiosity and stirred one's imagination. Marvelous relic-preservation of a prehistoric people looming like the dome of a cathedral from the level valley—the arena in which a vast race had lived and toiled, had come, seen and perhaps had conquered, achieved their ambitions and proudly expended their energies . . . .*

*As my companions were discussing the unsolved riddle of the past there came to our memory Volney's Meditations on the "Ruins of Empires"; seated amid the demolished architectural splendors of Palmyra in the Syrian plain of the historic Euphrates, there passed before his "mind's eye" the representatives of buried dynasties and dead faiths. What a chance was here at Cahokia for some historico-philosophic dreamer to "interrogate ancient Monuments on the wisdom of past times." Surely here were the remains of a vast and vanished empire. In this valley of the Mississippi had flourished, who knows how long ago, a mighty nation; they had built better than they knew, for their simple and stupendous structures had survived "the tooth of time and razure of oblivion."[4]*

A more long-lasting effect also came out of the St. Louis World's Fair: Cahokia became better known in international archaeological circles and aroused sporadic interest among scholars. Interrupted by two world wars and a severe national depression, study of the mounds picked up again in the 1960s and has intensified in recent years. Since local antiquarians, laypeople, and archaeologists working together founded the preservation movement, both their own investigations and the new appreciation of preservation they fostered had a profound effect on the Cahokia Mounds in the twentieth century.

One professional, William C. Mills, curator of the Ohio State Archaeological and Historical Society, wrote:

*I became interested in the Cahokia Mounds during the World's Fair in St. Louis and had several occasions to visit the mound with representatives from various parts of the world, and on one occasion I took a party of scientists numbering more than forty, and in a short address I gave them at the mound I urged upon the State of Illinois to take steps to secure this wonderful monument and preserve*

*it for all time. I explained that, in Ohio, where we have a great many interesting mounds, we had none so fine and beautiful as Cahokia Mound, yet we have taken steps to preserve them in their original form. Ohio has been, and is still, purchasing them. At present we have Fort Ancient, comprising some three hundred acres, made into a beautiful park; Serpent Mound, of over seventy acres, kept likewise; Big Bottom Park is another one of our possessions.[5]*

Right after the fair David I. Bushnell, an archaeologist at the Peabody Museum of American Archaeology and Ethnology at Harvard, published a scholarly account, "The Cahokia and Surrounding Mound Groups," in the *Papers of the Peabody Museum of American Archaeology and Ethnology,* which was read by all serious professionals. Bushnell, a native of St. Louis, had become interested in the mounds as a boy and continued his interest throughout his adult life.

A critical mass of public opinion about all American historical monuments was reaching the point where Congress felt enough pressure from several parts of the country to enact the first federal preservation law, the Antiquities Act of 1906. It enabled the president to proclaim certain sites national landmarks, establish permit requirements for archaeological work on federally owned or managed land, and penalize anyone who violated the law. It was watershed legislation. But Cahokia was not on the list.

Shattered, local supporters realized that legislation preserving the mounds had to be won first on the state level. As John E. Kelly wrote,

*Scholars at the Illinois Historical Society and elsewhere feared that the Ramey family heirs, the owners, would sell the land to a local brewery, who would buy it, honeycomb the mound with vaults for storing beer, and turn the site into a beer garden. Their fears were not groundless. Although Monks Mound was not turned into a storage vault, a tavern and beer garden called Schmidt's Mound Park did open east of Monks Mound. A discount store followed and later even a baseball diamond sprouted on the north side of the site.[6]*

Also, fields east of Monks Mound were platted for possible subdivisions.

In 1910 the Illinois Historical Society asked Warren K. Moorehead (1866–1939) to speak at an upcoming meeting. It was an astute invitation. Moorehead was renowned and well regarded. When he was only twenty-one he had exhibited his boyhood collection of Indian artifacts at the Centennial Exposition of Cincinnati in 1888 and soon thereafter was hired as an aide by Dr. Thomas Wilson of the Smithsonian Institution.

By 1891 F. W. Putnam of Harvard had put Moorehead in charge of excavations at the famous Hopewell site in the Scioto Valley to prepare an exhibition for the Chicago World's Fair of 1893. By working arduously, sometimes through the winter, Moorehead found many artifacts to exhibit—repoussé items in copper, effigies in stone, amulets, and pearl beads.[7] To accompany the exhibition Moorehead wrote a book, *Primitive Man in Ohio,* that was published in time for the opening of the fair. Books accompanying exhibitions were not as common in those days as they are today, and the tandem effort gained him a reputation as a prolific archaeologist. After the fair Moorehead joined Charles Peabody at Phillips Academy in Andover, Massachusetts, as curator and later served as director of the Peabody Museum for the rest of his career. In 1908, two years before the invitation to speak in Illinois, President Theodore Roosevelt had appointed Moorehead a commissioner of the United States Bureau of Indian Affairs.

More important than the speech he gave in Illinois, however, were the impressions Moorehead received. Like many brilliant people before and after him,

Moorehead was profoundly struck by the Cahokia Mounds. He returned to Cahokia eleven years later for serious work of his own. It was almost too late. Loss of the mounds was imminent. He had arrived in the nick of time.

Although loyal mound supporters had not been idle in the intervening years, their efforts to bring about government purchase—either federal or state—had been futile. After Cahokia was not included on the list following the Antiquities Act of 1906, dozens of groups organized themselves privately to try to save the site. The Monks of Cahokia boasted several hundred members from Madison and St. Clair Counties. They even met at "Schmidt's Mound Park," marched in the Madison County Centennial Parade, and otherwise made their presence felt, but to no avail.

Dozens of other existing civic groups also rallied to the cause of saving the mounds through purchase by the federal government, among them the Schubert Club of East St. Louis and the Federation of Women's Clubs in Granite City. A committee of eighty-four businessmen in St. Louis, including the Ramey brothers, the owners of the Monks Mound property, joined in the effort. In spite of all these pressures, a bill sponsored by local congressional representative Rodenberg in 1909 to make Cahokia a national park failed to pass. This crushing defeat forced the local people to realize that saving the mounds would once again be left to efforts in Illinois.

**Mounds Doubly in Jeopardy**

The mounds' destruction was imminent at every turn, and several did fall to the plow and the entrepreneur as the leveling continued. No sooner was one threat averted than another rose. Like a many-headed hydra, urbanization on all sides encroached on the old Indian ceremonial site. Developers coveted nearby land. St. Louis was a growing economic center, and with the railroad and the advent of the automobile, traffic engineers wanted direct access to the city. Mounds were doubly in jeopardy: they impeded national transportation routes, and they were readily available sources of much-needed cheap dirt for railroad and highway embankments across the swampy American Bottom.

When an electric railway company proposed building another spur across the mounds site in 1913, the local community was again aroused. Norman G. Flagg, the state representative in Springfield, sponsored a bill to make the mounds a state park. People in Edwardsville formed a Save the Mounds society, and they were joined soon thereafter by the Kickapoo Club of Bloomington. Everyone waited with bated breath for newspaper accounts of the debate in Springfield. At a crucial moment, Representative Burke from Cook County took the floor and stated bluntly, "My district needs parks for live people, and the guys in that mound are all dead ones." The bill died. Repeated attempts afterward also died.

## World War I Period

While national efforts were directed toward the war effort during World War I, the hiatus was a breathing space for Cahokia. Highway and railroad building and other urban encroachments abated for a few years. As soon as the war ended, however, real estate prices started climbing, and "empty" land was again eyed enviously. Acting quickly, the Ramey family and the Harding Brothers Syndicate bought the three hundred acres across from Monks Mound, known as Brooks Pasture. But later the *East St. Louis Daily Journal* reported:

*Hope for the preservation of the mounds of Cahokia . . . passed this week with the transfer of this tract to a real estate syndicate . . . . Fred Harding [of the syndicate] said, "We are merely adding to our present holdings . . . in the Washington Park factory district. We are not buying it with the idea of making it either a state or private park. There is not enough general enthusiasm to make the latter pay, and the mounds have been held by the Rameys and Brookses for many years, during which time they exhausted every effort to make it a state park. Even with the scientists of the country indorsing their move nothing was ever done by the state of Illinois towards making this a state park. We have been pushing the development of East St. Louis in that direction, and with one or two other holders have, what we believe, is the greatest factory and residential district in the East St. Louis district . . . . We have been after this property for over a year. It will most certainly be a home and factory district. Factories could be located along the B. & O. Belt railways [on the southern border of the site], leaving the rest of the tract for homes for workers.*[8]

There were already two electric car lines reaching this district—the Washington Park and Collinsville lines. Perhaps Harding envisaged for East St. Louis the same type of development that had already occurred outside St. Louis. The spread of cities into outlying areas was the rule rather than the exception in the United States after the war.[9]

Fearing the worst, David Kinley, president of the University of Illinois, a man keenly interested in Cahokia, was open to Moorehead's suggestion that Moorehead come to Illinois again, this time for serious, long-term investigations, without any demand for a salary.[10] After two years of negotiations between Moorehead, the university, and the Illinois State Museum, a contract was finally signed in 1921 stipulating that the materials collected would go to the Illinois

State Museum and the University of Illinois. At last Moorehead arrived, but the climate of public opinion was so dangerous it was clear from the outset that his work could not be confined to serious archaeological research alone.

## Five Separate Battles to Fight

With full command of the situation, Moorehead saw at once that the mounds were threatened on five separate fronts. He needed to secure permission from the owners for limited exploration; interest the press in telling the story to arouse more interest in support of legislation "to make of these tumuli and other remains a state park"; ascertain through exploration and excavation the character of the Cahokia people so as to enlist support in preserving the monuments and artifacts of their culture; persuade the University of Illinois or some competent state institution to continue proper explorations on an extensive scale; and raise the necessary funds to support these battles.

In spite of realistic evidence that defeat in any one of the areas would spell disaster for the whole enterprise and that a successful outcome was therefore unlikely, the intrepid Moorehead began to fight with full intensity on all five fronts.

Hiring several local former servicemen, Moorehead directed the digging of a trench sixty feet wide into the north face of Kunnemann Mound, where artifacts were uncovered, settling once and for all the question whether the mounds were man-made. Until then the director of the Illinois State Museum, A. R. Crook— a geologist—had maintained that they were natural formations. Although Crook was in favor of making the area a state park, his position on the origins of the mounds had been a major obstacle in the campaign to save them. The Ramey family's full support followed

soon after, and a good working relationship between the family and the archaeologist lasted several years.

With characteristic vigor Moorehead then hired teams of horses to drag a slip to unearth shallowly buried artifacts (fig. 99), workers to trench (fig. 100), others to bore (fig. 101), and assistants to describe and classify the findings. He kept the artifacts he found in cigar boxes labeled according to the levels at which they were uncovered. Moorehead's methods seem crude to modern archaeologists, who pride themselves on more rigorous methods.

Moorehead also knew that publishing his findings was important far beyond the professional responsibility of disseminating information and maintaining his own reputation: a wider public would furnish much-needed support for preserving the mounds. His report

#123-a. Trench face at summit of Harding mound. 6-8-27. Looking east

Fig. 99. Archaeological methods in the 1920s. Warren K. Moorehead hired former servicemen to drive the horse pulling the slip across Harding Mound (later known as Rattlesnake Mound) to expose soil profiles and to whitewash to indicate stratigraphy.

Fig. 100. (top) Digging trenches, photographing, and storing artifacts. In those days Moorehead kept many of the objects he found in carefully labeled cigar boxes.

Fig. 101. (bottom) Boring deep into the mounds. A hand-augering method Moorehead used in 1927 enabled him to take samples from older layers.

on the 1921 excavation in the *University of Illinois Bulletin,* exhibited recently at the Cahokia Mounds Museum, summarized his results to date.

Just as it seemed the archaeological work was off to a good start, violation of Monks Mound came from an entirely unexpected quarter.

## The Ku Klux Klan "Appropriates" the Site

On the night of May 26, 1923, 12,000 masked members of the Ku Klux Klan rallied in full regalia at Monks Mound (fig. 102). Attracted by the enormous size of the site, and hoping to appropriate its monu-

Fig. 102. Rally for the Ku Klux Klan. Row after row of parked cars (A) attest to the presence of a large crowd that gathered at Cahokia in July 1923. They built a large wooden cross (B) and set it high atop a mound for burning later under the night sky (C).

mentality for their cause, the Klan burned a huge cross on top of the great pyramid as a "guiding beacon" for arriving Klansmen. The meeting culminated in a midnight ride through the streets of Collinsville with participants "sounding their horns and creating a din which was heard all over the city." Some of the automobile drivers and their riders wore white witchlike caps; others carried pieces of white cloth.

Cars blocked the road for three miles on each side of the meeting place. Two newspaper reporters were denied admittance to the grounds, but they later crossed a field on the edge of the place where the ceremony was in progress by "pursuing a circuitous route." They were prevented from seeing the event by four unmasked men armed with clubs, but they heard cheering at intervals.[11]

Who were these Klansmen, and why were they at Cahokia? There were three separate Ku Klux Klan movements: one from 1840 to 1865, a pro-slavery group that was federally outlawed in 1871; another in the 1920s; and a third after World War II that was against civil rights. The nearby city of East St. Louis had experienced race riots in 1917, but the thrust of the 1920s resurgence of the Klan was not just antiblack. Members organized attacks against parochial schools, burned convents, humiliated drunkards, and railed against "Irish bigots who took their orders from Rome and practiced other forms of Papist idolatry." Part of the cause of the resurgence was the wave of southern European immigrants into the United States in this period and the perceived threat of job loss for native-born Americans.[12]

At the time, the "invisible empire" boasted that it was "the most powerful fraternal and nativistic organization in American history." The Klan was on record as being against "aliens, wets, and urban and priest rule." Its members helped to defeat unions attempting to organize southern textile workers. They were strongly in favor of "immigration restriction, restoring the Bible to primacy in the schools, restricting the Catholic Church, returning the Negro to rural docility, and stopping neighborhood transition."[13]

Conscious of the power of symbol and the allure of ritual, the Klan devised elaborate rites to captivate members; for example, Stone Mountain, outside Atlanta, Georgia, was an imposing granite butte, and it was here that the second Ku Klux Klan held its founding ceremony on Thanksgiving night in 1915.[14]

Monks Mound is strikingly similar in silhouette to the Georgia butte, and the likeness was no doubt a factor in Cahokia's being chosen as a rallying point for the Klan in East St. Louis.[15] To Moorehead and others this scenic borrowing or theatrical hijacking must have seemed a desecration of the mounds, but it also underscored the urgency of preserving the site by making it a state park where regulations for its use could be imposed.

As if he didn't have enough problems, local support for Moorehead's efforts was meager, and funds were perilously short. But Moorehead was no narrow scientist: he was up to the challenge. Becoming a public relations expert and fund-raiser, he ordered the local printer to make up impressive letterhead stationery (fig. 103), elegant calling cards, and even slips to be inserted by the distributor of his previously published books. "You have been kind enough to order some of my books. Will you please consider the appeal with reference to saving Cahokia—the largest mound group in the world." He solicited from local, statewide, and national groups, agreeing to countless speaking engagements in the cause. He even took advantage of the back of his calling cards, inscribing them, "This work is done in the interest of the State Museum at Springfield, also with the approval of the Smithsonian Institution, Harvard, New York, Chicago, Philadelphia and other museums" (fig. 104).

From the beginning of his work, Moorehead also constantly cultivated the press. He sent out releases

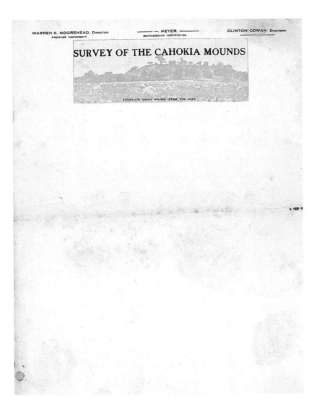

SURVEY OF THE CAHOKIA MOUNDS

WARREN K. MOOREHEAD, Director
ANDOVER UNIVERSITY
— MEYER. —
SMITHSONIAN INSTITUTION
CLINTON COWAN, Engineer

CAHOKIA'S GREAT MOUND, FROM THE PAST

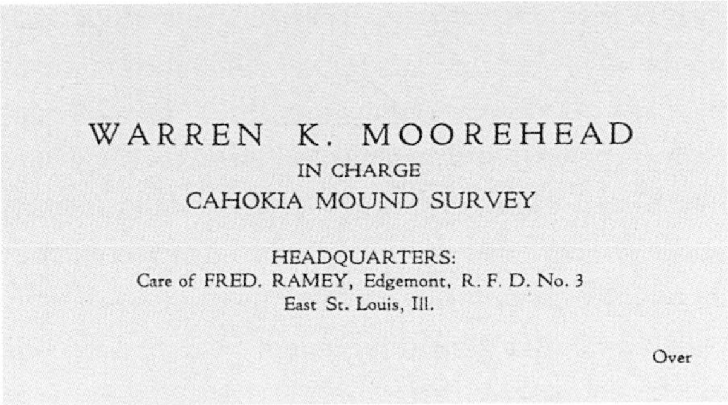

WARREN K. MOOREHEAD
IN CHARGE
CAHOKIA MOUND SURVEY

HEADQUARTERS:
Care of FRED. RAMEY, Edgemont, R. F. D. No. 3
East St. Louis, Ill.

Over

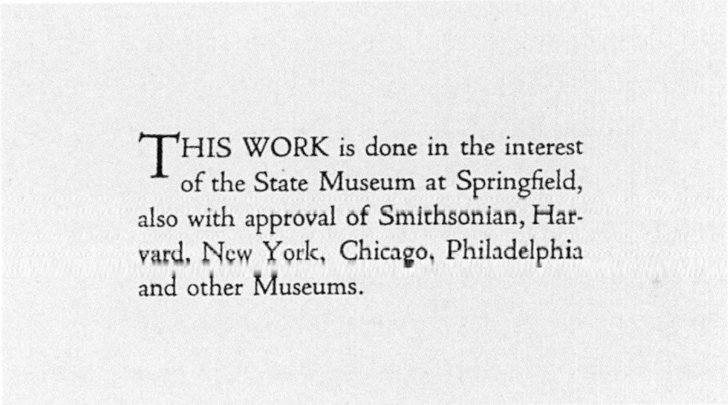

THIS WORK is done in the interest of the State Museum at Springfield, also with approval of Smithsonian, Harvard, New York, Chicago, Philadelphia and other Museums.

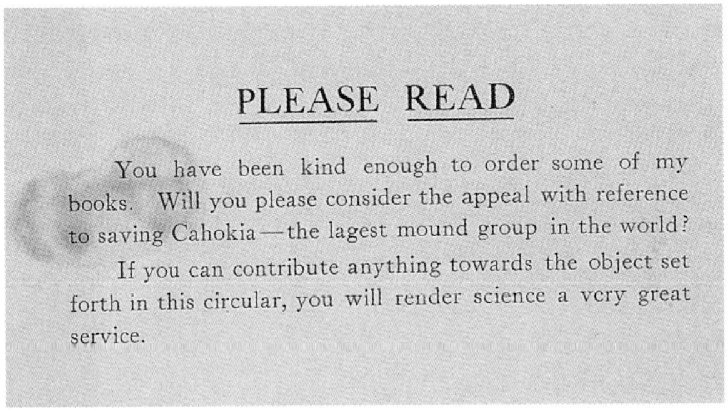

PLEASE READ

You have been kind enough to order some of my books. Will you please consider the appeal with reference to saving Cahokia—the lagest mound group in the world?

If you can contribute anything towards the object set forth in this circular, you will render science a very great service.

Fig. 103. (top, left) Moorehead became a public relations expert and a fundraiser. To help save the Cahokia Mounds, the archaeologist took upon himself all the duties that would now be assumed by a support staff, such as having letterhead and calling cards made up at the local printer.

Fig. 104. Moorehead's calling card. To make an impression on everyone he met, Moorehead let it be known on the back of his calling cards that several distinguished institutions supported his work at Cahokia. He also provided fund-raising pleas as inserts in his published works.

tirelessly, and articles appeared in numerous newspapers around the country, including the *Kansas City Star, Boston Telegram, Chicago Tribune, Chicago Post, Chicago Daily News, New York Sun, Atchison Globe, Christian Science Monitor, New York Times, Cincinnati Commercial Tribune,* and all the local papers as well.[16]

Finally, in 1923 Representative Thomas Fekete and Senator R. E. Duvall of East St. Louis introduced a bill in the Illinois State Legislature in Springfield calling for

the state to purchase two hundred acres around Monks Mound for $250,000. Under Moorehead's direction, all the stops were pulled and an all-out effort ensued. By this time newspaper editors were well informed, and twenty rallied in support of the state park.

Letters streamed into legislators' offices in Springfield. Distinguished scientists from several states endorsed public ownership. In testament after testament local people called on their representatives and senators. Letters and testimony from previous efforts were resubmitted, and new supporters added their voices to the cause. George S. Mephan, of the corner of Twentieth and Lynch Avenue, East St. Louis, wrote: "I have had an opportunity of showing this mound to several scientific gentlemen from Europe who are very familiar with Egypt and its archaeology. Their universal expression was that something should be done and done quickly to preserve this mound."

Philip Hinkle, curator of American archaeology at the Cincinnati Museum Association, wrote:

*The Cahokia Mound is one of the wonders of the world in the belief of many, and it would be almost a crime to neglect an opportunity to preserve it forever. Ohio has parked her Fort Ancient and her Serpent Mound, and Cahokia is just as well known the world over. Men and women come from all over the country to see the Serpent and Fort Ancient and they also come to Cahokia. Interest in the mounds is not centered in a few, but in tens of thousands, and anything that can be done to preserve the mounds should be done.*

Moorehead himself made many speeches. As he retold it in a speech to the National Research Council a few years later, he even *shamed* the Illinois state legislature into appropriate action.

*A friend of mine told me about how the late and genial Mr. Barnum had saved Stonehenge and told me to follow that idea but carry it further and make the people mad. So I prepared a very severe statement for the press and it was printed simultaneously in a number of large cities. It cast reflections on the intelligence of southern Illinois folk who preferred filling stations, hot dog stands, dance halls and bungalows to the greatest monument north of Mexico. I stated that in any other state but Illinois the mounds would have been included in the state parks long ago. The*

*reaction to this tirade was immediate. I was roundly denounced by the press. But politicians hurried from East St. Louis to Springfield and a bill to make the state park was passed in forty-eight hours.[17]*

The dream had come true, but various political negotiations en route to passage had severely compromised the effort. The legislature appropriated only $50,000 for the measure and purchased only 144.4 acres. Condemnation hearings had to be held to determine the value of the land, because the Ramey family wanted $140,000. Eventually a judge ruled that $52,119 was a fair price. The Ramey family's suit for more money was denied, and 144.4 acres, basically Monks Mound and a small surrounding area, became the Cahokia Mounds State Park in 1925. The rest of the ancient Indian site was still in private hands.

Important as the victory was, the land purchased was a woefully small portion of the original Mississippian site, which was over 4,000 acres, including more than one hundred mounds. Today over 2,200 acres of land is preserved.

In 1926, as the state park employees began plans to plant grass, lay out driveways, and set up a "tourist camp" on the newly acquired land, new threats loomed on all sides of the site where land was still in private hands.[18]

A housing developer touted the merits of living in "State Park Place," just east of Monks Mound. Dividing up the land between new streets with names like West Point Avenue, Yale Avenue, and Harvard Avenue, the realtor offered 283 lots for sale at $500 apiece.

*With its wonderful surroundings and accessibility for such a small outlay of cash and on such convenient terms, this wonderful subdivision lays between the newly created Cahokia Mounds State Park, a wonderful state development,*

*and the beautiful Fairmount Jockey Club property . . . .*
*It is out just far enough to be away from the smoke, dirt*
*and noise of the city, where you can have clean, pure air*
*and clear skies, yet close enough for you to enjoy the city's*
*conveniences and amusements. It is close enough to the*
*Collinsville coal fields to insure cheap fuel . . . . It is on a*
*paved State Highway (Collinsville Road) and the East St.*
*Louis and Suburban Electric Line which assures you of*
*proper transportation facilities.[19]*

A later map and an aerial photograph (figs. 105 and 106) of the area indicate that several lots were purchased and very small houses built, some of them on top of existing mounds, preventing any further archaeological examination there. Other intrusions included a church and a golf course. The whole area, however, was on such low-lying land that flooding was a constant danger.

On August 23, 1946, the Red Cross provided shelter for 253 victims of the "state park flood," and the Illinois Department of Health began inoculating six hundred residents against typhoid fever.[20]

Today people still live in the area, but maintenance has been deferred on many of the buildings, and no one would recognize the neighborhood from the descriptions in the 1920s advertisements. Building with modern construction methods on cheap land subject to flooding is problematic in several ways compared with indigenous Indian methods. Shingled roofs, concrete foundations, driveways, and paved streets exacerbate runoff and flooding. Also, the roots of the grass typically planted for suburban lawns have less than half the runoff absorption of the deep prairie roots of the native plants that surrounded much of Cahokia.[21] In addition, the Mississippian houses had frames of wooden poles set in trenches dug directly in the ground—that is, they had no concrete basements—and were roofed and clad with thatch.

While State Park Place was still going up the Powell family, who still owned Mound 86 (Powell Mound), which was outside the state property line on the western side of the site, wanted to fill a nearby swamp with dirt from the mound so they could farm both the swamp and the land underneath the mound. Mound 86, a large ridge-topped mound, was considered the "marker mound" for the western edge of the site, and the focus of the West Mound group. As such its potential historical importance was deemed immeasurable.[22] Never one to rest on his laurels, Moorehead continued to work for the purchase of the rest of the mounds by the state of Illinois.

The Powells offered $3,000 to any institution willing to remove the mound. When no takers came, either from the state or private donors, the Powells secretly began to dig up the northern part of the mound in late 1930. Dr. P. F. Titterington, a St. Louis physician and an avocational archaeologist, alerted the scholars he knew to what was happening. The group included A. R. Kelly of the University of Illinois, Will McKern of the Milwaukee Public Museum, and Thorne Deuel of the Illinois State Museum. They all dropped everything and came to the site at once.[23] Their sad duty was to record and salvage what they could while the great mound was razed to clear the way for farming (figs. 107 and 108). As demolition continued, they alternately worked frantically and watched in dismay. When Powell Mound was finally gone, Moorehead declared it "a tragic loss, the greatest destruction since the St. Louis group sixty years ago."

When the assembled archaeologists retreated to the ranger's cottage at the base of Monks Mound, with its little "relic room," later known as the "old museum," they must have been deeply discouraged. The Great Depression that began in 1929 was worsening, and though they did not know it, the small exhibition area in the relic room would be the only interpretive center

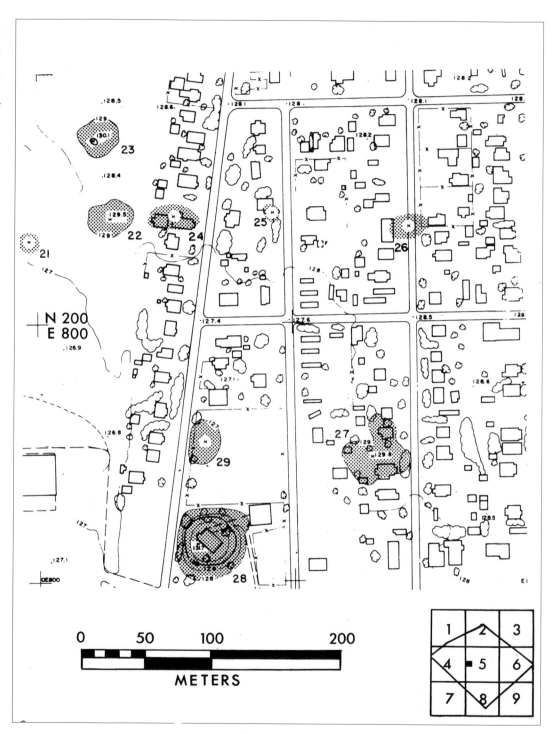

Fig. 105.
Single-family homes
spring up on the
Cahokia landscape.
Many very small
houses were built in
the area east of
Monks Mound in
the 1930s.

Fig. 106. (top) Housing development south of Monks Mound. Today all but two of these houses have been removed, helping to restore the original landscape.

Fig. 107. (bottom, left) Powell Mound as it was in 1922. This low, oblique air photo shows the mound before its destruction.

Fig. 108. (bottom, right) Destruction of Powell Mound. Suffering the greatest loss since the St. Louis mound group was destroyed sixty years before, archaeologists watched in dismay as the demolition continued in January 1931. Scholars from Illinois, Missouri, and Wisconsin dropped everything and came to Cahokia for last-minute efforts.

at the mounds for decades to come. Local people lent parts of their private collections for small exhibitions, but the park was mostly used for picnics, camping, sledding, and other recreational activities. A long hiatus began, but there was one other legacy besides Moorehead's from the period that would prove valuable in the distant future: aerial photographs.

## The Fly on the Rug versus the Fly in the Air

If Moorehead had been in the field in the winter of 1921–22 and had looked overhead, he might have glimpsed a small single-engine airplane flying back and forth over the site. In the cockpit were the pilot and photographer team of Lt. Harold R. Wells and Lt. Ashley C. McKinley, two Army Air Service pilots stationed at Scott Field in Belleville, Illinois. Owing to heavy smoke from surrounding industries burning soft coal, the pictures they took were not very clear, but they were the first aerial photographs ever published of an archaeological site in North America.[24] Less imaginative people might have been discouraged by the smoky results, not dreaming that something built over eight hundred years earlier, and invisible to the archaeologist on foot, might show up clearly in a photograph taken from three thousand feet in the air. But only a few months later, in April 1922, another team, two more young Army Air Service lieutenants, George W. Goddard and H. K. Ramey, proved the point in photographs that revealed possible archaeological features that there was no other record of and that no one was of aware until they were restudied years later.[25]

Amazing as it may seem, although eight centuries of deposits have covered the traces of the Mississippian civilization at Cahokia, including the disturbances of the soil caused by intensive farming and building, what is under the ground still affects the surface appearance.

Aerial photographs show the surface manifestations of subsurface features. Light linear lines were visible in the dark soil of plowed fields on Goddard and Ramey's photographs, revealing by the different soil color the exact location of what later turned out to be ancient palisades (fig. 109). Their presence was confirmed in 1966–67 on subsequent excavations by James P. Anderson and Melvin L. Fowler, and later radiocarbon techniques put the date at 1200. The first clue to a ceremonial area west of the palisade was also in these photographs.[26]

The land over an old trench or ditch may slump slightly, gathering more water, which will make the soil softer and the vegetation above it more abundant, so it differs slightly in tone from the surrounding area. On the other hand, the soil on an embankment becomes more compact and less suitable for plant life, with sparser growth. These effects may be imperceptible on the ground, making it difficult for the archaeologist to know where to dig, but in an air view the various tonalities or markings may form a significant pattern. Also, sometimes lighter subsoils were thrown out when trenches were dug, and this greater concentration shows up in aerial photographs. As a pioneer aerial photographer put it, "A fly walking on a rug would have difficulty in recognizing the design, but upon flying above the rug, the pattern would become distinct."[27]

In the decades following the two-day flight of Goddard and Ramey, which produced photographs taken from a conventional oblique or "pictorial" angle, new technology became available. In 1933 Lt. Dache M. Reeves used a "vertical" angle; that is, he placed the camera lens axis at right angles to the ground so the resulting pictures were exactly parallel to the ground. This technique made it possible to make an accurate map from photographs. Both methods are still valuable. The "pictorial" angle view is too distorted for mapmaking but has greater three-dimensionality.[28]

Fig. 109. Daring new aerial photography in 1922 yields results decades later. Amazing as it seems, a stockade built eight hundred years earlier still leaves surface traces. Although these are not visible from the ground, they can be seen from the air. The white streak visible in this old aerial photograph enabled archaeologists to begin digging right over the ancient stockade in 1966.

Wells, McKinley, Goddard, Ramey, Reeves, and others all make up a long line of photographers, some of them distinguished in the field. It seems that Cahokia attracted talented flier-photographers the way it attracted gentlemen scholars, fine artists, and brilliant archaeologists.

Why was Cahokia a cynosure for aerial archaeology? Although it was unknown to most, a few devoted people in influential places knew that it was the largest archaeological site in the United States, containing the largest group of mounds and the largest man-made earthen pyramid on the North American continent.[29] Inspired by their knowledge, they were emboldened to

ask for and get the means to validate it and promote it to a larger audience. Someone asked Gen. John J. Pershing for the favor of a flyover photographic flight; someone else asked for funds from the Smithsonian Institution for a thorough vertical stereoscopic series. In the 1970s one archaeologist, Melvin L. Fowler, climbed one-handed into a Cessna 172 behind the pilot with a Rolliflex hanging on a cord around his neck and a Crown Graphic in his other hand. All the photographs these men produced remain valuable tools for archaeologists to this day, and the work of Goddard and Ramey led to the use of aerial photography in other areas. Of course modern technology has added many other techniques to the photographer's kit: new lenses, new film stocks, satellite altitudes, infrared cameras, zooming scales, computer modeling, and even virtual reality. But the pioneers of the early twentieth century got them off to a flying start.

Just two years after Dache Reeves's flight, the federal government extended some aid and encouragement to Cahokia scholars when the Historic Sites Act was passed in 1935. It established the preservation of historic sites, buildings, and objects of national significance for public use and the "inspiration and benefit" of the American people. This time Cahokia was placed on the list within a year, owing perhaps to the influence of John Collier, head of the Bureau of Indian Affairs. Cahokia's status was immediately improved by its meriting federal protection. No money for improvements accompanied the legislation, however, and no immediate changes occurred as a result.

A look at the USGS map of 1974 (fig. 110) confirms that "Cahokia State Park" stayed the same for nearly forty years, although the surrounding area changed markedly. By the 1960s the state of Illinois had acquired several houses on the site east of Monks Mound, which were used over the next few years in an "improvise, improve, or make-do" fashion as the need arose. Sometimes a house became a temporary archaeological laboratory or field headquarters. Sometimes it became an exhibition preparation and storage area, other times an office or exhibition space. Laypeople, staff members, and archaeologists worked together in this atmosphere for decades, diligently pursuing their digging, mapping, classifying, analyzing, and interpretive work.

Most of the knowledge we have from archaeology is cumulative, like pieces put together by scores of diligent people working patiently over decades on a giant three-dimensional jigsaw puzzle, until at last someone perceives a meaningful pattern. What we know is based on the work of these laborers in the field, guided from time to time by the insights of a few leaders. Just as wars may be directed by generals but are won by armies, so our knowledge of the past is gained by the combined efforts of those who dig and those who direct the dig and interpret the findings.

Just before the outbreak of World War II, Harriet M. Smith, of the Field Museum of Natural History in Chicago, made a significant interpretation from the excavation she was directing at Murdock Mound (Mound 55), southeast of Monks Mound. After finding a true east-west line in a Mississippian-period house there, ascertaining that the mound itself paralleled the sides of Monks Mound, and finding architectural facets at the corners of the mound, Smith followed up her significant discoveries with significant interpretations. "I consider this shift a reflection of an intensified concern with agriculture," she wrote, "and a more sophisticated body of astronomical knowledge related to the farmers' seasonal almanac, based on the sun."[30] Twenty years later, salvage archaeology operations in advance of new highway construction would unearth a woodhenge, supporting Smith's observation.

## City Planning in Earth Architecture

Smith's careful reading of the strata she unearthed also revealed that all the houses after the lowest or earliest level were also oriented on a north-south axis (consistently 7.5 degrees east of true north at Cahokia) that exactly paralleled the sides of Monks Mound, including four others in this same row of subsidiary mounds. "It is so consistent an orientation as to foretell a city plan for at least the stockaded central area around Monks Mound."[31] Smith went on to clarify her position with fastidious detail.

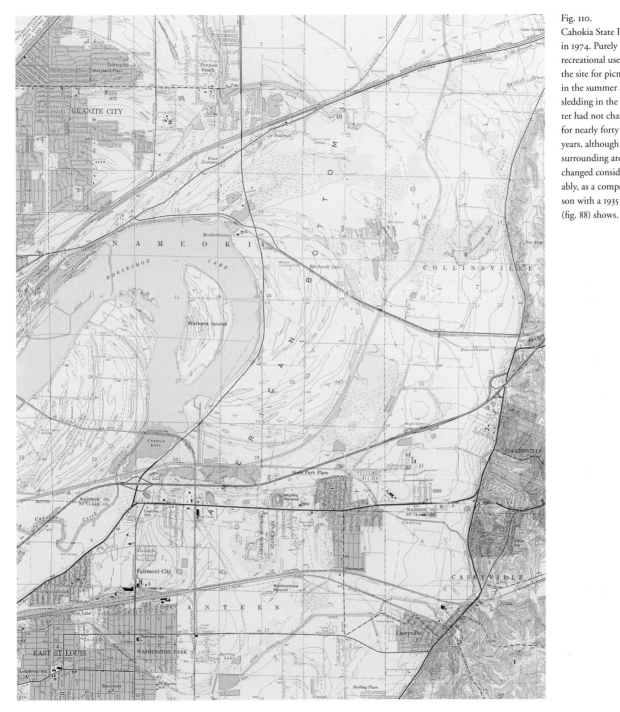

Fig. 110.
Cahokia State Park
in 1974. Purely
recreational uses of
the site for picnics
in the summer and
sledding in the win-
ter had not changed
for nearly forty
years, although the
surrounding area
changed consider-
ably, as a compari-
son with a 1935 map
(fig. 88) shows.

*One striking exception in the orientation of the Sub-mound Platform conclusively ties in the time of the finishing of the Murdock Platform with the presence of Monks Mound, at least with the east side of its low southern terrace. The east side of the Murdock Platform as well as the east edge of the Monks Mound terrace are oriented identically at N 7 degrees 30′ E and the north and south sides of the Murdock Platform are placed at right angles to this orientation. But the west edge of the Platform is not on the orientation and diverges another 5 degrees east, lengthening the south side of the Platform by a conspicuous 5 ft. [But] the west baseline for the Platform was lined up* optically *[italics in original] parallel with the east terrace face of Monks Mound, a block to the north and an avenue's width west. This must have been done by standing at various spots along the south edge of the Platform and sighting past the (necessary) pole at the NW corner until this line of sight seemed parallel rather than convergent (because of perspective), with the alignment of the east face of the big mound. This spot was actually 5 ft too far to the west, thus giving the Platform a west baseline oriented 5 degrees further east of north rather than the standard orientation of all other Murdock building lines and of the east terrace of Monks Mound itself. This human error testifies to the presence of Monks Mound as the focal point of the Cahokia complex for some time prior to the building of the Murdock Temple Mound, for the latter's underlying Platform is worn from long use.*[32]

## Architectural Subtlety in Earth Architecture

Smith found earth-formed facets at several corners of Murdock Mound and went on to assert that these were purely aesthetic in intention, as was the site planning, two features that ennoble the Mound Builders' work as high forms of the art of architecture. Like the ancient Greek builders of the Parthenon, the architects of the mounds even took into account the fallibility of human perception, or optical illusion. (The Greeks' uses of entasis and differential intercolumniation are examples.)

*In practice then the facet was an* architectural feature. *. . . . The Murdock architect dealt conspicuously with harmonious proportions and applied principles of good design, especially adapting them to the material in which they would be executed. The facet was the aesthetic invention of architects designing for construction in* earth. *I can't think of any parallel in stone or mud brick. The facet was a device for cutting down the squatty appearance inherent in earth constructions and producing the most impressive setting possible for the temple [to be erected on its platform summit]. It stopped the eye directly behind the base of the temple, so that this crowning structure seemed more towering without a long diminuendo stretching back behind it. The minor side facets from terrace to platform led the eye up a more vertical-seeming panel made to look the same width as the temple platform. The combination of squared front terrace and high, faceted rear presented a more imposing facade that was intensified by an effect of forced perspective to the rear. This pattern was designed to make earth architecture as impressive as possible [fig. III] . . . .* [33]

*I am confident that at least the east face of the terrace of Monks Mound existed in its present form when the final consolidation of the Murdock Platform was lined up with it, by optical illusion . . . . [as] black as coal, even when dry, Murdock Temple Mound must have looked quite handsome when completed.*[34]

To the discerning eye, the site planning of the Cahokia community is indeed sophisticated. A few examples will make the point. Forced perspective to make an architectural ensemble impressive was a noteworthy feature of Michelangelo's design for the Capi-

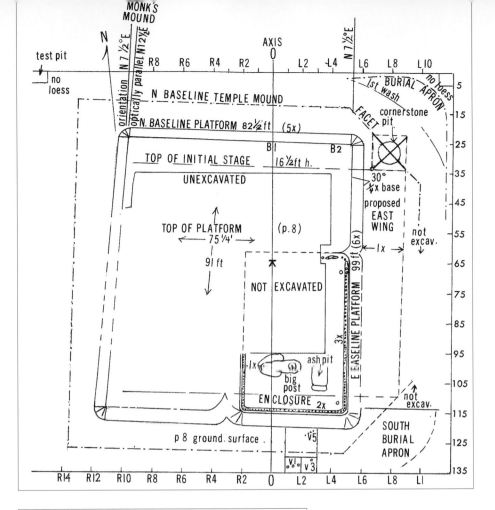

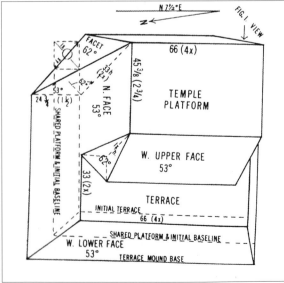

Fig. 111. Sophisticated and subtle city planning and architectural details. In the late 1930s archaeologist Harriet Smith argued that alignment with the cardinal directions, splayed perspective, subordination of one part to another, positive use of optical illusion, and creation of highly charged negative spaces made Cahokia architecture rank with the highest human architectural achievements, as shown in this 1941 plan and isometric of Murdock Mound.

toline Hill in Rome five hundred years later. The Cahokians also employed other highly developed urban devices. Choosing one major focus for their ceremonial center, the great pyramid, they lined up other mounds to be subordinate to it and to contribute to its monumentality by their very subordination. In Washington, D.C., the buildings along Pennsylvania Avenue are kept low, subordinate, so the Capitol dome may dominate the vista, a legacy from Pierre-Charles L'Enfant's city plan of eight hundred years after Cahokia. Even the capital city's mall, the long green space stretching in front of the Capitol, recalls the Grand Plaza in front of the great pyramid. All these factors—orientation to the cardinal directions, a hierarchical order of elements, splayed or forced perspective, the positive use of optical illusion, and the creation of meaningful, charged negative spaces like plazas—argue for community planning and organization on a highly artistic, civilized level.

The entry of the United States into World War II in 1941 halted Smith's excavations soon after her discoveries were made, but for decades other archaeologists would substantiate many of her conclusions. Smith's view that planning was an important feature of the civilized life of the Mississippians came far too late to prevent the Collinsville Road from cutting across the site between Monks Mound and the ceremonial grounds to the south. The road had been there at least since the early nineteenth century. On Patrick's map it was called the Collinsville Plank Road, and it later became part of the "national highway" known as U.S. 40. No one would have guessed the number and complexity of roads that would affect the Mississippian site in the next century. Soon after World War II was over, the Cahokia landscape was marked by the profound effects of America's escalating fascination with the automobile and the airplane.

## New Buildings Mark the Landscape

New modes of transportation bring clusters of new buildings in their wake, and even new building types—drive-in banks, restaurants, soft-drink stands, and theaters. An aerial photo (fig. 112) shows Cahokia swathed in the gigantic ribbons of white concrete roadways that still affect the site. Today combined Inter-states 55 and 70 are to the north; Interstate 255 just to the east; and State Highway 111 to the west. In addition, there are the numerous paved local streets, alleys, and byways.

A host of corollary structures also sprang up along new roadways—fast-food restaurants, motels, and gas stations, to name just a few. The aerial photograph also shows the ribbons of concrete around Monks Mound expanding into a vast apron of white just to the west—a drive-in movie theater, still a relatively new idea in the 1950s.[35]

Usually drive-ins had several graded ramps, with room enough for a few hundred cars, and Cahokia's Falcon was typical. The acoustics featured a speaker for each car. This private sound system allowed people to talk, smoke, or eat in their own cars without disturbing others. The drive-in meant no more stumbling in the dark, no more stepping on toes "in the blind quest for a seat."[36]

Among its manifold advantages the drive-in was touted as "a boon to invalids and elderly people . . . as there was no danger of contagion from infectious diseases, while the debutante is securely protected from close contact with undesirable neighbors."[37] The structures usually included a large stage, a screen, a projection booth, and entrance pillars of some kind. Most took only eight weeks to build and install.

By the later 1950s drive-ins were as ubiquitous in popular culture as hula hoops, pinball machines, and the enormous gas-guzzling cars of the Eisenhower era. Collinsville had its share of this culture with the Falcon, but it was not going to last.

Ironically, the automobile that gave birth to the drive-in was also the number one factor in the creation of the suburban malls and the multiplexes that forced drive-in movies into a downward spiral. The Falcon at Cahokia, like many others, eventually became a venue for X-rated movies. In the end its bad reputation made

Fig. 112. Cahokia site swathed in concrete and sporting a drive-in movie and an "airpark." The aerial photographs show where future archaeologists may find the old concrete footings for the screen and the foundations of the projection booth of the Falcon drive-in theater to the west and asphalt chips from the runway of the airpark (upper right) to the east. Both structures were built in the 1950s and demolished by the 1980s.

it easier to condemn it and acquire the site as state property, to be annexed to the Cahokia Mounds State Park. The old drive-in was finally demolished in 1983.

### A Unique Small Airplane Culture

Another relic of the postwar years, the Downtown Airpark, also appears at the east edge of the USGS map.

What is an airfield doing in this swampy region? Operating from the late 1950s to the late 1960s or early 1970s, this "airpark" reflects a small-airplane culture that was widespread in the United States but unique to the period.

The airpark was always a small, private airport, but it is still hard to imagine why it was built in the first place. There was a better airport, Lakeside (sometimes called Nickols), only three miles to the north. Lakeside, founded by Omar Midyett, was first used largely as a CPT (civilian pilot training) airport. It still exists, though it has been reduced to RLA (restricted landing area) status. A better airport is a few miles to the southwest in the town of Cahokia, the St. Louis Downtown Airport, or Parkside, also known as Parks. Why were there so many airports in such an underpopulated area?

The romance with airplanes touched all Americans in the 1920s and 1930s with Charles Lindbergh's first translatlantic solo flight and Amelia Earhart's daring expeditions and tragic end. Even "airmail" had an adventurous aura. Only special letters were sent by air, and having an airplane stop to pick up mail was a rarity for small midwestern towns. Collinsville was no exception. (The Cahokia Mounds State Historic Site has recently been annexed into the town of Collinsville.) It was front-page news in the *Collinsville Herald* when a mail plane was scheduled to stop on May 19, 1938.

*As the time for Air Mail Week is drawing near, may we ask you to join those who have responded so generously to the appeal to the public asking them to help make a success locally of Air Mail Week.*

*Pledges are coming in very nicely and we have the assurance that a plane will land here on May 19 and pick up the air mail . . . the pledges from the citizens promised that it would be worth while to make Collinsville one of the pickups, as Collinsville people always do honor for our city. This will be the outstanding event of the year. The cost of airmail is 6 cents an ounce or fraction thereof, while ordinary mail is 3 cents an ounce. So, won't you join the air mail boosters club?*

*In connection with observance the employees of the Post Office are sponsoring a cachet [seal] which will appear on all out-going air mail letters from May 15 to 21. The cachet, showing two Indians before a tepee with mounds in the background has been declared one of the*

*outstanding of the nation. Many favorable comments have been received by Postmaster D. R. Luebbe.[38]*

The importance of air power in securing victory in World War II was reflected in the stirring words of the Army Air Corps anthem: "Off we go, into the wild blue yonder . . . . we live in fame or go down in flame, nothing can stop the Army Air Corps!" The whole nation was convinced that an air industry boom of unprecedented scale would accompany the coming of peace: "airwaves are the waves of the future." Even before the war ended, Ben Regan of Chicago, chairman of the Illinois State Aeronautics Commission, declared to a Collinsville audience:

*The postwar aviation industry with its unlimited commercial and pleasure possibilities will result in the establishment of hundreds of small and large airports all over the nation, and one of the best sites for a major airport to serve this entire metropolitan area is right here at your back door . . . . [It has a] several thousand acre tract of level ground sufficient for runways to take care of the larger type planes, and it has the further advantages of adequate drainage, minimum fog and smoke and close proximity to downtown St. Louis, closer even than any airport development being seriously considered on the Missouri side of the river.[39]*

He was referring to a site in Lakeside near Horseshoe Lake, a suburb of ancient Cahokia, not far north of Monks Mound. "A community without adequate service facilities in a few years will be almost as far behind as a town is now that has no auto sales or repair shops." Regan also predicted that the aviation boom to come not only would apply to large planes for shipping and passenger travel "but also will include small privately owned pleasure craft for which several of the better known manufacturers in this field are expecting a big demand. Sale of these small planes at prices around $1000 is envisioned in a few years."[40]

## Rampant Optimism: Fifty-three Airports for Two Counties

Not to be left behind, the Illinois state legislature passed the Illinois County Airport Law in July 1945, even before the Japanese surrendered. The law provided that any two contiguous counties could act jointly in preparing their airport plans. The county line that runs just south of Monks Mound separates Madison County on the north and St. Clair County on the south, and a joint committee submitted a report five days after the end of World War II. Optimism was rampant: "53 Air ports for Two Counties Plan of Air Committee: Report of Two-Year Study Is Submitted This Week," the headline declared. The committee hoped for an airport for every community in both counties.

*The law provides that airport development should closely parallel in general the experience which has been gained in highway development . . . .*

*Consideration was given to the three operating fields of aviation: trunk airline operation, local airline operation and personal flying . . . to look forward in order to determine the part that each of these three branches of aviation could be expected to play in the economic and social activities of the various communities throughout Madison and St. Clair counties.*[41]

The rage for airplanes and airplane travel consumed the whole country. Not only was the airport built near Horseshoe Lake, another was erected just a few hundred yards southeast of Monks Mound. It was called the Downtown Airpark. Billy H. Greer, a pilot, described the situation to me.

*In those wild blue yonder days there was a clique of local businessmen, and when one of them learned to fly the others had to follow suit. When one of them bought his own airplane, the others had to follow. They flew on business, and they flew for pleasure, and they especially liked to go to the races at Fairmount Park, just half a mile from the airpark. To meet this demand, two local pilots who worked at Lakeside wanted to start a flying school and buy and sell used airplanes to businessmen. Finding negotiations with the Lakeside people difficult, they decided it would be cheaper and easier to start their own airport. The costs were not high. In those days it was usually just purchase of the land, in this case a useless swamp, and construction of one or two runways, some T hangars, perhaps an office and a tool shed.*[42]

In this way the Downtown Airpark began. Two runways were built in the swampy area east of the Tippetts Mound group, one running west-northwest to east-southeast and the other north to south. There was also a hangar and a small office building. As Greer reported, it was

*a poor choice of location, because of surrounding obstructions, and homes immediately up to the ends of the home-made runways. I am amazed that they got it certified. Today there would be no way it would be approved . . . . It was a very hazardous place to fly in and out of . . . . They traded in aeronautical objects d'junque till they closed it down and sold it to the state of Illinois for some obscene price . . . . It should have been called Travesty Airport.*[43]

For some time in the early 1960s the airport was active as a flying school, with an average of twenty students at a time and two or three instructors, but the main business of owner Claude Cleveland and his successor Bill Fisk was selling used airplanes.

Dale Rust of the Illinois Department of Aeronautics, who taught flying at the Downtown Airpark in 1964, agreed with Greer's account: "The swampy ground was frequently flooded and had to be pumped constantly when it rained to keep the runways dry. There were obstructions on all sides—Highway 40 on the north, and a railroad embankment on the south, and buildings to the east and west."[44] Eventually the state of Illinois bought the Downtown Airpark, and it is now part of the interpretive center's nature/culture hike trail, where ecological interpretation of prairie wetlands takes place.

There are still traces of the old runway on the western edge of the freshwater marsh at the site. But at the end of the century, some forty years after the heyday of the airport, this deserted marsh is more like it was in the year 1000 than what it was as a suburban airport in 1960. Smartweed, arrowhead, great bulrush, and milkweed have seeded down in cracks in the old asphalt and done their patient work—breaking the manmade surface into pieces small enough to be carried away by the wind. Cattails, spike rush, slough grass, and other prairie plants have taken the place of the old airpark, and nature has so nearly completely regained control that only occasional bits of asphalt, the jetsam of the old runways, still surface from the marsh. This remnant of Spring Lake now is home to a beaver lodge and is visited frequently by blue herons and other birds.

## The Rise and Fall of the Housing Subdivision

A similar fate awaited the sixty houses that had sprung up at the foot of Monks Mound across Collinsville Road—the Ramey subdivision. The first houses in this tract were probably built just before the United States entered World War II, sometime in 1941. (One or two houses appear in the background of photographs taken of Harriet Smith's excavation of Mound 55 in 1941.) The Great Depression had lifted somewhat, and new homeowners were attracted by the prospect of building right on the border of a state park, with the distinctive presence of Monks Mound as part of their vista.

Further building was interrupted by World War II, but soon after the war a variety of houses sprung up in the four long rectangular blocks off Ramey Street. Most were single-story frame houses, some in the new ranch style with partial brick facing, others of concrete block with stucco cover. Most of the basements had problems with cracking and leaking because of the high water table in the low-lying locale.

## From State Park to State Historic Site

In the late 1970s the state of Illinois reclassified the Cahokia Mounds from a state park to a State Historic Site. From this moment forward the state bought up the houses in the Ramey tract as they came up for sale and auctioned them off to the highest bidders, with the proviso that the new owners had to move them. By the time the new interpretive center opened in 1989 only four were left; two were removed a few months later, and the last two were used as residences for site managers. In the Mississippian period a part of this area was also residential, but the houses were clad and roofed with thatch, not brick and shingles.

The postwar years saw some promising changes in the field of archaeology that were portents of the immense progress in understanding the site that would occur in the last third of the century. Money from foundations became available for serious, sustained work. The reclassification of the Cahokia Mounds from state park to State Historic Site had other far-reaching implications, the subject of the next chapter.

## Summary

By 1900 the Cahokia landscape was so changed by farming, canals, ditches, clear-cutting, railroad construction, housing, erosion, highways, streets, telephone lines, and rogue vegetation that only shadows of its past remained. Fortunately the mounds and their shadows were still momentous, for the landscape was otherwise so transformed that all possibility of recovering its secrets might have been lost.

The early twentieth century began with a rousing interest in the St. Louis World's Fair of 1904, which magnified popular support for and professional interest in Cahokia. But intermittent interest from afar, however respectful and devoted, was not sufficient to sustain preservation, and intrusions on the site occurred in many forms. Had it not been for Warren K. Moorehead, the prime mover of Cahokia preservation, there is little doubt that mounds would have been leveled for the dirt needed to fill the surrounding swamps—for railroads, highways, or farmland.

Although the original purchase of 144.4 acres by the state of Illinois was only a fraction of the site needing preservation, it heartened supporters and gave them a focus for their energies. When highways, drive-ins, housing developments, and even an airport intruded on the mounds in the early twentieth century, there was a symbolic place to retreat to, the legacy of at least some statewide recognition. The presence of Monks Mound, protected at last, must have given strength to the small band of supporters who continued their work through the coming years. Archaeologists too were beginning to find new financial resources for their work—foundation grants and federal money. They were going to need all the help they could get to meet yet another deluge of problems unimaginable at the time.

FIG. 113. CAHOKIA TODAY. THE RAKING LIGHT OF AN
EARLY DAWN FLIGHT CAPTURES THE MYTHIC PRESENCE
OF THE ANCIENT MOUND CITY IN OUR TIMES.

# Modern Cahokia

## A Critical Mass at a Critical Time

For about forty-five years Cahokia was tended by a site superintendent whose main duty was to monitor the picnic grounds. Not until 1971 did the state of Illinois hire professional archaeologists to oversee the Cahokia site. At first only two were employed, James P. Anderson and William R. Iseminger, but from the start they worked together with university archaeologists, anthropologists, preservationists, scholars from related fields, and a variety of state-employed experts.

Sometimes these people had different agendas for the site, and sometimes they were at cross-purposes with each other. Overall, however, Cahokia inspired them, and for the most part they put themselves at the service of something higher than self. That "something higher" also varied: it might be the pursuit of knowledge through archaeology, saving the site for posterity, gaining the recognition they felt the place deserved, or finding continuing meaningful, life-fulfilling work.

All these motives were probably present at one time or another in the roster of people who served Cahokia in the late twentieth century, but together they at last secured it with a firm institutional foundation. As time went on, their efforts would gain international recognition for Cahokia's historical value, its place in the global story of human achievement.

Looking back, it is sometimes hard to believe it happened. The necessary critical mass for major change developed and was effective only because the efforts of these various groups finally became mutually reinforcing at a critical time. A kind of circular, self-sustaining, and expansive social chain reaction was set up.

Archaeological findings began to reinforce interpretive efforts, and interpretive efforts helped preservation, which encouraged volunteerism, which freed the state interpreters to spend more time on investigative and preservation work, on encouraging Native American participation, and on obtaining funding and recognition. In 1971 no one would have dared hope that within eleven years UNESCO recognition would occur and within eighteen years a world-class interpretive center would open to welcome visitors from all over the globe.

## Difficult Beginnings

When they first came to work in 1971, James P. Anderson and William R. Iseminger set up shop in a former model home on the site. Later Bea Robertson joined them as an assistant. Getting started in this converted headquarters-office was challenging. Space for exhibit preparation, mimeographing, mailing, and other tasks had to be squeezed into the small house. There were other problems. Anderson had to devote his complete attention in the first few months to the final excavations at Mound 72 (discussed below), while Iseminger began to set up some interpretive programs.

The beginnings were necessarily modest. Iseminger approached visitors, scout troops, and schoolchildren he encountered on the site, inviting them to ask questions. Later he prepared a slide program and sent out letters to local school superintendents informing them of his availability. It was the beginning of the educational programs he would continue to develop for more than twenty-five years.[1]

Anderson had studied under Melvin L. Fowler, an eminent archaeologist at the University of Wisconsin–Milwaukee, and Iseminger, just finishing his master's degree in anthropology at Southern Illinois University at Carbondale, had also worked as a student with Fowler and Anderson in a dig on the south stockade in 1968.

## The Old Museum

Also on the site was a small pueblo-style museum that had been erected in 1929 as a combination ranger's residence and "relic room." At the time only one small room was devoted to exhibits, and some of the display cases were empty. As Iseminger later recalled:

*Our first goal was to improve some of the existing exhibits . . . . We gradually ripped out some, improved some, and installed others. During those first few years it was not unusual for us to work six and seven days a week, and sometimes I think Jim lived there. He did most of the carpentry and I helped bend more than a few nails.*

*We also knocked holes in walls and enlarged doorways to create passageways. We begged for and salvaged materials, as we had a very limited budget. One of our greatest assets was Jim Houser, curator at the St. Louis Museum of Science and Natural History (and a founding member of the Cahokia Mounds Museum Society) . . . . Whenever they dismantled displays or were getting rid of cases, equipment and other materials, he gave us a call and we picked them up as a gift or for nominal cost . . . . In order to help fund our operations we also set up a small gift shop . . . through the Illinois State Museum Society.[2]*

At times it seemed that troubles accumulated more rapidly than successes. A sales counter, built in Springfield, was delivered but was too large to get around a corner in the small house, so they had to remove a window to bring it in and "just barely made it." The shop could not be closed without affecting visitor flow, and the old building plagued the young men with other difficulties.

*The poor building had severe cracks in many areas which would spread open in dry seasons as the building settled, and close up in wet seasons. Roof leaks were common. The wiring was an electrician's nightmare, although mostly done by electricians . . . . The furnace was the worst . . . . the original old boiler for the steam heat had been converted from coal to oil and the pipes were held together by encrustations and rust. It amazed many a furnace repairman, who made frequent calls. A recycled air conditioner struggled to cool the building . . . and then there were the poisonous brown recluse spiders, birds in the ceiling and mice in the walls (and everywhere).[3]*

Far more troublesome than all the spiders, birds, and mice, however, were the political changes in the Illinois capital at Springfield. When the park was first established in 1925 it was managed by the Department of Parks and Memorials, which later became the Department of Conservation (DOC). In 1971 the DOC went into a joint operation with the Illinois State Museum (ISM). The DOC managed the land, and the ISM managed the museum and the interpretive programs. The joint management went smoothly for the first five years Anderson and Iseminger worked there. In 1976, however, the DOC resumed total management, effectively ousting the ISM, which had supported the professional, or archaeological, aspects of site operations.

*This was a very unstable and unsure time for me . . . . We did not know where we stood in the reorganization. Conservation did not have job titles or classifications equivalent to our positions, but we were assured that we would be kept on at or near our salary levels. The [Illinois] State Museum was unsure of the future of the museum and archaeology at the site, and this prompted a movement to Springfield of a large amount of archaeological materials and field equipment that had been stored at the site. The Field School program was also canceled that year.*

*Our job security gradually eroded, and it was not until June 30, the last day of the fiscal year, that we heard that we still had jobs the next day when Conservation took over . . . but at substantially lower pay scales. However, we decided to stay, as we had built up the museum and programs and wished to continue to do so. We gradually weathered the uncertainty of that transition. For my part, I had never considered working anywhere else, a feeling I still hold today.[4]*

When Anderson and Iseminger arrived in 1971 the state owned approximately 650 acres. Persuading, cajoling, contributing, begging, litigating, and other land acquisition tactics (fig. 114) occupied everyone concerned with the site.

*Large portions [of the present holdings of 2,200 acres] were included in two major tracts of land that had been in litigation for many years, the Kunnemann tract at the north edge of the site, and the Rattlesnake Mound tract at the southern edge. Complicated negotiations and some condemnation were required to finally obtain these properties, which include major mound complexes and habitation areas. I recall one meeting in which a railroad representative had asked if it would be possible to move the mounds![5]*

All concerned agreed simply not to renew the lease of the Downtown Airpark in the mid-1970s, and the Falcon drive-in theater was finally acquired and demolished in 1983, "a welcome elimination (for us) of some X-rated entertainment." Perhaps the most important acquisition was the Ramey subdivision. The sixty houses in this tract across from Monks Mound were slowly purchased by the state of Illinois as they came up for sale.

Added to the problems of coping with bugs, rodents, politicians, railroad men, private property

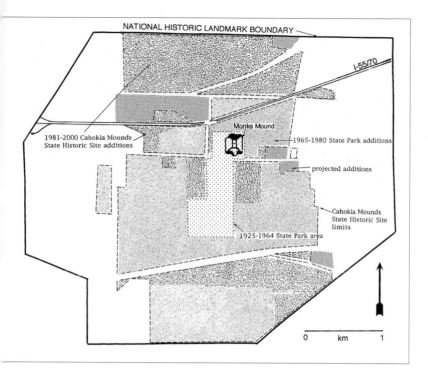

NATIONAL HISTORIC LANDMARK BOUNDARY

I-55/70

Monks Mound

1981-2000 Cahokia Mounds State Historic Site additions

1965-1980 State Park additions

projected additions

Cahokia Mounds State Historic Site limits

1925-1964 State Park area

0    km    1

Fig. 114. From 144 acres in 1925 to over 2,200 by 1985. Many methods were used to preserve more of the original Native American site.

rights, and lack of funds were the physical problems of maintenance. They plagued the two young professionals right from the beginning.

## The Scarred Earth Moves

Iseminger recalls that "for years the principal access up Monks Mound was an old trail up the west side that had first been made by T. Ames Hill in the 1830s when he built his house on top. Over the years erosion had deepened his original cut in some areas, but the lower portion of the path had been partially paved. Secondary trails were rampant all over the mound, especially on the west, south and east slopes. Many of these trails had eroded into gullies five feet deep."[6]

The recreational use of the site for so many years had also left its scars. Picnic tables and shelters to the south of Twin Mounds (Mounds 59 and 60), playground equipment to the north, and a park road running between them attracted thousands of people yearly, which contributed to severe erosion. A campground near an old borrow pit seemed to invite destruction. Funds were not available for security guards, and this area was subjected to vandalism of all kinds, including the torching of one of the pit toilets. More and more trails intruded on the mounds with each passing year.

*We tried many methods over the years to reduce the trails. A snowfence was erected around the top edge of Monks [Mound] which helped a little, but it was often torn down. Barricades and signs were destroyed or stolen . . . .*

*In the mid 1970s we began a program of stabilization by filling in the gullies using the yellow loess soil from the Collinsville bluffs. This would contrast with the dark clay soils of the mound so future archaeologists would not be confused. First, a secondary service road up the west side which joined Hill's old road was filled, then many of the gullies. This was repeated many times over the years as we gradually made progress. The difficulty is that people tended to climb where there was less vegetation, which was where we had just filled. But, I guess it was better there than on the true mound soil.[7]*

Less than a decade later a more severe challenge would face the staff. In the meantime, the vegetation cover on Monks Mound was a constant challenge. Indians did not have trees on their mounds, which obscure the silhouette, the geometry, and thus the sacred meaning of the structures. In addition, the extensive and deep root systems of midwestern trees can destroy valuable archaeological evidence. By the 1960s the neglected mounds were covered with trees (fig. 115). But clearing is not a one-time operation. Iseminger re-

Fig. 115. Trees and other vegetation obscure Monks Mound. Cutting down the trees and clearing away other plants is not a one-time operation. In Illinois's lush climate, year after year it has to be done all over again.

called: "I can remember at least two occasions when Monks Mound was clear cut in the mid and late 1970s. This had to be done all by hand with chain saws, axes and machetes. Usually, by the following year it was again overgrown."[8]

It was a great day in the late 1980s when a new machine, a Slopemaster mower, arrived in Cahokia. It could operate on steep land, and its frequent use solved the excessive growth problem and reduced the man-hours necessary to maintain the original appearance of the mounds. A judicious use of herbicides and pest control (e.g., gassing the groundhogs) also helped to maintain the site.

The threat of sprouting trees and other rogue vegetation is not the most serious problem of maintaining earth mound architecture, however, as later events would prove.

While constantly coping with maintenance problems, Anderson and Iseminger were also actively assisting archaeological investigations. Although archaeological knowledge usually accumulates gradually, there are occasional dramatic breakthroughs, and luckily for the history of Cahokia, the 1960s and 1970s saw some remarkable discoveries. All together they fueled a newly unfolding preservation movement that dramatized the site and helped save it.[9]

## In the Path of History

Once again in its thousand-year history, Cahokia's special geographic position played a role in its fate. Situated as it was near the converging waterways that defined the nation's first transportation network, Cahokia was also affected, as we have seen, by the railroads that followed the waterways, and it was to be affected once again by new federal highways that followed the railroads. But this time there was an ironic twist in Cahokia's favor.

Responding to new pressures from people in the historic preservation movement, in 1956 Congress passed the Federal-Aid Highway Act, which contained a provision for salvaging archaeological remains that would be destroyed by the construction of highways and, more important, made funds available for the work.

In 1960, when plans were under way for the construction of four major federal expressways outside St. Louis, Missouri, and East St. Louis, Illinois (Interstates 55 and 70 and their respective bypasses, Interstates 255 and 270), it was apparent that the highways cut across what had once been part of the Cahokia complex. Archaeologists would be needed to ascertain what was in the path of the proposed work. In their turn, the archaeologists would be able to salvage what they could. It opened a critical period in Cahokia's history.

## Highway Salvage Archaeology

At Cahokia "highway salvage archaeology," as this newly funded work was called, opened a new era of exploration and intensive investigation. The astonishing discoveries seemed to justify both the legislation and the preservation movement, which in turn reinforced Cahokia archaeology.

## Warren Wittry Excavates a Solar Calendar

After two seasons of fieldwork in 1960 and 1961, trying to keep ahead of the bulldozers, Warren Wittry, of the Illinois State Museum, began to study his excavation maps. He observed that the numerous large oval pits he had excavated seemed to be arranged in arcs forming circles. That the circles were not just his imagination was attested by the subsequent discovery of additional post holes of these circles by Dr. Robert L. Hall of the Illinois State Museum in 1963. Wittry asked himself: Would any of these pits line up with the rising sun at the summer and winter solstices or the spring and fall equinoxes? If they did, he might have discovered a solar calendar. Logically, some way of measuring the seasons would be vital to an agricultural people, who needed to know the right times for spring planting and fall harvesting, when to schedule the ceremonies to ensure their success, and when to hold other important rituals. Also, there were precedents for solar calendars in many other ancient civilizations.

With three posts recently erected in the original post positions, at the fall equinox in 1978 Wittry observed a phenomenon that must have thrilled him as it had thrilled people hundreds of years before and continues to thrill people to this day. When the sun rose in the east on September 22, it aligned with the central observation post and the empty space in front of the slope between the first and third terraces of the great pyramid, Monks Mound, so that it seemed the pyramid itself was giving birth to or embracing the sun. Wittry was spectacularly right. Or so it seemed to many scholars. He named his discovery the American Woodhenge, after Stonehenge in England. Some scholars believed the circle had other functions as well, such as predicting both lunar cycles and solar eclipses, and possibly served as an engineering device to lay out the placement of the mounds, but these uses have not been firmly established.[10]

Other evidence substantiated Wittry's discovery. A beaker fragment found in a pit near the winter solstice post bore a circle and cross symbol that for many Native American cultures symbolizes the earth and the four cardinal directions (fig. 116). Radiating lines probably symbolized the sun, as they have in countless

other civilizations. On the beaker, Wittry believed the open path on the lower right represented the winter solstice sunrise position and the closed path on the lower left the winter solstice sunset position, essentially a map of the Woodhenge and a cosmological symbol.

A possible offertory pit was also found near the winter solstice post, suggesting that a fire was lit to emulate the sun and encourage its return to renew the annual cycle of birth and rebirth on earth. Later excavations would uncover five rebuildings of the Woodhenge at this location, probably erected at the height of Mississippian civilization.[11]

## In the Heart of Darkest Illinois

Wittry's discovery was heralded in the press, with one interpretation revealing that anti-midwestern bias extends even to prehistoric times. In an article titled "Cahokia: Corn, Commerce, and the Cosmos" in a popular astronomy journal, E. C. Krupp, an eminent astronomer, commented:

*A prehistoric astronomer within the megalithic ruins of Stonehenge, or perhaps an ancient Maya sky watcher seated by the upper tower windows of Chichen Itza's Caracol, does not particularly strain our imaginations in this era of intense interest in archaeo-astronomy. An astronomer among 30 foot posts and earthen mounds in the American Midwest, one thousand years ago, is, however, much harder to accept. The Mississippi Valley just doesn't seem exotic enough to hold ancient mysteries. In fact, it is difficult enough to imagine monumental architecture*

Fig. 116. A cross within a circle, symbolizing the cosmos and its four cardinal directions. Warren Wittry believed that the open path on the lower right of this beaker fragment represented the winter solstice sunrise position (where the shard was found), as the closed path on the lower left represented the winter solstice sunset position. The design was both a map and a symbol.

*there, let alone a rich, complex society complete with as-tronomers. Yet Cahokia Mounds, in the heart of darkest Illinois, is one of the largest earthworks in the world, and includes the third largest artificial structure in the New World, Monks Mound. There is also evidence that the ancient astronomers of Cahokia planned their city according to astronomical principles and observed the sun's annual progression through the solstices and equinoxes.[12]*

It should be noted here that Monks Mound is the largest *totally* earthen structure in the New World. Also, a woodhenge is strikingly similar to the dance circle erected in countless Amerindian communities, both in the past and in the present. From another perspective, Robert L. Hall, an anthropologist at the University of Illinois Chicago, also recently challenged the standard interpretation of the Cahokia Woodhenge as an astronomical instrument.

*From time to time questions have arisen concerning the need for a complete circle of posts to define a woodhenge . . . if the function was primarily astronomical. For observing the sun you would only need posts between azimuths 60 to 120 degrees and 240 to 300 degrees. The answer, of course, is that the function was probably not primarily astronomical. The purpose of the Mount Chicoma world center shrine [near the Tewa pueblo in New Mexico] was to gather and direct powers of nature and to serve as a location for communication with the forces of nature at the time of pilgrimages. The function of the woodhenges [at Cahokia] was probably very similar. Their function was probably not as passive observatories but as active instruments to direct the powers of nature into the heart of the community. And this function was enhanced by their design. In the same way the central post and pit features of the Emergent Mississippian Period plazas were probably a design to enhance some similar function. They surely represented symbolic world centers as well.[13]*

One use does not negate or exclude other uses. Communication and observation may have gone hand in hand. Also, the Mississippians may have been interested in other heavenly bodies besides the sun, as are the Omaha and the Osage.

## Success Builds on Success: Melvin L. Fowler

When he began work in Cahokia in 1966, archaeologist Melvin L. Fowler realized that "no one since Moorehead's time had attempted to deal with the Cahokia site in its entirety, nor had anyone since Patrick attempted to work out a detailed map of the site."[14] A scientist who could think about large-scale problems while he dealt fastidiously with the small-scale issues that would lead to their solution, Fowler set to work simultaneously on three fronts: mapping, excavating, and interpreting the results.

Using old maps, old aerial photographs, and old field notes and commissioning new photogrammetry and surveying, Fowler's team from the University of Wisconsin–Milwaukee (UWM) carefully put together a detailed map of the entire Cahokia site. The map was produced at a scale of 1:2,000 with a one meter contour interval. Too large to be printed on a single sheet, the UWM map is divided into nine numbered sections. Now indispensable to all Cahokia studies, this large-scale map, using more precise surveying techniques, made it possible to locate mounds not noted by any of the earlier investigators. And by comparing the UWM map with the 1876 Patrick map, for example, and subtracting the "new" elements, it is possible to determine the changes made to the land in this past century when so much has happened.[15]

Looking again at the Goddard-Ramey photographs, Fowler also noted a disturbance in the earth that photographed as a light streak east of Monks Mound.

Using their new maps, Fowler and his crew were able to plot the place on the ground exactly, and they started to dig. Before the 1966 field season was over, the team has discovered traces of an enormous Mississippian stockade system under the disturbed ground. Several more years of digging were necessary to piece together its original form, because four stockades had been built in the same general location (fig. 117).

Trench lines also indicated that defensive towers or bastions had been built into the stockade every sixty-five feet. Subsequent excavations and projections eventually suggested a two-mile-long stockade surrounding the central portion of Cahokia.

Fig. 117. Anatomy of a stockade. The mighty rebuilding efforts and careful engineering of the Mississippians were revealed when archaeologists excavated their protective wall.

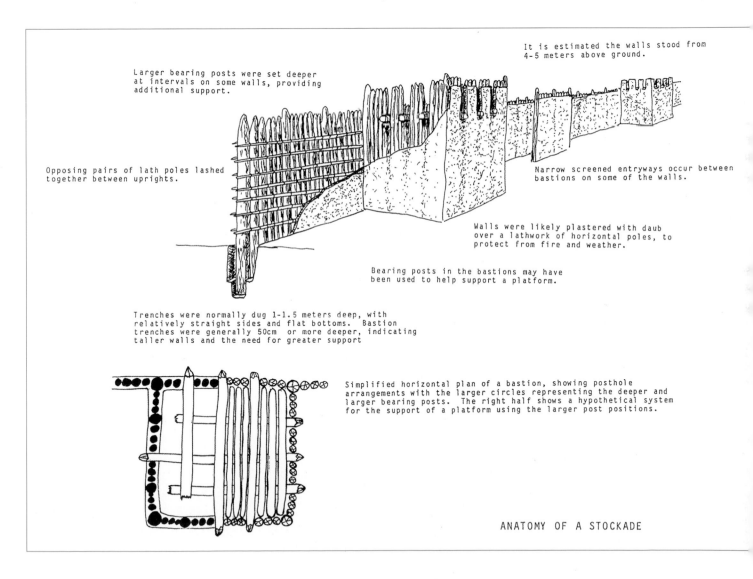

It is estimated the walls stood from 4-5 meters above ground.

Larger bearing posts were set deeper at intervals on some walls, providing additional support.

Opposing pairs of lath poles lashed together between uprights.

Narrow screened entryways occur between bastions on some of the walls.

Walls were likely plastered with daub over a lathwork of horizontal poles, to protect from fire and weather.

Bearing posts in the bastions may have been used to help support a platform.

Trenches were normally dug 1-1.5 meters deep, with relatively straight sides and flat bottoms. Bastion trenches were generally 50cm or more deeper, indicating taller walls and the need for greater support

Simplified horizontal plan of a bastion, showing posthole arrangements with the larger circles representing the deeper and larger bearing posts. The right half shows a hypothetical system for the support of a platform using the larger post positions.

ANATOMY OF A STOCKADE

What deductions can we make from the presence of this prehistoric stockade? It appears the wall was built and rebuilt four times between 1150 and 1550. Each time it was built, the Indians felled more than 15,000 oak and hickory trees, Each log had to be at least one foot in diameter and about fifteen feet long, and it had to be dragged, carried, or floated from the forest, sometimes three to five miles away. Since the society was without the wheel or beasts of burden, intensive human labor had to be organized for the massive pub-

lic works of erecting four separate stockades on such a large scale.

Archaeologists agree that the stockade probably had a dual purpose. No evidence has yet been discovered that Cahokia was ever invaded, but three things about the stockade suggest that its primary purpose was defensive: the height of the wall (ten to twelve feet above the surface); the presence of projecting bastions from which archers could shoot (fig. 118); and some "evidence that portions of the wall were hurriedly built, cutting

Fig. 118. The stockade wall protected the central ceremonial precinct, including Monks Mound, sixteen other mounds, and the Grand Plaza.

through residential areas, as if danger was imminent."[16] The stockade may also have functioned as a social barrier separating the elite from the lower classes.

Spanish accounts of the lower Mississippi testify to enmity and warfare between Native American groups in a later period, and many of the communities were fortified before the Europeans arrived.

How many hours of labor were needed for cutting and preparing the trees, transporting them to the site, digging the trench foundations, erecting the posts, filling and tamping around them, collecting and preparing cordage to lash them together, and other finishing touches such as applying the final coats of daub plaster? Iseminger estimates the total labor could be as much as 190,300 person-hours.[17] The stockade (fig. 119) was clearly the work of a highly organized society, with a disciplined workforce of specialists and laborers, all working together for a common purpose under the direction of a powerful paramount chief.

## Another Pattern Perceived

As he continued to study the 1966 UWM maps and other data, Fowler began to perceive another pattern. He knew from Harriet Smith's work on Murdock Mound that individual mounds were based on mathematical calculations. If the Mississippians built pieces of their community this way, couldn't they have built their whole community on a mathematical model? In a later project devoted to classifying the mounds according to size and shape, Fowler noted that most were platform or conical, but a few were ridge-topped. He also noticed that two of the ridge-topped mounds were at the westernmost and southernmost points of the site (Powell and Rattlesnake Mounds)—both at the outer "boundaries" of the community. Wondering if ridge-topped mounds were "marker mounds" or had some

Fig. 119. A highly organized society. The erecting of the stockades revealed the necessity for a disciplined workforce.

other special significance, Fowler began to look for others. When he noted another ridge-topped mound (Mound 72) in the southern part of the site, so small (only six feet tall) that it had been ignored by earlier

*The location and distribution of mounds at Cahokia form a rough diamond with Monks Mound at its center. Canteen Creek, right, joins Cahokia Creek, which flows into the Mississippi River.*

Fig. 120. A diamond-shaped city plan. This schematic drawing, based on Fowler's map (fig. 55), shows the location and distribution of the principal mounds in Cahokia.

mapmakers, his educated intuition told him he had found something important. But even he had no idea at first of the tremendous significance that lay in the excavations ahead.

Predicting that if there was any validity to his theory he might find a ceremonial post hole that lined up due south of the southwest corner of Monks Mound, Fowler began to dig there. When the unmistakable circular stain of a post hole began to emerge in exactly the spot Fowler predicted, his thesis gained credibility. Furthermore, a straight line drawn from this post and extended through a small mound on the first terrace of Monks Mound intersected ridge-topped Rattlesnake Mound on the south and another mound in the Kunnemann group to the north. Fowler felt he had might have found the north-south axis of the site and termed his hypothesis the "Cahokia baseline." A line drawn from Powell Mound, a ridge-topped mound at the west edge of the site, through the small mound on the southwest corner of Monks Mound and extended equidistant east forms an east-west axis also intersecting Mound 2. Connecting the four points forms a roughly diamond-shaped site plan, with Monks Mound at the center (fig. 120). Since the complex was constructed over a three-hundred-year period, further evidence is needed to demonstrate an intention at any one time

Skeptics might argue that people connecting point markers sometimes make patterns completely unrecognized by the people who placed the markers in the first place, but Fowler's subsequent excavations of Mound 72 surprised him and many others in the archaeological community. The discoveries he made later, based on this hypothesis, lent weight to his argument, as did the later discovery of several post holes associated with eight of nine rebuildings of a small mound on the southwest corner of the first terrace of Monks Mound. It had to be more than coincidence that these occurred at the predicted Cahokia baseline intersection points on this corner of Monks Mound.

The cultural evidence Fowler was about to uncover in Mound 72 was of great importance. To the uninitiated, Mound 72 looks like a natural rise of the earth. Putting together the spatial picture in his mind's eye, however, Fowler saw three clues to a more intriguing possibility. Mound 72 lay on the north-south baseline of the complex, but unlike all the other mounds, it had a unique diagonal axis, northwest to southeast, aligning with the summer solstice sunset and the winter solstice sunrise. It belonged to the special category of the few ridge-topped mounds ever found in Cahokia. His conclusion: dig here (fig. 121). The results were dazzling.

For the next five years one wonder after another was unearthed. Mound 72 was complex; it contained three smaller mounds and several surface and burial pits as well (fig. 122). When it was all over, Fowler had discovered tens of thousands of spectacular grave goods and the skeletons of nearly three hundred people. Under the southeastern primary mound was a chief in his early forties lying on a blanket of 20,000 whelk shells from the Gulf of Mexico. Around him were the skeletons of six attendants, and six more were nearby. On top of them were placed a roll of sheet copper, stacks of mica, fourteen beautifully shaped chunkey stones (one disintegrated), and two caches of more than eight hundred perfect arrowheads, many made from exotic cherts. Under the central primary mound Fowler found the skeletons of four decapitated men, their handless arms overlapping each other, clearly sacrificial victims. Next to the men a deep pit held fifty-three women, arranged in two rows and buried two or three deep at the west end. Associated with the third primary mound at the northwest end were three burial pits containing nineteen, twenty-two, and twenty-four women respectively. One of these pits had been partially redug and included

Fig. 121. Excavating an unassuming ridge-top mound reveals spectacular finds. Melvin L. Fowler's educated guess that Mound 72 might be important was the beginning of the most significant discoveries in Cahokia's history.

an offering of over 36,000 shell beads and another four hundred perfect arrowheads, numerous bone and antler artifacts, and several broken vessels. Around these primary mounds were several other pits containing "bundle burials," or burials of disjointed bones, suggested that the remains of other people had been prepared and set aside awaiting the death of a chief, whom they would then accompany into his grave (fig. 123). Another deep pit had two burial layers, the lower one containing some forty people tossed in and perhaps violently dispatched. Above them were fourteen people who had been ceremoniously carried there on litters with frames of cedar poles. Such differential burial treatment indicates different social rank and status.

The knowledge gained from the dig confirmed that the Mississippians had direct or indirect trade relationships as far away as Oklahoma, Tennessee, southern Illinois, Wisconsin, Lake Superior, the southern Appalachians, and the Gulf of Mexico.[18]

**MOUND 72 CROSS-SECTION**

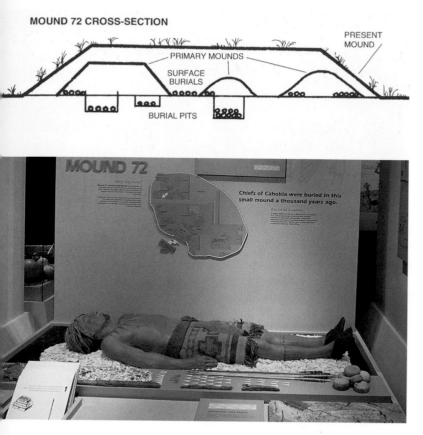

Fig. 122. (top) Three mounds in one. The complexity of Mound 72 is clarified in this schematic drawing, which also shows that it was built over several years.

Fig. 123. (bottom) Offerings of 36,000 shell beads and over eight hundred perfect arrowheads. This re-creation of the burial of a leader in Mound 72 shows him resting on a bird-shaped blanket of some 20,000 marine shell beads. The cache of offerings also included a copper staff, a large pile of mica, fifteen chunkey stones, and more shells.

All together Fowler's contributions to Cahokia archaeology are inestimable, but even more important is his legacy endorsing the age-old wisdom of archaeology: deciding where to dig comes from intuition based on knowledge, years of fieldwork, careful examination, and thought. Informed imagination can ignite the spark that illuminates the larger meaning of a whole culture.

## Other Significant Contributions

Just as important as the astonishing discoveries made by Wittry and Fowler, however, are the cumulative results of less dramatic findings. Slowly but surely dozens of smaller studies enabled scholars to assemble pieces of the Cahokia puzzle so that gradually a clearer, larger picture emerged providing the whole context of the Mississippian tradition at Cahokia. Iseminger's account provides the details of the record (see box).[19]

When all is said and done, it is remarkable that we have such a vivid picture of this Amerindian complex at the end of the first millennium. Robert Hall's 1975 analogy is still apt.

*But no matter how refined we may think archaeology has become, considering the size of the Cahokia site proper, approaching six square miles, and considering the length of the Mississippian occupation, at least three centuries, let's say 25 generations, and considering the small area explored archaeologically, less than one percent of the site, just the ambition to make a definitive statement at this time about Cahokia presumes the confidence a scholar might assume who seeks to understand the operations and inner workings of the United States Congress by monitoring the archaeologically visible activity of one legislator's wastebasket.[20]*

## Painstaking Archaeology, Painstaking Preservation

As the painstaking work of archaeology continued, the painstaking work of preservation at last began to show results. In 1964 the Cahokia Mounds had been declared a National Historic Landmark, reinforcing the efforts of Illinois supporters to get recognition of the site's importance. Many times this story has been re-

### Contributions of Other Researchers

Robert Salzer brought field schools from Beloit College to dig for three seasons (1969, 1971, and 1972) on the Merrell Tract, in an unsuccessful search for the West Stockade, but the work revealed important information about residential use of that area. One of his former students, John E. Kelly, served as field director and later earned his Ph.D. from the University of Wisconsin. He was hired as a field director for the University of Illinois on the Interstate 270 (now I-255) project around Cahokia and later worked on American Bottom projects with Southern Illinois University at Edwardsville. He has conducted research at numerous sites on the fringes of Cahokia, contributed knowledge about site layout and the history of Cahokia's occupation, developed the concept of the Emergent Mississippian period in the region, and "rediscovered" remnants of the East St. Louis mound group. He is currently affiliated with the Central Mississippi Valley Archaeological Research Institute (CMVARI) and coordinates field schools through Washington University, St. Louis, and the university of Missouri–St. Louis. With both, he has worked all around the Cahokia area as well as at the Cahokia site, often in cooperation with other institutions.

Washington University has had a long association with the Cahokia site since the 1920s when Robert S. Terry studied human remains recovered by Warren K. Moorehead. In the 1950s, Preston Holder conducted important tests on the Kunnemann Mound at the north edge of Cahokia and at the Wilson Mound, probably an elite burial mound just west of the Cahokia site in Fairmont City. In the mid-1960s Nelson Reed, John Bennett, and James Porter conducted soil coring tests on Monks Mound that revealed the mound had been built in a number of stages, roughly from 900 to 1150. Later, teams working under Reed discovered that a large building 104 feet long by 48 feet wide had been built on top of Monks Mound about 1150 and that a stairway had been placed up the front of the south ramp of the first terrace.

James Porter had been responsible earlier in the 1960s for the highway salvage excavations at the Mitchell site, about seven miles north of Cahokia, for Southern Illinois University at Carbondale. His work later formed part of his dissertation on the Mitchell site at the University of Wisconsin. He conducted a considerable amount of work at Cahokia and the region in the 1960s and 1970s and was best known for his pioneering petrographic and thin-section work on Cahokia ceramics.

University of Illinois projects, under the direction of Charles J. Bareis, learned much about mound construction techniques and prehistoric soil engineering through excavations on the first terrace of Monks Mound and found extremely well-preserved flora and fauna in the Submound 51 borrow pit to the southwest of Monks Mound. The pit was discovered by Bareis, Porter, and Wittry while they were attempting to salvage information from the overlying Mound 51, which had been sold for fill by its owner. Bareis and his field schools also excavated residential areas at the Powell Mound at the western end of the site and the Dunham Tracts just south of the Woodhenge. Bareis and Porter directed the extensive multiyear salvage excavations on the I-270 (now I-255) project, which provided invaluable information about prehistoric settlements in the American Bottom and gave us a new look at Cahokia "from the outside in" and a better understanding of settlement patterns in the American Bottom through time.

Several people under Fowler's tutelage at the University of Wisconsin–Milwaukee were involved in projects at Cahokia. James Anderson directed excavations on the East Stockade, South Stockade, and Mound 72. After he and Iseminger came to Cahokia, working for the Illinois State Museum (ISM), they expanded excavations of the East Stockade in a joint effort between ISM and UWM, and later as the focus of the Cahokia Mounds Museum Society field schools, learning much about this defensive system and the residential sequences it traversed. Elizabeth Benchley revealed a complex sequence of ceremonial structures and small mound construction on the southwest corner of the first terrace of Monks Mound, as well as the presence of the mid-1700s French chapel and associated historical Indian occupation there. She also did some testing on Merrell Mound (Mound 42) and conducted preliminary testing at two proposed new museum construction sites. Ken Williams, who began his work at Cahokia as a high school student working on Monks Mound under Bareis and Porter, supervised the East Lobes excavations on Monks Mound, where the famous "birdman tablet" was found, and also exposed a well-preserved stratigraphic sequence that was instrumental in developing a modern ceramic chronology for the site.

Timothy Pauketat, now with the University of Illinois and formerly with the University of Oklahoma and State University of New York–Buffalo, has been involved in numerous research projects in the area, and his research emphasis is understanding Cahokia's sudden expansion during what he terms "the Big Bang," starting about 1050; he is currently examining sites in the adjacent uplands dating to this time. He has also examined Mound 49 at Cahokia and monitored waterline installation transects through the Grand Plaza, revealing important information about its artificial construction. Pauketat also led a team of researchers reexamining the materials recovered by Bareis's work on the Submound 51 borrow pit, revealing new information about ceremonial feasting and ritual, and he has published and expanded on Preston Holder's work on the Kunnemann Mound as well as that by Wittry and Robert Hall on Tract 15-A.

Robert Hall has long been involved in Cahokia research, conducting the second year of woodhenge excavations (Tract 15-A) in 1963 for the Illinois State Museum. While with the University of Illinois Chicago (then called the University of Illinois at Chicago Circle) in the 1970s, he codirected the work with Wittry in later excavations at the Woodhenge and had his field schools test the large, once deeper borrow pit south of the Twin Mounds, assist in the East Stockade excavations, and use remote sensing to examine a potential museum construction site on the Dunham Tract. He was also instrumental in establishing the chronology for the site, using both ceramics and radiocarbon dates, and in developing interpretations of symbolism and meaning from the artifacts recovered here and elsewhere and possible links to earlier and later Native American cultures.

In the late 1980s the site staff and the Cahokia Mounds Museum Society wanted to establish a research relationship with an institution that would conduct field schools and other projects at the site. Southern Illinois University at Edwardsville filled this role through the Contract Archaeology Program under the direction of Neal Lopinot and William Woods. With Lopinot, George Holley, James Collins, and many others, Woods had previously conducted the excavations at the site of the new interpretive center. For eight years several small but important projects were conducted under the supervision of Lopinot, Holley, Rinita Dalan, and Woods. They did extensive remote sensing and coring around the site, revealing much subsurface data about natural and man-made features. They expanded the South Stockade excavations, producing new information about its construction, and tested in the Grand Plaza, showing that it had been artificially leveled; Warren K. Moorehead's excavation trench in Mound 56 was relocated and partially reopened; shallow testing was conducted around the Roach Mound group, the Little Twin Mounds, several small "promontory" mounds that extend out into borrow pits, and the Tippetts Mound group, yielding new data about the construction and use of these areas; large test pits were placed around Mound 48, revealing some high-status use of that area; and several education field school programs for teachers were conducted. Additionally, this team pioneered new techniques of examining the particle size and magnetic properties of slopewash soils to determine the original shapes of mounds. In the late 1990s, groups from Southern Illinois University at Edwardsville conducted excavations before the installation of the per-

manent steps up Monks Mound and monitored the installation of a drain system in the west side of the mound. The step project revealed new data about mound construction techniques and also uncovered some refuse pits dating to the mid-1700s, when it is believed there was a small Illini village on the first terrace. Horizontal drilling for the drains encountered stone cobbles some 32 feet in extent 40 feet under the second terrace and 150 feet into the mound. Remote sensing and coring tests are continuing at this time in an attempt to identify the dimensions and nature of this enigmatic and unique feature.

In the late 1990s a new relationship was forged when the Cahokia Mounds Museum Society decided to support a commitment from an institution for long-term, multiyear projects at Cahokia, specifically to determine the route of the stockade wall around the western and northern portions of central Cahokia. An agreement was reached with CMVARI to coordinate this and other projects. Mary Beth Trubitt, then of Northwestern University, agreed to direct the project, although her institutional affiliation later changed to Western Michigan University and then to Henderson State for the Arkansas Archaeological Survey. As a result, southern portions of the West Stockade route along the Grand Plaza have been identified. At this same time, CMVARI, under the direction of John Kelly, also worked with James Brown of Northwestern University and field schools from Washington University to reopen a 1950s excavation by the Gilcrease Institute (Tulsa) into Mound 34, to reexpose the profiles and features and reexamine them with the technology and knowledge we have of the site today.

George Milner, who was a student in Salzer's Beloit College excavations at the Merrell Tract and was one of the site directors for Bareis and Porter on the I-270 project, is now affiliated with Penn State University. He has studied the human remains from around Cahokia and mound sites nearby as part of his dissertation research, developing information about nutrition, trauma, and disease. He has also done some intensive studies of the natural environment and produced important information about the terrain and wetland resources throughout the America Bottom, which has recently been published by the Smithsonian Institution Press. Although he sees Cahokia in a more conservative light than many Cahokia researchers, he has provided some important information about the human and natural history of the site.

Tom Emerson, another of the I-270 project site directors, now directs the Illinois Transportation Archaeological Research Program at the University of Illinois. His research at sites surrounding Cahokia has given him insights into developments at the main center as reflected in its suburbs and the role of political and religious power in cultural developments at Cahokia and areas under its influence. As a result of his work with the figurines from the I-270 project, he has developed a special interest in the Mississippian figurines found throughout the American Bottom region as well as the distribution of the distinctive Ramey incised pottery that originated at Cahokia.

Although the preceding are often considered the principal investigators of Cahokia archaeology, many others have been involved in specialized studies. Lucretia Kelly has done extensive work with the analysis of faunal remains from Cahokia and surrounding sites, building on earlier work by Paul Parmalee and developing concepts on exploitation strategies. Brad Koldehoff has made major contributions with his lithic studies and analysis of materials from Cahokia and numerous other American Bottom sites. Another I-270 veteran, Mark Mehrer, has published on the relationship between Cahokia and sites in the countryside around the center. Botanical studies by Neal Lopinot, Katie Parker, Gayle Fritz, Leonard Blake, and Hugh Cutler have provided important insights into the use of wild and cultivated plants in the diet and nutrition of prehistoric peoples throughout the region, especially at Cahokia.

This is not an exhaustive list, since many other archaeologists have been involved in Cahokia research, some at the site, some working elsewhere in the Cahokia sphere, and still more reexamining or reinterpreting the work of others and developing new perspectives on Cahokia archaeology.

William R. Iseminger

peated in the history of preservation: national recognition propels local recognition.

Since 1976 was the bicentennial of the American Revolution, interest in all aspects of the country's past was at an all-time high. Congress appropriated funds for books, films, exhibitions, scholarly symposia, and other projects. In this atmosphere of a new appreciation of our ancient roots, the state of Illinois began its reclassification of Cahokia from a state park to a State Historic Site, which became official in 1981. The long-term consequences were immeasurably beneficial.

An explicit change in management priorities from a *recreational* to a *cultural* emphasis enabled the staff to order the removal of picnic tables and playground equipment and to focus more on interpretive work. They were able to cut more trees to reveal the geometry of the mounds and to recreate the panoramic vistas of the old mound complex.

In another irony favoring the long-term preservation of the site, when the sponsorship of the Illinois State Museum and the Illinois State Museum Society were lost in this shift, Anderson had to instigate the founding of the separate Cahokia Mounds Museum Society. This group grew vigorously over the years. Since both its work and its financial resources could be focused on just on one place, in the end its contributions to the preservation of Cahokia were probably greater than what the older institutions could have mustered.

## Institutionalized Salvage Archaeology: The Office of Contract Archaeology

In 1974 the United States Congress passed the Archaeological and Historic Preservation Act, providing funding for archaeological data recovery at sites affected by federal undertakings, and appropriated funds for archaeological work. By 1985 enough momentum and Illinois support had built up to enable William I. Woods, together with Sidney Denny and Neal H. Lopinot, to found the Contract Archaeology Program at Southern Illinois University at Edwardsville to fill this role. The sponsorship of work at Cahokia by the Department of Conservation (and later the Illinois Historic Preservation Agency) made publication of the re-

sults possible and helped disseminate knowledge to a wider community. Later, when plans for a new interpretive center materialized, the Office of Contract Archaeology was able to investigate various sites to determine the most suitable, or least invasive, place to build.

## The Power of Big Plans

The decade of the 1980s also saw another effect of the institutionalization of preservation in Illinois. Anderson and Iseminger were asked to help Sue Wydick and several others at the Department of Conservation to produce a "Master Management Plan" to give form to their shared vision for Cahokia's future. Fifty-six pages long, the report was cogently divided into meaningful parts. The "conceptual plan" section, for example, identified three separate activities at the site and the spaces to be devoted to them: cultural interpretation, natural interpretation, and archaeological resources. Starred prominently in the cultural area was a new interpretive center (fig. 124). The "land acquisition" section was detailed and specific, naming adjoining lands to be acquired and listing them in order of priority, with the proviso that "as parcels become available they should be considered [for purchase] at that time." The "natural interpretation" section listed over seventy plant species to be protected on the site. A detailed, realistic development budget concluded the document.

The power of ideas, especially big ideas, embodied in a far-reaching printed document with effective graphic presentation cannot be overestimated. For the next two decades this Master Plan helped steer the fate of the Cahokia Mounds State Historic Site toward fulfilling its potential. The illustrations helped legislators, foundations, preservation commissioners, and the public visualize the future of the site (if properly developed according to the vision of the plan) and en-

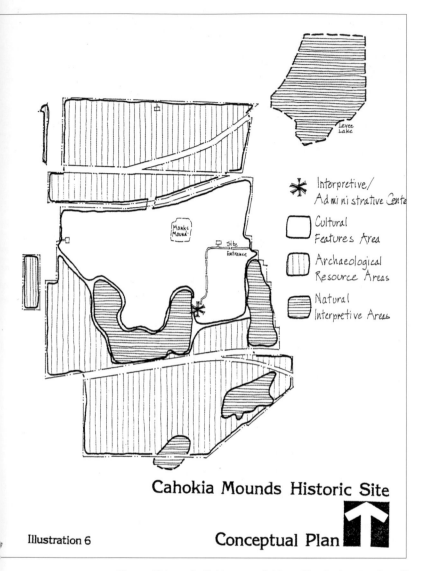

Levee Lake

✳ Interpretive/ Administrative Center

☐ Cultural Features Area

☐ Archaeological Resource Areas

☐ Natural Interpretive Areas

Monks Mound

Site Entrance

# Cahokia Mounds Historic Site

Illustration 6

# Conceptual Plan

Fig. 124. Vision embodied in a masterly Master Plan. In the 1980s the staff outlined its dreams for the future of the site, including more land to be acquired, a new interpretive center, and plant species to be protected.

listed their support at crucial turning points. The Master Plan stressed the larger issues, and the holistic presentation in maps and diagrams made it easier for laypeople as well as specialists to grasp the fundamental ideas. It was planning in the best sense.

## International Preservation Efforts Help Cahokia

About the time the Master Plan was published, Larry Aten, of the National Park Service, decided that Cahokia was worthy of inclusion in the UNESCO World Heritage List, a designation established by UNESCO in 1972 to highlight the most important monuments of the human heritage all over the planet. Aten worked closely with Iseminger and Anderson at the site, and with Alan Downer, archaeologist for the Department of Conservation in Springfield, as the group set about proving their case. Since this list includes the Taj Mahal, the Great Wall of China, and the Pyramids of Egypt, success would depend on making the argument that Cahokia was a masterpiece of worldwide, timeless human achievement. Although Cahokia was not part of the well-known canon of great architecture, they believed it should be. At the time only one other Amerindian archaeological site in the United States was being considered—Mesa Verde, Colorado.

Although Cahokia was state owned and most UNESCO landmarks were national property, the nominators went ahead vigorously. (Until recently, Cahokia was the only state-owned property on the list.) UNESCO landmarking proceeds by a painstaking nomination process. The nominators carefully study the criteria established by the sponsoring organization, research the site's historical, cultural, and architectural significance, and analyze all the evidence in terms of these criteria.

Using the Master Plan and other materials, the two-man team prepared the lengthy nomination form including accurate descriptions, dimensions, and characteristic, measured features. Overall, the UNESCO convention states that to be listed sites must be the "works of man or the combined works of nature and of man, and areas including archaeological sites which are of outstanding universal value from the historical, aesthetic, ethnological or anthropological points of view."

In addition, each property nominated should meet one or more of six criteria. The team argued that while only one criterion was necessary for inclusion, Cahokia met four, numbers ii, iii, iv, and v, as follows:

ii.  *Exhibit an important interchange of human values, over a span of time or within a cultural area of the world, or developments in architecture or technology, monumental arts, town-planning or landscape design; or*

iii. *Bear a unique or at least exceptional testimony to a cultural tradition or to a civilization which is living or which has disappeared; or*

iv.  *Be an outstanding example of a type of building or architectural or technological ensemble or landscape which illustrates (a) significant stage(s) in human history, or*

v.   *Be an outstanding example of a traditional human settlement or land-use which is representative of a culture (or cultures), especially when it has become vulnerable under the impact of irreversible change.[21]*

For criterion ii the nomination brought forth evidence of both site planning and landscape design in Cahokia's residential and public areas and the presence of mounds and palisades.

For criterion iii the nomination argued that the American Bottom was a unique environment, quite different from other prehistoric population centers. That the civilization was unique and has disappeared was self-evident.

For criterion iv it focused on the three outstanding structures that illustrate the evolution of political and social organization and technological thought at Cahokia: Monks Mound, Mound 72, and the Woodhenge. In this way the authors used the dramatic and recent archaeological discoveries to make their case: "Monks Mound . . . is the largest earthen structure in the New World, and the largest prehistoric man-made structure north of central Mexico. Only the Pyramid of the Sun at Teotihuacan and the Cholula Pyramid [both of stone] are larger."

For criterion v the nomination argued that the influence Cahokia exerted over vast areas of the North American continent made it outstanding, citing its central role in a regional trade system and its dense population.

In summarizing the arguments for placing Cahokia on the list, the authors added:

*Cahokia consisted of a large population center that provided goods and services for the surrounding communities in the American Bottom. The American Bottom is unusual in its ecological abundance, allowing the largest concentration of prehistoric people to occur in North America. The resulting social, economic and political system that arose in the American Bottom reaches its peak at Cahokia. Elite groups rose in power and status as seen in Mound 72. A labor force was organized to construct large public works projects, of which Monks Mound represents the most conspicuous example. Trade materials from thousands of miles away were processed and distributed from Cahokia . . . . Cahokia contains many exciting insights into the evolution of prehistoric society from a simple egalitarian organization into one of increasing complexity— a foundation of the modern nation-state.[22]*

## Cahokia Becomes a UNESCO World Heritage Site

Although the 1972 nomination did not succeed (Mesa Verde's did), it was revised and resubmitted, and in 1982 the international commission at UNESCO approved Cahokia for listing with other World Heritage Sites with the following citation: "Through the collective recognition of the community of nations expressed within the principles of the convention concerning protection of the world culture and natural heritage, Cahokia Mounds State Historic Site has been designated a World Heritage Site and joins the select list of protected areas around the world whose outstanding natural and cultural resources form the common inheritance of all mankind. December 14, 1982."

The benefits this success set in motion are manifold, and now for the first time the beneficence seemed to move downward from international to national to state level as well as upward.

## National Preservation Efforts Help Cahokia

The national preservation movement in the United States was in full swing at the time, but it was focused almost exclusively on saving old buildings. Perhaps because the center of activity was at first on the East Coast and dominated by architectural historians, little attention was paid to landscape or archaeological sites. One other benefit of the UNESCO nomination is that it, together with the Master Plan, may have influenced the Board of the National Trust for Historic Preservation (a nonprofit organization chartered by Congress in 1949) to help Cahokia at a critical time. The mission of the National Trust is to provide "leadership, education, and advocacy to save America's diverse historic places and revitalize our communities."[23]

When the Kreider Truck Company building and lot just east of Monks Mound came up for sale, the trustees were asked to contribute part of the money to purchase it for the site. Once again Cahokia inspired those who came in contact with it to higher thoughts

and actions and to a larger vision. For the first time in its history the National Trust financially supported an archaeological site.[24] Later the building became the site's maintenance building.

## State Preservation Efforts Help Cahokia

Responding to the phenomenal growth of the preservation movement nationwide, in 1985 the state of Illinois created a new department, the Illinois Historic Preservation Agency. It combined the old Historic Sites Division of the Department of Conservation, Preservation Services, and the Illinois State Historical Library. The shift put a new emphasis on historic sites. No longer would they have to compete for funds with the recreational and wildlife operations of the Department of Conservation; they would have funds of their own for cultural and historic interpretation. More than anything else, Cahokia needed a new visitors' center, and the process that had begun in 1984 accelerated, including excavations to find an appropriate site (fig. 125). New support came from the new agency, from Governor James R. Thompson, and from a growing body of ardent, devoted volunteers.

While all this success was happening at the preservation level, however, a new threat to the existence of Monks Mound occurred from an old quarter—midwestern rainfall. It seemed for a time that the geometric appearance of the mound might be lost at last and its meaning obscured.

## The Great Mound Moves

In a 1997 article in *Historic Illinois,* William R. Iseminger described the impending catastrophe this way:

Fig. 125. More patient excavations. Test diggings for the new interpretive center uncovered ancient Mississippian houses, revealing a new aspect of Cahokia's history.

*In 1984 a large crack formed at the top of the north side of Monks Mound following some of the rainiest seasons we had seen for several years. A second crack on the east side turned out to be the worst, however, and a major slump there created a gash about 20 feet deep near the top, and a mass of soil bulldozed its way slowly down the side. This was the exact location of one of the two "east Lobes" on the mound and indicated that these features, and similar ones around the mound were the result of ancient slumps, several likely occurring while the Indians were still here . . . . The following year, after another unusually wet season, another slump formed on the west side of the mound.*

*Slumping probably began as early as Mississippian times, and has continued off and on until the present day. Monks Mound may look as immovable as any mountain, but in battles with nature, it has sometimes yielded. William Woods believes that originally Monks Mound had only one platform, now deeply buried, but it had been enlarged several times, probably before the addition of the first terrace. Several additions on the south side later produced the present lower or first terrace. Around the same time, caps on the summit defined a third and fourth terrace. These originally extended farther west, making the mound's west side originally a mirror image of the east side. The present second terrace, according to Woods, was created by a massive slump, which was later patched, but then eroded away.*

*Slumping can be caused by internal water buildup during wet years, exacerbated by a high water table within the mound. Following three very wet years in the early 1980s, together with the closing of nearby steel mills which allowed the water table to rise, the mound became saturated, and major slumps occurred on the east and west sides in 1984 and 1985. This was not surface erosion; large masses of the mound slowly moved downslope as a unit, a giant land slide. Modern equipment and new engineering methods are helping to control the problem. New soil, of a different color, was bulldozed up the east slope to fill in the scarred areas left after that area slumped.*

*When a slump occurred on a projecting ridge of the second terrace, the center dropped downward two to three feet, like a saddle, and flowed into adjacent valleys. At the same time the entire mass moved westward as it pulled away from the main body of the mound, and a roll of earth formed at the toe of the slope. After its initial movement, this slump seemed to stabilize, and it was left alone. However, it reactivated in 1994 and 1995, dropping dramatically, as much as eight feet in places. The crack expanded northward across two more ridges for nearly half the length of the mound, and the roll at the bottom grew to almost six feet in height.*

*Engineering studies following the 1984–85 slumps offered several possible solutions, but all of them would have adversely affected the mound more than the slumps. Fortunately, a new technology of drilling horizontal drains into the mound has been perfected since then, and this technique was used to install five drains into the slump area in an attempt to remove some of the internal water, a project which began in August, 1997.*

*The major cracks and scarps have been filled with sand, special soils, sealed with a geosynthetic clay liner or erosion-control mats, and capped with a fine-grained fill to stabilize these areas and prevent the penetration of sur-face water. Also, low profile earthen berms have been placed above the slump area to divert surface water away from the problem areas.*[25]

While drilling horizontally to install interior drains in the west side of Monks Mound, contractors under the direction of William Woods drilled through 32 feet of stone cobbles about 150 feet into the mound and some 40 feet below the surface of the second terrace. This discovery of stone in earth architecture is a new finding whose meaning has yet to be fully investigated and interpreted.

Another maintenance problem has been the stairs to the top of Monks Mound. In the past visitors forged their own way up the mound, creating myriad trails over the entire surface. Some eroded, leaving gullies up to five feet deep in places. In 1980 a wooden stairway was constructed to direct traffic up and down in one place, but these steps deteriorated, partly because of the same water problems. Water seeped under the steps and eroded the surface beneath the support beams, causing the stairway to shift. A stairway of concrete steps was determined as the best solution, and after archaeological testing by Southern Illinois University at Edwardsville, the new permanent steps were installed in 1998.

## Volunteer Strength: Time, Work, and Money at Critical Times

The Cahokia Mounds Museum Society (CMMS), which had been founded in the turbulent changes of 1976 when the site lost its sponsorship by the Illinois State Museum Society, expanded exponentially in size and scope in the next decade. When it was first organized the group had about forty members; today there are over four hundred. Since the state of Illinois does not print more than basic brochures for its sites, the CMMS has published scores of brochures, guides, audiovisual materials, reprints, newsletters, and books. It also took over publication of the quarterly newsletter the *Cahokian*. Funds for an annual lecture series, special conferences, tours, archaeological explorations, and field schools have come from its dues, donations, and the profits of its museum shop. The organization has purchased audiovisual equipment, computers, cameras, and other equipment for the site. The board of directors, a mix of citizens interested in promoting Cahokia, hired an executive director, Chris Pallozola, to manage the society's daily affairs and a museum shop manager.

## Cahokia Gains New Values in a New Age

The Cahokia Mounds State Historic Site also sponsors a volunteer program that has itself transformed the meaning and power of the landscape. As they discover and communicate old meanings of the site, the volunteers also create new meanings for themselves and others. These new meanings bring renewed identity through service to something higher than self and create fellow feeling in the community devoted to that service.

After an intensive training program, members of the "volunteer corps" take on the work of lobby greeters, gallery guides, information desk resource people, tour guides (who take additional training), library and clerical aides, and assistants to the museum shop staff.

*Continuing education is provided in two ways: volunteers are welcome to attend the annual lecture series, and we have training sessions to update the skills in each volunteer category. We sponsor trips for our volunteers; last year, for example, an excursion to Fort de Chartres and an overnight canoe trip. Of course additional training can be*

*done on their own by reading the* Cahokian *or other materials available in our shop or in the library. Morale is high; people love to work here, and they often continue to come for many years. We celebrate their contributions with an annual volunteer appreciation banquet where we hand out certificates and service awards.*

*Volunteer events are wholly funded by volunteers. For example, volunteers sell soft drinks at special events. I am very proud of our program. It is now a well-established, on going institution, and I rarely have to make more than two or three phone calls to fill the monthly work schedule. Considering that the volunteers do the work of sixteen full-time people, and most of them work half a day a week, I think that is remarkable.*[26]

## A Bridge of Feeling

As long-time volunteer Don Dillow, a former teacher of vocational agriculture and a local junior high school assistant principal, put it:

*Indian culture has been of interest to me since I was a child. We had so very many Indian artifacts on our and the neighboring farms, about 22 miles west of Mill Creek, Il. Most of these were chert and arrow heads. In fact, there were so many that, would you believe, I kept none of them. At the time they were a nuisance to the farming operations . . . . My granddad, who lived on the adjoining farm, once plowed up what is now called a "Stone Box Grave." He placed the stones back and continued on with the plowing.*

*While I was still home and since that time I have tried to imagine what life was like in that valley where we lived with the big drainage creek running through it while the Indians lived there. I remember an area approximately 30' by 30' where arrow heads and chert pieces were 4 to 5 inches deep. I've been told by archaeologists that it was what is called a blank shop [workshop]. Instead of carry-*

ing the chert a great distance, they would rough out the arrowheads and then finish or refine them at the destination.

I have reflected so many times, and still do, on what that valley must have been like back then. What kinds of people, dwellings and other structures were there during the Indian habitation. I have been told they were Shawnee, probably the last Indians to inhabit that area.

I have been very pleased to volunteer at the Cahokia Mounds World Heritage site. Being a Gallery Interpreter and Tour Guide has given me the opportunity to continue to meet and work with people from all over the world while I continue my interest in Indian Culture. Just as I still try to visualize what life was like for the Indians around my home and neighboring farms during my youth, I try on my tours to get people to visualize what life was like at the Cahokia Mounds. I like to call it an attempt to create a bridge of feeling. Instead of just seeing mounds, plazas, borrow pits and woodhenges, I hope the people see and feel human aspirations and dedications to something outside themselves that bound them together in such an amazing endeavor to create the largest city north of Mexico.

The longer I give tours the more I see a dedicated people striving against what must have seemed impossible odds. At the end of the tour when people thank me I tell them the Spirits of thousands of Indians who labored here now thank them for coming to listen and learn about their magnificent city and culture, because each time we tell the story their city is pulsating back to life just a little more. I try to get them to feel as the Spirits of the Indians must have felt when the settlers began moving into the area. The farmers and construction crews began to erase, destroy and alter their city. The Spirits of those from the past must have wept as they saw the evidence of their existence being destroyed. But the archaeologists arrived. Appreciative people pleaded a cause for preservation to willing listeners. Archaeologists began to reconstruct the city. The State began to acquire and protect a greater part

of the city. Surely the Spirits of those Cahokian Indians must have been gladdened as the corner was turned. Their magnificent city was not lost. Someone noticed. Now someone is telling the story on the tour. Now you came. You listened. Hopefully you will tell others so they will come and we will tell them the story. Each time we tell the story we can feel the city pulsating back to life just a little bit more . . . . I think it helps people to be more thoughtful and tolerant of all cultures . . . to see ourselves in a continuing changing time sequence.[27]

## Everyday Pleasures

There are also everyday pleasures in volunteer work—the sociability of being with others, the sense of being useful, the fun of meeting people from all over the world, and the satisfaction of having been a meaningful part of their American experience.

You see people from all over the world standing here in awe . . . . This is the only chance they will have in their whole lives to see this magnificent site and hear this story . . . the astronomy professor from Arizona, the doctor from Sweden, the farmer from New Zealand, a college professor with graduate students . . . people with visiting relatives to entertain . . . . They look at me when they thank me, and they shake my hand and I can tell by their touch, by the pressure of their hand, by the look in their eye what it has meant to them. As you get older you want something that continues to add meaning to your life. I like to feel I did a little bit to make this whole thing happen . . . much as some of the original Indian inhabitants must have felt about making the mound city . . . we give up something of ourselves to see something bigger develop. . . . No matter how tired I might be at the end of the day, if you ask me if I will continue, the answer is "you betcha!"[28]

If Don Dillow is right about how some of the original Indian inhabitants might have felt about making the mounds, some of their descendants would agree.

## Contemporary Native Americans

Since 1977 Native Americans and other visitors have come from all over the United States to participate in programs at Cahokia. These programs include dancing (fig. 126), storytelling, crafts, and music. The names of the festivals have changed throughout the years, from "Rediscover Cahokia" to "Heritage America" to "Prehistoric Lifeways," and the audiences have increased from a few hundred in the beginning to over 30,000 in the early 1990s. Representatives from the Cherokee, Choctaw, Chickasaw, Comanche, Creek, Ponca, Cheyenne, Apache, Nez Percé, Sioux, Osage, Hopi, Navajo, and other tribes travel hundreds of miles to participate. Tommy Wildcat, a Cherokee from Park Hill, Oklahoma, summed up the feelings of his tribe in a recent interview. "Whenever I say that it is time to make plans to go to Cahokia there is an uplift in people's spirits. For the Cherokee, it is like going home. We have a strong spiritual connection to Cahokia, for we sense that the Mound Builders were our ancestors, and this is our ancient home." Also, the late Wood Bell, a Choctaw who had been coming to Cahokia every year for many years, said that he appreciated the work the people at the site were doing, keeping the area where he does his dancing well maintained and clear.[29]

The Native American and other craft specialists teach visitors how to carve a bow, attach an arrow

Fig. 126. A continuing uplift for Native American spirits. Frequent festivals at the Cahokia Mounds site celebrate the crafts, storytelling, music, and dancing of many tribes, both ancient and modern. Native American dancer Jay Mule, a Choctaw from Haskell Indian Nations University, Lawrence, Kansas, performs in the annual celebrations.

point to a shaft, knap flint, make gourds into bowls, form pottery, make cordage, finger weave, engrave shells, and tool copper. They also demonstrate basketry, food preparation, archery, flute making, ceramics, silverwork, beadwork, kachina modeling, and contemporary art forms. Sharing their heritage with others who clearly value what they are experiencing is spiritually strengthening, and these artisans are grateful to the site and its interpreters for making it possible. "After all," Tommy Wildcat continued,

*when the Europeans first arrived here as colonists trying to escape from oppression they saw that we were living as a free people. The idea of freedom lived amongst us, and they experienced this freedom. America is based on freedom. I hope the staff continues to educate more people who come to this continent about the legacy of the Cahokians and their descendants. They are doing a wonderful job, and I trust the government will continue to fund them, because the site is as important to our history as Mt. Rushmore is to the whole of the United States.*

Taken together, the events symbolize a return of *spiritual* value to the ancient Indian ceremonial site. "To the Cherokee, Cahokia is one of the most important historic sites in America, like the Statue of Liberty. It is a symbol of the society that was here before the Europeans came, a symbol of a free people."[30]

As a staff member put it, "It is somewhat unique to have Native American participation on such a large scale at an archaeological site such as Cahokia, but they have expressed their pleasure with the way the site displays and gives dignity and respect to the prehistoric Indians who lived here."[31]

Things have not always gone smoothly, but considering the difficulties that have arisen at other archaeological sites when members of the American In-

dians against Desecration (a division of the American Indian Movement) protest the digging up and display of Native American remains, disputes at Cahokia have been settled relatively peacefully. The ceremonies continue, and the accent is on the affirmation of Native Americans' values and customs at the site of one of their most notable achievements.

The occasional troubles may be a symptom of a deeper chasm that remains in both Native Americans and contemporary Americans about their joint past. Although it is beyond the scope of this book to investigate or interpret the consequences of the nineteenth-century genocide, the ambivalence on both sides may be due to unresolved psychological and spiritual issues and point to a national need to address our history in this area in greater depth. The Native American Graves Protection and Repatriation Act (1990) decreed that human remains, and in some circumstances grave goods, must be returned to the appropriate tribes, if it is possible to figure out who they might be. This momentous legislation will have far-reaching consequences, including forcing many archaeologists and museums to discuss linkages between specific sites and specific contemporary Indian tribes.

Only time will tell how these issues will be resolved, but this much is certain: many aspects of the contribution of Native Americans to American life continue to be overlooked, and establishing new links is educational. Some museums with large Native American collections, for example, now have Native American advisory boards.

As Charles Hudson wrote in 1976, "At the time Europeans first came to the New World, the Southeastern Indians lived on the fruits of an economy which combined farming with hunting and gathering; they organized themselves into relatively complex political units; they built large towns and monumental ceremonial centers; and they possessed a rich symbolism and an expressive art style. But hardly any of this has left an impression on our historical memory."[32]

The Amerindian community is keenly aware of this historical amnesia about the contributions of the ancient tribes to the history of our continent. Americans of other ethnic backgrounds may know a lot about their own roots, but they usually have only narrow and superficial positive notions or negative stereotypes about our Indian heritage. They know about the supportive role of the Indians that the Pilgrims celebrated at Thanksgiving, or about the pueblo builders of the Southwest, but the most common image is of the "marauding frontier Cherokee or Creek . . . savagely bloodying the heads of idyllic pioneers." On the other hand, there are some people who boast that they have Indian blood or an Indian grandmother and extol Indian spirituality and herbal medicines. Whether positive or negative, the tendency to think in stereotypes comes from prejudice, ignorance, or romanticizing. Native Americans have been inadequately studied and portrayed. The sad irony is that justifiably angry feelings may erupt in just those settings designed to alleviate prejudice and ignorance, such as the celebrations at Cahokia. Once again, Cahokia is not immune to the larger forces in American history.

For the most part, however, the mingling of Cahokia's volunteers, staff, and other visitors at special events in the past has suggested a harmonious intermingling of various strands of Amerindian life in the larger life of the people of the United States. You can hear French, English, and various Indian languages spoken within yards of each other.

Indian words and phrases abound in American life, especially in the names of our cities and rivers. Mississippi means "great waters"; Iowa, Missouri, Arkansas, and Illinois are named for the tribes that once inhab-

ited regions touched by the great river. At the Cahokia get-togethers people boast of their mixed blood and admire Indian ceremonies and crafts. Children carry back stories to their scout troops, where Indian imagery is an integral part of the program. Scout dens are named after animals, Indian fashion, such as Wolf Den or Bear Den, and one of the highest camping honors a Boy Scout can receive is the Order of the Arrow.

People need special places, those that architects designate as conveying "a sense of place." But as J. B. Jackson once argued, a sense of place has less to do with characteristics of a particular setting or an architectural style than with a sense of recurring events.[33] We all know what this means. The annual family picnic in a grove by the river is meaningful because every time we go there we have a heightened experience of love passing from one generation to another. The sameness of the place is as important as the sameness of the menu. Together they symbolize continuity. Ham, corn on the cob, baked beans—the ritual repetition of what we eat is something familiar, something we can count on, in a place we know and love because we have been having a good time there since we were children. The value of "a sense of place" can accrue to many locales—a church or synagogue, a theater, a lake, a levee, or a dance circle in the shadow of a mound. "A sense of place makes possible a sense of community based on shared experiences."[34]

## A Meeting Place for Scholars

The annual lecture series sponsored by the CMMS also provides continuity for the scholarly community, both archaeologists and those from other disciplines, and establishes links with the volunteers and other members of the lay public. Conferences in the past have created an opportunity and a place for such diverse experts as palynologists and archaeoastronomers to share their findings, pool their resources, and discover connections that lead to new insights.

In this vital landscape, it seems that everyone involved with Cahokia is transformed. The place makes everyone who experiences it an ardent devotee. And at last the energy, the status of the UNESCO listing, and the institutional structure were in place for the crowning achievement of these twentieth-century stewards of Cahokia: the building of a world-class interpretive center.

## The Design Team Turns Problems into Solutions

In 1984 Margaret Brown, an experienced archaeologist and a hands-on professional, took Anderson's place as site superintendent. That same year, two years after the UNESCO designation, Illinois governor James R. Thompson released $6 million for the construction of a new interpretive center at Cahokia. This was a historic opportunity, and Brown and Iseminger seized it, but the work ahead was also painstaking. Great care was needed in selecting the right site and assembling the design team.

Choosing the site for the new building was especially nettlesome. The CMMS began pushing for a new museum in the late 1970s, and testing of possible locations was begun by the University of Wisconsin–Milwaukee under Fowler and Elizabeth Benchley. Later a tract (Interpretive Center Tract I, or ICT-I) was tested by Benchley and later by Michael Nassaney of Southern Illinois University at Carbondale. That area then flooded several years in a row, rendering it unsuitable. Just to the north, however, there was an area on slightly higher ground. To proceed, the team had to be sure the building would minimize impact to the

noteworthy archaeological material. Excavations in the new area (called ICT-II) began in 1985 under the direction of William I. Woods of the Contract Archaeology Program (now the Office of Contract Archaeology) at Southern Illinois University at Edwardsville. Day after day more artifacts and other features were discovered. By the end of 1987, remains of more than eighty structures and several hundred pits had been excavated from ICT-II, from four phases of occupation—all of them Mississippian. What was to be done? There was literally no spot at Cahokia that lacked signs of past occupation.

People feared that instead of finding a clear spot for the building, the archaeologists had found another archaeologically rich area. Would this be another irony? Would looking for another site result in discoveries that would delay construction once again? By a stroke of creative inventiveness, this situation was changed from a lose-lose roadblock to a win-win solution.

Since the area was rich in materials that would provide insights into a particular neighborhood and its evolution, the new interpretive center would *incorporate* the new discoveries. A new theme would provide further enrichment: deeper understanding of changes in a Cahokia neighborhood. It would include shifts in the orientation, size, and floor depth of Mississippian houses over time. An obstacle had been transformed into an opportunity for the design team, Gerald Hilferty and Associates. Limitations are challenges, and sometimes, in inspired hands, they can be turned into a vehicle of expression. To get around the limitations the archaeological discoveries imposed, the design team would capitalize on them! Once again, as so often in its history, the site inspired and brought out the best in its designers, enhancing the spirit of teamwork and cooperation.

The local Collinsville architect, Charles Morris of Architectural Associates, suggested building up the construction area five to six feet so that it would be above the flood zone. The building was also designed so it could be fitted into a basic footprint provided by the archaeologists, between two newly discovered mounds on the south and east and a borrow pit on the west.

### EXTERIOR OF THE VISITORS' CENTER

Care was exercised in every aspect of the design. The architect gave the interpretive center a low profile (fig. 127) so the gently sloping angle of the roof is like a subdued echo of the surrounding mounds. It does not look like a mound and does not compete with them; rather, it seems to complement them, to enhance the contemporary entrance to the mounds site. The shape of the mass, like an open boomerang, pulls visitors toward its earth-warm beige brick walls.

Anchoring the whole structure, the base, like the low patio wall in front, is of dark brown brick. The walls are a greenish beige, and the roof is also beige so that walls and roof harmonize with each other and the whole takes its place gently in the color scheme of the surrounding grassy fields.

Fig. 127. A fitting interpretive center for a UNESCO World Heritage Site. Here the roofline echoes the shapes of the surrounding mounds, and the beige brick cladding fits unobtrusively into the surrounding prairie.

Prairie grasses wave in the breeze alongside the semicircular entrance portal, which seems to advance toward visitors in a welcoming gesture. The surfaces are gently modeled with protruding courses and punctuated by the windows of the office wing. The entrance is strongly articulated by large brick piers, with two courses of "capitals" that support the sweeping overhang. It is all horizontal, in earth colors and at home in its spacious midwestern environment that looks out over the prairie, the American Bottom, and also encompasses the nearby woodlands and the bluff to the east.

The problem of what to do about the houses outside the building became the solution of providing a transition between the building and the surrounding grass: a patio surrounded by a low wall.

### THE PATIO

The outlines of the houses and pits uncovered in the excavations that preceded construction are painted in "ghost plans" on the concrete patio floor. A marker captioned "What Was Here?" lies at the patio entrance ready to enlighten curious visitors. Various colors— browns, grays, and blues—indicate different periods of habitation.[35]

The patio is spacious to accommodate several ground plans. The average house here was about twelve by sixteen feet, but a few were larger. In one place the foundation trenches of four houses intersect. With some effort of the imagination, you can reconstruct what was here and when. In another place a small structure was torn down and replaced by a larger one fifty years later, as you can deduce by the colors of the lines. The dates are finely tuned—fifty-year intervals— making everyone marvel at how the archaeologists figured it all out.

As soon as you enter, curving picture windows on the north wall give you a wide, expansive view of Monks Mound and the Great Plaza. To the left of the entrance is a large mural by L. K. Townsend depicting the central area about 1100 (fig. 41). The complex appears as if seen from the top of a nearby mound. In the foreground the geometric shapes of Twin Mounds set the stage of the sacred landscape. In the middle ground, stretching as far as the eye can see to the east and west, are other mounds, with thatched houses scattered thickly among them. To the left of the palisade wall is the ancient Woodhenge. In the center, at the heart of the complex, is the Grand Plaza. In the distance, dominating the skyline and rising far above the horizon, is Monks Mound, a verdant acropolis. The place seems alive, and the mural makes a fitting overture to the experience of the interpretive center, bringing together so many aspects of the site in one holistic image. Together the huge window, with its vista of the site as it is today, and the mural depicting it as it was a millennium ago provide a stunning sense of entrance.

Off to the left a stairway leads to the theater for the multimedia orientation, an award-winning program by Donna Lawrence Productions of Louisville, Kentucky, and the theater exit opens to a carefully planned path through dioramas and exhibit islands.

To reflect the old neighborhood that was underneath, Hilferty thought of including part of it in the building. "Since we wanted to explain how archaeologists worked, I had the idea of incorporating five of these small domestic sites right in the building. The new interpretive center would incorporate the old house foundations, preserving them and their artifacts in situ, at the same time converting them into explanatory material."[36]

Five of the old Mississippian house foundations that had been discovered on the building site were incorporated into "sunken wells" inside the building, along the visitors' walkway. Painted with house and pit patterns like the exterior patio, these "wells" are some of the most moving parts of the interpretive center, hung as they are with gossamer, life-size drawings of Indians going about their everyday life, right in the same spot where they lived a thousand years ago. Architecturally they provide a dynamic vertical counterpoint to the spatial experience in the otherwise horizontal walk through the galleries.

The designers and the staff worked intensively together throughout the design and production phases. Records of their correspondence, memos, and telephone calls fill several file drawers and attest to the attention to detail these professionals brought to their work.

At the end of the orientation program the lights in the theater dim with the setting sun in the slide show, and other lights slowly go up on a life-size village diorama behind the screen, which rises at the end of the show. By the clever use of two-way mirrors, the ancient complex seems to spread out in infinite dimensions, drawing visitors to come in and take part. Exiting at the front of the theater (so others may come in at the back), visitors walk through darkened galleries, gazing as the life-size figures go about the work of their daily lives in thatched houses and sunny plazas. The designers thus achieved the effect of a large, dense, busy place in a small space.

We walk in wonder through an ancient neighborhood. A young girl grinds corn outside her house while her mother cooks a pot of stew over an open fire. We see foods stored in an old granary and watch a potter forming bowls and a flint knapper shaping a knife while in the distance a young man butchers a newly killed deer. An old man hobbles about with a staff, an old woman tends a baby, and a little girl chases her brother, who has grabbed her cattail doll. Behind all this the mirrors repeat the images into the distance, giving the effect of a huge complex.

The exhibits in the perimeter of this wing of the interpretive center are devoted to seven aspects of Cahokia: time, culture, city, structures, life, products, and knowledge. They are suitable for all ages, so small children can enjoy the lively illustrations painted on the walls and pull out drawers to find hidden artifacts. Large paintings give a context to the many items on display—pottery, tools, and other crafts. Deeper levels of meaning are embodied in the extensive labels for adults who want to go further into the subject. Everyone can have a turn at trying to drill a hole in a shell bead with a bow, a rawhide string, and a stick tipped with a chert microdrill.

We see dioramas of the four seasons, Woodhenge, and Monks Mound and view artifacts of stone, wood, shell, bone, cloth, pottery, and other materials. Finally, in a charming finale, we learn how archaeologists know about ancient societies from their material culture. We see a display and even sit in a small mock-up of a "drive-in movie," a witty reminder of the Falcon in its better days; we watch a videotape of how archaeologists work and analyze what they find, use computers, and see how a flint knapper makes a hoe.

Toward the end a "sunken well" diorama replicates what was going on recently in exactly that spot. Mannequins representing the contemporary archaeologists work in an excavation pit. At the edges are panels explaining how they gather bones, pottery, and other artifacts, how they date things, how they use evidence from other disciplines.

Finally, the team took on the question of what happened to the mighty civilization. Speculations about its demise include climate change, shorter growing seasons leading to repeated crop failures, and migration of a large part of the population. Or perhaps in more than three hundred years overpopulation and its consequences—depleted local resources—caused the end to come. Another possibility was failure of leaders to solve the problems, so that people lost faith in their society, and increasing conflict with others. Cultural change may have begun a return to older tribal ways or promoted a move to new lands.

Recent scholarship has proposed more positive reasons for the shift away from Cahokia. Considering their remarkable history of adaptation to change, it is equally possible that the Mississippians left Cahokia to take advantage of newly available resources elsewhere or to capitalize on better hunting or growing conditions in another part of the land.

Visitors see the large entrance mural again at the end of their interpretive tour, when it serves as a summary of the experience within the center and also as a prelude to a walk outdoors with a volunteer guide or a self-guiding tape cassette or booklet.

Visiting the interpretive center, you feel the shared inspiration of the archaeologists and the design team. You sense that people's commitment grew as they worked together. The teamwork had an energizing effect on them all. Each talent was willingly subordinated to their common cause: preserving and interpreting the history of Cahokia. In this creative atmosphere, dedicated professionals from three disciplines—archaeology, architecture, and exhibition design—melded their talents, and the effect of the whole design was more than the sum of its parts. As Gerald Hilferty put it, "Our goal was to create an atmosphere for visitors that would take them back to this vibrant, booming, capital city."

At the equinox on September 23, 1989, a host of dignitaries gathered at dawn, as people had gathered nearly a millennium before, to celebrate the rising of the sun—and this time also to celebrate the opening of Cahokia's splendid new interpretive center. The crowd, awestruck by the cosmic event in the sky, so appropriate to the occasion, cheered exuberantly when Margaret Brown and Ettus Hiatt, then president of the Cahokia Mounds Museum Society, cut the bright red ribbon opening the doors to a wider audience. A few weeks later Governor Thompson officially dedicated the interpretive center, with a blessing by Native American elder Evelyne Voelker.

## Summary

The meaning and value of the land at Cahokia—from a hunting and gathering site, to a religious center, to a picnic spot, to a world-class interpretive center—has continued to change for nearly three millennia. We can imagine the simple hunting value of the camp of prehistory. We have seen what Cahokia was like in the heyday of its expansion, from about 1050 until its abandonment in the fourteenth century, when the sacred value of the land was expressed by the great terraced pyramid, Monks Mound. In addition, the geometry of the ensemble of the mounds, their orientation to the cosmos, their carefully scaled relation to each other, and the enhancing powers of ceremonial space and vista made them symbols of spiritual perfection.

We know that French priests valued the site for their Christian chapel and the celebration of mass. The farmers who tended the land in the nineteenth century valued the site solely for its rich agricultural potential, except for the Ramey family, who protected it and cautiously and selectively welcomed archaeologists. But the sacred meaning of the mounds was lost. In this vacuum the exploitation of railroad tycoons, highway engineers, and other developers threatened the very existence of the old ceremonial center. When a new meaning emerged in the late twentieth century with a fresh appreciation of history and preservation, a new *historical* value accrued to the site, appreciated by Americans of all ethnic backgrounds.

In their stewardship of the site, as people today share their knowledge with others from all over the world, the meaning of their lives is immeasurably enriched. With the establishment of institutions to support those who preserve, interpret, and protect it, Cahokia has gained continuing *humanistic* value.

FIG. 128. CROSSING THE MILKY WAY. IN A.D. 1066 THE
NATIVE AMERICANS IN CAHOKIA SAW HALLEY'S COMET WITH
UNAIDED EYES AS IT STREAKED THROUGH THE SKY. THIS RECENT
PHOTOGRAPH WAS TAKEN WITH THE AID OF A TELESCOPE.

# Epilogue

This has been a long story, from the Big Bang to the present, a tale stretching over about 13 billion years. It has also been a big story in space, stretching with human migration from Asia over the Bering land bridge to encompass the repercussions of European politics, which influenced the history of the Cahokia landscape for several centuries.

To look at this small piece of the earth through different lenses, over as long a period and from as great a distance as possible, has required the help of astronomers, geologists, geographers, archaeologists, anthropologists, preservationists, historians, humanists, and a host of other experts. Since we lack written evidence from Cahokia or even handed-down stories, we have sometimes borrowed speculative accounts from archaeologists, based on data they have recovered during years of work in the field. For similar reasons we have used reconstruction illustrations based on measured research. The experts all applied their own frames of reference to the subject, and very different pictures have emerged. Our job has been to put them together.

Sometimes there were overlaps in the physical evidence. When accounting for the extreme weather change known as the Pacific Climate Episode, for example, we encountered the views of the palynologist, the paleontologist, and the climatologist. One area of general agreement among the physical scientists, however, has been clear: Cahokia occupied one of the richest ecological areas on earth.

There were also overlaps in the historical evidence. We know from written records that a seventeenth-century French king was interested in his New World colonies. We know that French missionary priests built a chapel in Cahokia, with its characteristic *poteaux en terre* support system, and even left behind a brandy bottle as part of the archaeological evidence. The French monks who followed left records in letters and newspaper accounts. Later in the nineteenth century the Illinois Central Railroad lured farmers to western Illinois, and the increase in population eventually led to a housing development and even an airport on the Cahokia grounds.

After the period we anthropocentrically called the "prologue," as if the *real* story dealt only with what human beings did to the land at Cahokia, we found that over the centuries, as people built buildings and shaped and reshaped the landscape, they endowed Cahokia with very different values.

To early Amerindians, the south bank of Canteen Creek had *hunting and gathering* value. It was near forests and prairies, streams, lakes, sloughs, and marshes: it was a valuable campsite.

The Mississippians of (1000–1400) made the same spot an awe-inspiring, powerful mound city, a holy landscape—the heart of a vibrant ceremonial center, crowned with a monumental terraced pyramid, endowing the land with *sacred* value.

When the Mississippians left, the land was without human stewardship, becoming a desolate, overrun ruin. Three hundred years later, in their brief tenancy (1730–50), French priests and later French monks (1809–13) gave the place *Christian* value, imprinted with a log chapel topped by a wooden cross.

For a time aspiring entrepreneurs maintained the Cantine Trading Post on the banks of the creek, giving the land *commercial* value. After their departure, however, the site again reverted to fallow ground.

When the settlers of the early nineteenth century arrived, their *agricultural* values turned the land into plowed fields, and in the 1830s Monks Mound became a homesite for one of the first farmers, T. Ames (Amos) Hill. Later railroad tycoons and real estate developers, coveting the land for its *economic* value, leveled many mounds and turned parts of the old Amerindian grounds into embankments, levees, and drainage ditches. In the twentieth century new economic motives brought housing subdivisions, a drive-in movie, and even an airport to the site.

Finally, a small piece of the original site was declared an Illinois state park. On the old ceremonial plaza, local inhabitants picnicked in the shady groves in summer, children played on seesaws and swings in the fall and sledded on Monks Mound in winter. A piece of Cahokia had been preserved by giving it *recreational* value.

Always, it seems, the presence of the mounds made most visitors aware, even if only dimly, that in the distant past the site had been a holy place with meanings they were only vaguely aware of but ought somehow to respect.

With the arrival of professionals on the staff of the Cahokia Mounds State Park in the 1970s, and by their sustained efforts, the site finally gained recognition of its *historical* value—it was declared a State Historic Site, and finally a UNESCO World Heritage Site, with cultural resources that belonged to the "common inheritance of all mankind."

The monumentality of the great pyramid, the plazas, and the subordinate mounds built by the Cahokia Indians transformed this landscape into an awe-inspiring sight that resonated with the dreams of idealists and visionaries for centuries. At times the chords it struck in the souls of those who beheld it were religious, commercial, or opportunistic. Off and on over the next two hundred years it inspired artists and scholars, including a German prince, to investigate and document its hidden secrets. On some occasions it served as a rallying point for the dark forces of violence, war, and prejudice. Ultimately this same monumentality became both sign and cynosure of the history of the preservation of the great pyramid.

But historical value is not enough. Value is a living, dynamic quality. Unless a building, or a place, or buildings in places and landscapes can attain contemporary value, the efforts of the preservationists have been in vain. The value of a place may shift and change; it may be regained or lost entirely. When contemporary Native Americans revisit Cahokia, for example, the land regains some of the *spiritual* value it had long ago. Today the people of the site staff, their support group the Cahokia Mounds Museum Society, and visitors from all over the world have endowed Cahokia with a continuing *humanistic* value.

For me Cahokia also has *personal* value. After five years spent researching this book, I came to the site a day early for the equinox celebrations being held during the weekend of March 21–23, 1997. I had looked forward to this experience for a long time, and I did not want to rush.

To prepare myself, I spent the evening before the daybreak ceremonies wandering around Kunnemann Mound on the north side of the site. I wanted a view of the view— to see what it might have been like for an ordinary person standing near the edge of a crowd of thousands. How would America's great terraced pyramid look from the vantage point of one of the border mounds?

As I stood there in the stubble of last fall's corn crop while the noise of the last car faded from Sand Prairie Lane, all my senses were heightened. I was awed by the immensity of Monks Mound in the distance; the smell of warm earth filled my nostrils and the cool breeze freshened my cheeks; my ears vibrated to an enchanting humming, chirping music. "This cornfield is singing!" I said it aloud to myself. I stood entranced. Later I learned that I had heard thousands of male western chorus frogs courting thousands of females in their annual spring mating ritual.

The temperature dropped during the night, to good effect. As I drove down Collinsville Road at 5:30 A.M. and the cool air met the soft exhalations of the warm earth, the mounds seemed to rise out of the mist. Then, as if this were not enough, a radiant orb appeared out of the clouds in the west and moved gently down in the sky. It was the full moon setting. There was a brief pause, a moment of complete darkness: the eastern sky turned from black to deep purple. Seconds later the brilliant rim of the newborn sun blazed through the arms of America's great terraced pyramid, turning the world to gold.

That night I climbed to its heights again. There was to be a partial eclipse of the moon. As if a cosmic denouement were in order, when the star-studded sky darkened it gave greater brilliance to a sight seen once in six thousand years—the streaming tail of the Hale-Bopp Comet. I knew that in 1066 the Cahokians had seen Halley's Comet crossing the sky. As I stood gazing at the stars above me and the mound city below, a Native American poem I had memorized came to my mind:

*There is purity and strength*
*In places sacred to the people*
*Places strong in the*
*Oneness of earth and sky and of all things.*

# Notes

INTRODUCTION

1. Archaeologists vary in their estimates of the population of Cahokia. The reasons are complex. Part of the problem is that not enough has been excavated. Still another aspect is that the population itself probably varied seasonally or even ceremonially. Since estimates range from 10,000 to 20,000, the comparison with eleventh-century London seems reasonable. A recent reference states: "In the late 11th century, shortly after the Norman conquest, when the building of the Tower of London was a tangible manifestation of the city's importance, it held between 14,000 and 18,000 persons" (s.v. "Population," in *The London Encyclopaedia,* ed. Ben Weinreb and Christopher Hibbert [New York: St. Martin's Press, 1983], 613). Also, London was probably somewhat smaller before the Norman Conquest of 1066. See also Timothy R. Pauketat and Thomas E. Emerson, *Cahokia: Domination and Ideology in the Mississippian World* (Lincoln: University of Nebraska Press, 1997).

2. Sarah Bradford Landau and Carl W. Condit, *Rise of the New York Skyscraper, 1865–1913* (New Haven: Yale University Press, 1996), 57–58.

3. The seven other cultural sites in the United States are Mesa Verde, Independence Hall, La Fortaleza and San Juan Historic District, the Statue of Liberty, Chaco Culture National Historical Park, Monticello and the University of Virginia, and Pueblo de Taos. UNESCO also lists ten natural sites in the United States: Redwood National Park, Yellowstone National Park, Grand Canyon National Park, Everglades National Park, Mammoth Cave National Park, Olympic National Park, Great Smoky Mountains National Park, Yosemite National Park, Hawaii Volcanoes National Park, and Carlsbad Caverns National Park. In addition the United States shares four natural sites with Canada, for a total of twenty-two. The four shared sites

are Tatshenshini–Alseki/Kluane National Park; Wrangell–St. Elias National Park and Reserve; Glacier Bay National Park; and Waterton Glacier International Peace Park.

4. William N. Morgan, *Prehistoric Architecture in the Eastern United States* (Cambridge: MIT Press, 1980), is a notable exception. Morgan, an architect, has also provided some handsome drawings.

CHAPTER ONE

1. Lynda Norene Shaffer, *Native Americans before 1492: The Moundbuilding Centers of the Eastern Woodlands* (New York: M. E. Sharpe, 1992), 7–10.

2. Christopher J. Schuberth, *A View of the Past: An Introduction to Illinois Geology* (Springfield: Illinois State Museum, 1986), 48.

3. Ibid., 58.

4. Douglas C. Ridgley, *The Geography of Illinois* (Chicago: University of Chicago Press, 1921), 95.

5. Although the meltwaters of the fourth and last glacier, the Wisconsinan, affected the landscape around Cahokia, a complete discussion is beyond the scope of this book.

6. Ridgley goes on to describe "a slope so gentle as to be imperceptible to the eye and difficult of detection by instruments . . . but everywhere except in some river valleys sufficient to insure good drainage" (*Geography of Illinois,* 37); Schuberth, *View of the Past,* 133, also talks of this favorable tilt.

7. Conversation with William I. Woods, July 1998. I am indebted to Woods for many helpful suggestions as well as for his indispensable online bibliography (www.siue.edu/CAHOKIAMOUNDS).

8. As Schuberth goes on to tell us, "The origin of loess has been a matter of some conjecture, but it is now generally agreed that the silty sediments were stripped by winds from the bare, wide, glacial outwash floodplains of the Mississippi, Illinois, and Missouri rivers as the ice melted away. So much fine-grained sediment [ground down by the glaciers from boulders to gravel] was carried down these rivers by meltwater during the spring and summer thaws that the lesser discharge during the winter season could not sweep most of these sediments onward. Strong winter winds blowing eastward swept tons of this glacial silt from the dried out, unprotected, and wind-exposed floodplain surfaces. Since the prevailing wind direction was toward the east, loess thickness is greatest along the eastern side of the river

floodplains and decreased rapidly farther to the east as the ancient winds quickly dropped their sediment load" (*View of the Past,* 136).

9. Ibid., 137.

10. Schuberth, *View of the Past,* 165.

11. Ibid., 168.

12. *Oxford English Dictionary,* 1937 edition.

13. A satellite photograph combines information from seven separate sources, from visible light down to infrared heat rays. Warm vegetation appears red, built-up areas are violet, water is blue, and bare fields appear white. David Buisseret, *Historic Illinois from the Air* (Chicago: University of Chicago Press, 1990), 3.

14. William I. Woods, lecture, Field School, Cahokia Mounds, July 1996.

15. Ronald E. Yarbrough, "The Physiography of Metro East," *Bulletin of the Illinois Geographic Society* 16 (June 1974): 12–28. The 1927 flood, which crested at thirty-six feet at St. Louis, "awakened national and local conscience as to the dire need for flood control. Congress passed the Federal Flood Control Act in 1928 . . . . By the mid 1970s a complete system of 200–year levees 'walled-out' the river to a flood stage of 52 feet. These levees are sometimes called '200 year levees' because they were built higher than any crest for the last 200 years of recorded flood marks."

16. Ibid., 20.

17. Ibid., 24.

18. Charles Horton Cooley, *The Theory of Transportation* ([Baltimore]: American Economics Association, 1894), quoted in Ridgely, *Geography of Illinois,* 249.

19. Ridgley, *Geography of Illinois,* 66.

20. Ibid.

21. Ibid., 68.

22. The climate, or the weather average in Illinois over the years, is so favorable that "if the average rainfall were the actual rainfall in Illinois year by year, season by season, and month by month, there would be no crop failures of any kind; there would be neither swollen streams nor flooded farm lands; the larger precipitation of spring and summer would always suffice for the rapid growth of all crops; and the smaller rainfall of autumn and winter would give the best of weather for harvesting and threshing small grains, and for the ripening and gathering of corn . . . . there would be no drought years, no dust bowl eras, no crops destroyed by lack of water" (ibid., 82).

23. Stephen Sargent Visher, *Climatic Atlas of the United States* (Cambridge: Harvard University Press, 1954), 175.

24. Robert L. Hall, *An Archaeology of the Soul: North American Indian Belief and Ritual* (Urbana: University of Illinois Press, 1997).

25. Ridgley, *Geography of Illinois,* 110.

26. Ibid., chap. 6. See also Donald F. Hoffmeister and Carol O. Mohr, *Fieldbook of Illinois Mammals* (New York: Dover, 1972).

CHAPTER TWO

1. Bjorn Kurten and Elaine Anderson, *Pleistocene Mammals of North America* (New York: Columbia University Press, 1980), 354. Analysis of the stomach contents of the prehistoric animals tells us what they ate. We also know their diet from observations of caribou still living in Canada.

2. Brian M. Fagan, *Ancient North America: The Archaeology of a Continent,* rev. ed. (New York: Thames and Hudson, 1995). This standard text is the source of the dates in this chapter. Although there is general agreement with this dating system, some overlaps exist, and some local variations are inevitable. I have tried to arrive at dates consistent with the interpretation of specialists, but some are approximations and subject to change when further data are uncovered. Another useful system is Shaffer, *Native Americans before 1492,* 6, chart.

3. Fagan, *Ancient North America,* 81.

4. Ibid., 348.

5. Stuart Struever and Felicia Antonelli Holton, *Koster: Americans in Search of Their Prehistoric Past* (Garden City, N.Y.: Anchor/Doubleday, 1979).

6. Charles M. Hudson, *The Southeastern Indians* (Knoxville: University of Tennessee Press, 1976), 47.

7. Struever and Holton, *Koster,* 145.

8. Ibid., 146.

9. D. K. Charles and J. E. Buikstra, "Archaic Mortuary Sites in the Central Mississippi Drainage: Distribution, Structure, and Implications," in *Archaic Hunters and Gatherers in the Midwest,* ed. James Phillips and James Brown (New York: Academic Press, 1983), 117–45, quoted in Fagan, *Ancient North America,* 371.

10. Fagan, *Ancient North America,* 394.

11. Ibid.

12. Richard B. Lee, quoted in Struever and Holton, *Koster,* 258. This study is not in Struever and Holton's bibliography.

13. Struever and Holton, *Koster,* 161.

14. Fagan, *Ancient North America,* 394.

15. Bruce D. Smith, *The Emergence of Agriculture* (New York: Scientific American Library, 1994), chap. 8.

16. Robert Silverberg, *Mound Builders of Ancient America: The Archaeology of a Myth* (Athens: Ohio University Press, 1986), 11–13.

17. Gordon R. Willey, *Introduction to American Archaeology,* vol. 1, *North and Middle America* (Englewood Cliffs, N.J.: Prentice-Hall, 1966). This text gives definitions helpful for distinguishing traditions, periods, and cultures.

18. "Fort Hill," Ohio Historical Society site information flyer, 1997.

19. Fagan, *Ancient North America,* 419.

20. E. G. Squier and E. H. Davis, *Ancient Monuments of the Mississippi Valley* (1848), clarified by Arthur W. McGraw (n.p.: A. W. McGraw, 1992), quoted in Silverberg, *Mound Builders,* 88.

21. Silverberg, *Mound Builders,* 204–5.

22. Fagan, *Ancient North America,* 419.

23. Ibid., and Hudson, *Southeastern Indians,* 59.

24. "Serpent Mound," Ohio Historical Society site information flyer, 1997.

25. Fagan, *Ancient North America,* 21.

26. Frederick R. Eggan, "The Ethnological Cultures and Their Archaeological Backgrounds," in James B. Griffin and Albert C. Spaulding, "The Central Mississippi Valley Archaeological Survey, Season 1950—a Preliminary Report," *Journal of the Illinois State Archaeological Society,* n.s., 1, 3 (1951): 44.

27. Silverberg, *Mound Builders,* 14.

28. Pauketat and Emerson, *Cahokia.* Chapter 6, "The Construction of Mississippian Cahokia," by Rinita A. Dalan, contains a lucid account of earthmoving operations and the necessary connection of public works to social organization. See also Pauketat's *The Ascent of Chiefs: Cahokia and Mississsippian Politics in Native North America* (Tuscaloosa: University of Alabama Press, 1994).

CHAPTER THREE

1. John E. Kelly, "Redefining Cahokia: Principles and Elements of Community Organization," in *The Ancient Skies and Sky Watchers of Cahokia: Woodhenges, Eclipses, and Cahokian Cosmology,* ed. Melvin L. Fowler, Wisconsin Archeologist 77, 3–4 (Madison: Wisconsin Archeological Society, 1996), 97–119;

Martha Ann Rolingson, "Elements of Community Design at Cahokia," in Fowler, *Ancient Skies and Sky Watchers of Cahokia,* 90. The essays in this book provide the basis for the discussion that follows.

2. Paul Wheatley, *The Pivot of the Four Quarters* (Chicago: Aldine, 1971), 417, quoted in William G. Gartner, "Archaeoastronomy as Sacred Geography," in Fowler, *Ancient Skies and Sky Watchers of Cahokia,* 130.

3. Robert L. Hall, "American Indian Worlds, World Quarters, WOrld Centers, and Their Shrines," in Fowler, *Ancient Skies and Sky Watchers of Cahokia,* 120–25. Several examples are given in this article.

4. Gartner, "Archaeoastronomy," 128.

5. Frank Hamilton Cushing, quoted in Jesse Green, ed., *Zuñi: Selected Writings of Frank Hamilton Cushing* (Lincoln: University of Nebraska Press, 1981), 185.

6. Cushing, quoted in Green, *Zuñi,* 261–62.

7. John E. Kelly, "Redefining Cahokia: Principles and Elements of Community Organization," *Wisconsin Archeologist* 77, 3–4 (1996): 97.

8. Garrick A. Bailey, ed., *The Osage and the Invisible World: From the Works of Francis la Flesche* (Norman: University of Oklahoma Press, 1995), 40–42, quoted in Kelly, "Redefining Cahokia," 106.

9. William R. Iseminger, Timothy Pauketat, Brad Koldehoff, Lucretia S. Kelly, and Leonard Blake, "East Palisade Investigations," in *The Archaeology of the Cahokia Palisade,* Illinois Cultural Resources Study 14 (Springfield: Illinois Historic Preservation Agency, 1990), 35–37.

10. Ibid.

11. Another estimate for the labor required to build Monks Mound by the method of basketloads of earth from borrow pits was given in a recent paper by George Milner and Michael Wiant. They assigned a figure of 1,177,701 cubic meters of earth for Monks Mound and 555,780 for the other mounds at Cahokia for a total of 1,180,000 cubic meters. At this volume, and figuring one cubic meter in each basket carried on the back of a laborer, it would take a labor force of no more than five hundred working for ten five-hour days each year to erect the mounds at Cahokia (Wiant, "Platforms of Power," paper presented at Cahokia Conference, June 27, 1998). Rinita Dalan believes you would have to double Milner and Wiant's estimates of time involved in the public works labors to account for the plazas alone.

12. Timothy Pauketat, "The Place of Post-Circle Monuments in Cahokin Political History," in Fowler, *Ancient Skies and Sky Watchers of Cahokia,* 82.

13. Rinita Dalan, "The Construction of Mississippian Cahokia," in Pauketat and Emerson, *Cahokia,* 99–100. Dalan draws on sources as follows: Margaret R. Ehrenberg, *Women in Prehistory* (Norman: University of Oklahoma Press, 1989); Claude Meillassoux, "On the Mode of Production of a Hunting Band," in *French Perspectives in African Studies,* ed. Pierre Alexandre (London: Oxford University Press, 1973), 187–203; J. Woodburn, "Hunters and Gatherers Today and Roconstruction of the Past," in *Soviet and Western Anthropology,* ed. Ernest Gellner (London: Duckworth, 1980), 995–117.

14. Fowler, *Ancient Skies and Sky Watchers of Cahokia,* 152. Fowler is quoting T. Earle, "Chiefdoms in Archaeological and Ethnohistorical Perspective," *Annual Review of Anthropology* 16 (1987): 279–308.

15. Fowler, *Ancient Skies and Sky Watchers of Cahokia,* 154.

16. Ibid., 155.

17. Claudia Gellman Mink, *Cahokia, City of the Sun: Prehistoric Urban Center in the American Bottom* (Collinsville, Ill.: Cahokia Mounds Museum Society, 1992), 36.

18. Ibid., 57.

19. Ibid., 58.

20. Ibid., 56.

21. Ibid., 58.

22. Mink, *Cahokia,* 57.

23. Ibid.

24. Ibid., 47, 66–67.

25. William R. Iseminger, "Culture and Environment in the American Bottom: The Rise and Fall of Cahokia's Mounds," in *Common Fields: An Environmental History of St. Louis,* ed. Andrew Hurley (St. Louis: Missouri Historical Society Press, 1987), 38–57.

26. Michael Coe, Dean Snow, and Elizabeth Benson, *Atlas of Ancient America* (New York: Facts on File, 1986).

27. William I. Woods, "The Fall of Cahokia: An Unintended Suicide," paper presented at the Illinois History Symposium, December 7, 1996, Springfield, Ill. Quoted material is from the abstract, 1.

28. Iseminger, "Culture and Environment," cites Robert L. Hall, "Cahokia Identity and Interaction Models of the Cahokia Mississippian," in *Cahokia and the Hinterlands: Middle Missis-*

sippian Cultures of the Midwest, ed. Thomas E. Emerson and R. Barry Lewis (Urbana: University of Illinois Press, 1991), 25.

29. Mink, Cahokia, 67.

## CHAPTER FOUR

1. Charles J. Balesi, The Time of the French in the Heart of North America, 1673–1818 (Chicago: Alliance Française, 1991), 4.

2. Jolliet was the first person on record to see the possibilities of a canal connecting the Chicago River with the Des Plaines, but that is another story—the story of the Illinois-Michigan Canal. See Tony Hiss and Edward Ranney, Prairie Passage: The Illinois and Michigan Canal Corridor (Urbana: University of Illinois Press, 1998).

3. Relation descouvertes et des voyages du sieur de La Salle seigneur et gouverneur du fort de Frontenac, au delà des grands lacs de la Nouvelle-France, faite par l'ordre de Monseigneur Colbert, 1679 80 81, in Pierre Margry, Découvertes et etablissements des Français, 1:435–544, as cited in Balesi, Time of the French, 61. Balesi does not say he mentions them, but Walthall does in John A. Walthall and Elizabeth D. Benchley, The River L'Abbe Mission: A French Colonial Church for the Cahokia Illini on Monks Mound, Studies in Illinois Archaeology 2 (Springfield: Illinois Historic Preservation Agency, 1987). Walthall's source is Theodore Calvin Pease and Raymond Clarence Werner, eds., The French Foundations, 1680–1693, Collections of the ISHL 23 (Springfield: Illinois State Historical Library, 1934), and Charles Callender, "Illinois," in Handbook of North American Indians, ed. Bruce G. Trigger (Washington, D.C.: Smithsonian Institution, 1978–), 15:673–80; but the ultimate source of all of this subsequent scholarship is a report to Colbert. Note that La Salle does not mean the present site, but Dumont does in Dumont de Montigny, Mémoires historiques sur la Louisane (Paris: Bauche, 1753), 341. Also, readers are reminded of the distinction between the Cahokia, an Illini tribe, and their predecessors at Cahokia, the Mississippian people. The Algonquian-speaking Cahokia-Illini Indians were latecomers to the Cahokia Mounds area, even though the site was eventually named after them.

4. Margaret Kimball Brown and Lawrie Cena Dean, The French Colony in the Mid-Mississippi Valley (Carbondale, Ill.: American Kestrel Books, 1995), 2.

5. Richard White, The Middle Ground (Cambridge: Cambridge University Press, 1991), x–xi.

6. Ibid., 67–68.

7. Walthall and Benchley, River L'Abbe Mission, 8, quoting from Joseph H. Schlarmann, From Quebec to New Orleans; the story of the French in America . . . Fort de Chartres (Belleville, Ill.: Buechler, 1929), 290.

8. Anna Price, "The French Regime in Illinois, 1718–1740," Historic Illinois (Illinois Department of Conservation, Springfield) 5, 3 (1982): 3, quoted in Walthall, River L'Abbe Mission, 9. See also Price, "French Outpost on the Mississippi, Historic Illinois 3, 1 (1980): 1–4.

9. Price, "French Regime," 3, quoted in Walthall, River L'Abbe Mission, 9.

10. Excavations were carried out under the direction of Elizabeth Benchley, University of Wisconsin–Milwaukee, in 1968, 1969, and 1971.

11. Charles E. Peterson, "Notes on Old Cahokia," Journal of the Illinois State Historical Society 42, 1–3 (1949): 340, quoted in Walthall, River L'Abbe Mission, 27.

12. Pease, French Foundations, quoted in Walthall, River L'Abbe Mission, 10–11.

13. Archaeologists have not yet discovered the exact location of this trading post. We know from Land Books that in 1778 Isaac Levy and Jean-Baptiste La Croix "made an Establishment on the River L'Abbe [Cahokia Creek] at the lower side of the Great Nobb, near where the french Church stood"; KasKaskia Land Book A, 320, recorded December 25, 1804, St. Clair County, but sworn and subscribed before John Dumoulin, one of the justices of the Court of Common Pleas for St. Clair County, on July 19, 1799. The land was sold in 1799 but not registered in the Land Book until 1804.

14. Deed of May 1799.

15. Walthall, River L'Abbe Mission, appendix B, Cahokia Record A, 350, 37–38, quotation on 83.

16. Gilbert Garraghan, S.J., "The Trappists of Monks Mound," in his Chapters in Frontier History: Research Studies in the Making of the West (Milwaukee: Bruce, [1934]), 100, quoted by Iseminger, "The Monks of Cahokia," Journal of the Illinois Archaeological Survey 5, 1–2 (1993): 15.

17. Joseph P. Donnelly, S.J., "Letters from Monks Mound: The Correspondence of Dom Urban Guillet with Bishop Plessis, Quebec, 1809–1812," in Old Cahokia: A Narrative and Documents Illustrating the First Century of Its History, ed. John Francis McDermott (St. Louis, Mo.: St. Louis Historical Doc-

uments Foundation, 1949), 291, quoted by Iseminger, "Monks of Cahokia," 16.

18. Iseminger, "Monks of Cahokia," 8; the source is John Reynolds, *My Own Times, Embracing Also the History of My Life* (Belleville, Ill.: Perryman and Davison, 1855).

19. In discussing the geophysical history of Illinois (chapter 1), I noted that before the North American continent drifted north, vast tropical forests grew in what was to become Illinois. When these decayed, great layers of coal formed, a source of wealth during the Industrial Revolution. See Iseminger, "Who Were Those Monks?" *Cahokian,* summer 1993, 8, and J. C. Wild, *The Valley of the Mississippi Illustrated in a Series of Views,* ed. Lewis Foulk Thomas (St. Louis, Mo.: Chambers and Knapp, 1841). The value of these coal deposits to the future of Illinois is inestimable, since much of the industrial economy of the region depended on coal well into the twentieth century. It was largely the rich coal deposits that brought the thick grid of railroad tracks that cross parts of the Cahokia landscape.

20. Henry Marie Brackenridge, *Views of Louisiana Together with a Journal of a Voyage up the Missouri River in 1811* (1814; reprinted Chicago: Quadrangle Books, 1962), 287–88.

21. Iseminger, "Who Were Those Monks?" 40.

22. Ibid., 41.

23. Iseminger, "Monks of Cahokia," 19.

24. Georges-Henri-Victor Collot, *Voyage dans l'Amérique Septentrionale, ou Description des pays arrosés par le Mississippi, l'Ohio, le Missouri et autres rivières affluentes* (Paris: A. Bertrand, 1826), 4. This work is available on microfilm from Yale University Beineke Library, in both French and English. Although the Yale edition was not printed until 1826, the survey began in 1796, when the area west of the Mississippi was still French.

CHAPTER FIVE

1. Sibyl Moholy-Nagy, *Matrix of Man: An Illustrated History of Urban Environment* (New York: Praeger, 1968), 194–95.

2. Balesi, *Time of the French,* 319.

3. Ibid., 321.

4. Brackenridge did not have a commission from Thomas Jefferson as earlier scholars reported.

5. Henry Marie Brackenridge, *Journal of a Voyage up the River Missouri in 1811* (Baltimore: Coale and Maxwell, 1815), iv.

6. Brackenridge, *Views of Louisiana,* 187–88.

7. Ibid., 191–92.

8. Ibid., 192–93.

9. Edwin James, *Account of an Expedition from Pittsburgh to the Rocky Mountains: Performed in the Years 1819 and 20, by Order of the Hon. J. C. Calhoun, Sec'y of War: Under the Command of Major Stephen H. Long. From Notes of Major Long, Mr. T. Say, and Other Gentlemen of the Exploring Party,* 2 vols. with atlas, compiled by Edwin James, botanist and geologist for the expedition, under the command of Stephen H. Long (Philadelphia: H. C. Carey and I. Lea, 1823).

10. Ibid., 1:59.

11. Ibid., 1:311.

12. Milton W. Brown et al., *American Art: Painting, Sculpture, Architecture, Decorative Arts, Photography* (New York: Abrams, 1979), 224.

13. "Prince Maximilian," a biographical essay by Joseph C. Porter, from the catalog of an exhibition (p. 10) organized by the Joslyn Art Museum Center for Western Studies, 1984, which was shown later at the Metropolitan Museum, New York. The prince also donated nineteen cases of specimens to a German museum at the time of his death.

14. Robert Hughes, *American Visions: The Epic History of Art in America* (New York: Alfred A. Knopf, 1997), 190.

15. *The WPA Guide to Illinois,* with a new introduction by Neil Harris and Michael Conzen (Chicago: A. C. McClurg, 1939; reprinted New York: Pantheon, 1983), 30.

16. Ibid., 31.

17. Frederick E. Hoxie, ed., *Indians in American History: An Introduction* (Arlington Heights, Ill.: Harlan Davidson, 1988).

18. Charles Joseph Latrobe, *The Rambler in North America, 1832–1833* (New York: Harper, 1835), 2:18.

19. Wild, *Valley of the Mississippi.*

20. Ibid., v–vi, 70.

21. Ibid., no. 8, February 1842, the "north" view.

22. Ibid., 53.

23. Ibid., 54 (no. 3, September 1841, of original series).

24. J. Paul Goode, *The Geographic Background of Chicago* (Chicago: University of Chicago Press, 1926), 51–52. (Published from a speech to the Chicago Real Estate Board.)

25. Illinois Central Railroad, "The Illinois Central Railroad Company Offers for Sale," pamphlet published in 1857, now in the Newberry Library, Chicago, Case H94896.44.

26. Ray Allen Billington, "Americans on the Move," in *We Americans,* ed. Thomas B. Allen (Washington, D.C.: National

Geographic Society, 1975), 137. The source is dated 1835, but no other data are given.

27. Ibid., 138.

28. Frederick Gerhard, *Illinois as It Is: Its History, Geography, Statistics, Constitution, Laws, Government . . . Etc.* (Chicago: Keen and Lee, 1857), cited in *WPA Guide to Illinois,* 27. The source of the quotation is not given in the book's bibliography.

29. Stephen Williams, "Nineteenth Century Perceptions concerning Cahokia and Its Meaning," paper read at the Cahokia Symposium, Society of American Archaeologists meetings, New Orleans, April 26, 1991.

30. Charles Rau, "Indian Pottery," in *Annual Report of the Smithsonian Institution* (Washington, D.C.: Smithsonian Institution, 1867), 346–55. Rau's text reveals acquaintance with E. G. Squier and E. H. Davis, notable mound archaeologists of the Ohio Valley, and a personal conversation with Dr. Davis, who examined his specimens from Cahokia Creek. See also James B. Griffin, "The Cahokia Ceramic Complexes," *Proceedings of the Fifth Plains Conference for Archaeology,* Notebook 1 (Lincoln: University of Nebraska Laboratory of Anthropology, 1949), 44–58.

31. To mention just four examples, Rau cited Le Page du Pratz, *Histoire de la Louisiane* (Paris: De Bure, 1758); Dumont de Montigny, *Mémoires historiques sur la Louisiane* (Paris: Bauche, 1753); James Adair, *History of the American Indians* (London, 1775); George Henry Loskiel, *Geschichte der Mission der evangelischen Brüder unter den Indianern in Nordamerika* (Leipzig: Barby, 1789).

32. Paul Francis Titterington, *The Cahokia Mound Group and Its Village Site Materials* (St. Louis, Mo.: P. F. Titterington, 1938), 2. The stone implements that were found were gathered up and are now in the Missouri Historical Society.

33. Ibid., 3.

34. Clyde C. Walton, ed., *John Francis Snyder: Selected Writings* (Springfield: Illinois State Historical Society, 1962), 268–69. Includes a biographical essay by Phyllis E. Connolly and an appraisal of Snyder's archaeological work by Melvin L. Fowler.

35. Ibid., pl. 8.

36. Ibid., 272.

37. From an article in the *Chicago News-Record,* July 8, 1892, in Personal Scrapbook A, 274, quoted by Phyllis E. Connolly, "A Biographical Essay," in Walton, *John Francis Snyder,* 18. The scrapbooks are part of the Snyder Collection in the Illinois Historical Library in Springfield.

38. *Virginia Gazette,* January 15, 1897, in Personal Scrapbook B, 172–73, quoted in Connolly, bibliographical essay in Walton, *John Francis Snyder,* 19.

39. Founded in 1911.

40. *Chicago Record-Herald,* October 18, 1903, in Personal Scrapbook C, 99–101, quoted by Connolly, biographical essay in Walton, *John Francis Snyder,* 18).

41. Walton, *John Francis Snyder,* 267. Snyder is here reporting on Patrick's work.

42. Ibid., 268–69.

43. Stephen D. Peet, "The Great Cahokia Mound," *American Antiquarian* 13, 1 (1891): 3.

44. Ibid., 5.

45. William R. McAdams, "Archaeology," in *Report of the Illinois Board of World's Fair Commissioners at the World's Columbian Exposition, 1893* (Springfield, Ill.: H. W. Rokker, 1895), 286, 298–99.

46. Ibid., 231.

47. Ibid., 236.

48. Ibid., 237.

49. Ibid., 251.

50. Harlan Ingersoll Smith, "The Great American Pyramid," *Harper's Monthly* 104 (1902): 199–204.

51. Ibid.

**CHAPTER SIX**

1. Brochure, East Side Electric Railway System, about 1902.

2. Geri Weinstein-Bruenig, cultural geographer, conversation with the author, July 1998.

3. E. O. Randall, secretary of the Ohio State Archaeological Society, quoted in "The Mound Builders: The Greatest Monument of Prehistoric Man—Cahokia or Monks Mound," undated pamphlet, probably printed by the Ramey family about 1913 to help persuade the legislators to vote for state purchase when a bill to that end was introduced by Representative Norman G. Flagg.

4. Stephen D. Peet, quoted by E. O. Randall in *The Masterpieces of the Ohio Mound Builders* (Columbus: Ohio State Archaeological and Historical Society, 1908, 1–2. Randall is quoted in Ramey, "Mound Builders."

5. Ramey, "Mound Builders."

6. John E. Kelly, "Warren K. Moorehead," in *The Cahokia Mounds,* by Warren King Moorehead, Classics in Southeastern

Archaeology, ed. Stephen Williams (Tuscaloosa: University of Alabama Press, 2000).

7. Moorehead Collection, Ohio Historical Society, box 7.

8. *East St. Louis Daily Journal,* September 7, 1919.

9. For an account of one instance of such urban growth outside Madison, Wisconsin, see Michael P. Conzen, *Frontier Farming in an Urban Shadow* (Madison: State Historical Society of Wisconsin, 1971).

10. Ohio Historical Society, WKM Collection, C106, box 63.

11. *Collinsville Herald,* June 1, 1923.

12. This resurgence of the Klan was at its strongest from 1915 to 1944. Illinois had the fifth largest Klan membership in the United States. There were over 2 million members nationally, and St. Louis and East St. Louis had 5,000. Chicago and its environs had about 50,000 members. Kenneth T. Jackson, *The Ku Klux Klan in the City: 1915–1930* (Chicago: Ivan R. Dee, 1992), table 9.

13. Ibid., 237.

14. Nancy MacLean, *Behind the Mask of Chivalry: The Making of the Second Ku Klux Klan* (New York: Oxford University Press, 1994), 142.

15. The Klan was so active in the area that it even had a women's branch. See Kathleen M. Blee, *Women of the Klan: Racism and Gender in the 1920s* (Berkeley: University of California Press, 1991). See also Leonard J. Moore, *Citizen Klansmen: The Ku Klux Klan in Indiana, 1921–1928* (Chapel Hill: University of North Carolina Press, 1991).

16. Ohio Historical Society, C106, box 64, Moorehead scrapbook.

17. Ibid.

18. "Plans for State Park Being Made," *Collinsville Herald,* June 25, 1926, 1.

19. *Collinsville Herald,* July 29, 1927, and August 5, 1927.

20. *Collinsville Herald,* August 23, 1946; The photograph was taken by a photographer from the *St. Louis Globe-Democrat.*

21. Patricia Leigh Brown, "It Takes a Pioneer to Save a Prairie," *New York Times,* September 10, 1998, B6.

22. Melvin L. Fowler, *The Cahokia Atlas: A Historical Atlas of Cahokia Archaeology,* 2d rev. ed., Illinois Archaeological Survey Bulletin 7 (Urbana: University of Illinois, 1997), 198; first edition published by Illinois Historic Preservation Agency, 1989. Fowler also clears up some confusion in Moorehead's numbering in this area (153).

23. Titterington would later publish work on the site.

24. David I. Bushnell Jr., "Archaeological Reconnaissance of the Cahokia and Related Mound Groups," in *Explorations and Field-work of the Smithsonian Institution,* Smithsonian Miscellaneous Collections 72, no. 15 (Washington, D.C.: Smithsonian Institution, 1921), 92–105. Bushnell saw the possibilities in connection with his work on second-line communities.

25. Robert L. Hall, "The Goddard-Ramey Cahokia Flight: A Pioneering Aerial Photographic Survey," *Wisconsin Archeologist* 49, 2 (1968): 75–78.

26. Ibid., 78.

27. Dache M. Reeves, "Aerial Photography and Archaeology," *American Antiquity* 2 (1936): 104–5.

28. Melvin L. Fowler, "Aerial Archeology at the Cahokia Site," in *Aerial Remote Sensing Techniques in Archeology,* ed. Thomas R. Lyons and Robert K. Hitchcock (Albuquerque: Chaco Center, National Park Service, 1977), 71.

29. Ibid., 68.

30. Harriet M. Smith, "The Murdock Mound: Cahokia Site," in *Explorations into Cahokia Archaeology,* ed. Melvin L. Fowler, Illinois Archaeological Survey Bulletin 7 (Urbana: University of Illinois, 1968), 49–88a; quotation on 56–58.

31. Ibid., 69–70.

32. Ibid., 70.

33. Ibid., 82–84. Smith also adds, "That the facet also made it stronger (serving as a corner brace) may not [even] have been intentional." Smith found the final platform of Murdock Mound to be 33 feet high and 66 feet long by 45 feet wide. She also ascertained a modular unit of measurement in Murdock Mound that she termed the "Cahokian rod," a unit of about 162 feet.

34. Ibid., 86.

35. Kerry Segrave, *Drive-in Theaters: A History from Their Inception in 1933* (Jefferson, N.C.: McFarland, 1996). Perhaps the first drive-in was the Drive-in Theater of 1933 in Camden, New Jersey.

36. Howard E. Hall, "World's First Drive in Theater," *Architecture* (London) 136 (December 8, 1933): 286.

37. Ibid., 287.

38. *Collinsville Herald,* May 6, 1938, 1.

39. Ibid., July 20, 1945, 1.

40. Ibid.

41. *Collinsville Herald,* August 10, 1945, 1.

42. Telephone interview with Billy H. Greer, July 1996.

43. Billy H. Greer, letter to the author, November 13, 1996, and telephone call, November 10, 1996.

44. Telephone conversation with Dale Rust, July 1996.

CHAPTER SEVEN

1. William R. Iseminger, "Looking Back over Twenty Years: Recollections of Cahokia," *Cahokian,* winter 1990 and winter 1991. The two parts are a trove of information about this period. They contain detailed lists of personnel, archaeological excavations, land acquisition and improvement, the Cahokia Mounds Museum Society, the growth of education programs, and the opening of the interpretive center.

2. Ibid.

3. Ibid., 11.

4. Ibid.

5. Ibid., 13.

6. Ibid.

7. Ibid.

8. Ibid.

9. A number of midwestern universitites and institutions participated. The main ones were the University of Wisconsin–Milwaukee, under Melvin Fowler; Washington University of St. Louis, under Nelson Reed; the University of Illinois, under Charles Bareis; Beloit College, under Robert Salzer; the Illinois State Museum Society; and the Cahokia Mounds Museum Society, under Anderson and Iseminger.

10. Warren L. Wittry, "An American Woodhenge," *Cranbrook Institute of Science News Letter* 33, 9 (1964): 102–7. See also Wittry, "The American Woodhenge," in *Explorations into Cahokia Archaeology,* ed. Melvin L. Fowler, Illinois Archaeological Survey Bulletin 7 (Urbana: University of Illinois, 1969).

11. Mikels Skele, "The Cahokia Surveyor," unpublished manuscript, 1983, 8, available at the Office of Contract Archaeology, Southern Illinois University at Edwardsville.

12. E. C. Krupp, "Cahokia: Corn, Commerce, and the Cosmos," *Griffith Observer* (Los Angeles) 41, no. 5 (1977): 10.

13. Robert L. Hall, "American Indian Worlds, World Quarters, World Centers, and Their Shrines," in *The Ancient Skies and Sky Watchers of Cahokia: Woodhenges, Eclipses, and Cahokian Cosmology,* ed. Melvin L. Fowler, Wisconsin Archeologist 77, nos. 3–4 (Milwaukee: Wisconsin Archeological Society, 1996), 125.

14. Fowler, *Cahokia Atlas,* 2d ed., 36.

15. Ibid., 57.

16. Claudia Gellman Mink, *Cahokia, City of the Sun: Prehistoric Urban Center in the American Bottom* (Collinsville, Ill.: Cahokia Mounds Museum Society, 1992), 33.

17. William R. Iseminger, Timothy Pauketat, Brad Koldehoff, Lucretia S. Kelly, and Leonard Blake, "East Palisade Investigations," in *The Archaeology of the Cahokia Palisade,* Illinois Cultural Resources Study 14 (Springfield: Illinois Historic Preservation Agency, 1990), 35–37.

18. Fowler, *Cahokia Atlas,* 145.

19. Among other discoveries, Nelson Reed of Washington University excavated the Fourth Terrace and the South Ramp of Monks Mound (1972); an overall view of these various excavations appears in William R. Iseminger, "Looking Back," part 2, 6–11. Details are published in papers by the various authors.

20. Robert L. Hall, "Chronology and Phases at Cahokia," in *Perspectives in Cahokia Archaeology,* ed. James A. Brown, Illinois Archaeological Survey Bulletin 10 (Urbana: University of Illinois, 1975), 30.

21. Web site, www.unesco.org/whc Online, October 4, 1998.

22. Ibid.

23. Web site, www.nationaltrust.org, October 7, 1998; telephone interview with Alan Downer, December 3, 1998. Downer is now director of the Navajo Nation Historic Preservation Department and chair of the National Association of Tribal Historic Preservation Officers.

24. Later they were reimbursed by the State of Illinois. The state did not have the money in the right account, so in the meantime the National Preservation Loan Fund paid for it.

25. William R. Iseminger, "Monks Mound: A 'Moving Monument,'" *Historic Illinois* 20, 2 (1997):10.

26. Telephone interview with Paul Nixon, former assistant site manager, November 26, 1996. The volunteer organization is now managed by a volunteer coordinator.

27. Don Dillow, unpublished paper written at author's request and interview, July 13, 1996.

28. Ibid.

29. Tommy Wildcat, telephone interview with author, December 16, 1998.

30. Wood Bell, telephone interview with author, January 5, 1999.

31. William R. Iseminger, "Heritage America 1991," *Cahokian,* winter 1991–92, 2.

32. Charles M. Hudson, *The Southeastern Indians* (Knoxville: University of Tennessee Press, 1976), 3.

33. J. B. Jackson, *A Sense of Place, a Sense of Time* (New Haven: Yale University Press, 1994).

34. Suzanne Stephens, "Trailers, Wetlands and Boondocks: Two Historians of the American Landscape Take a Close Look at Sights Many of Us Might Just as Soon Avoid," *New York Times Book Review,* November 27, 1994, 7. The article consists of reviews of John Brinckerhoff Jackson, *A Sense of Place, a Sense of Time* (New Haven: Yale University Press, 1994), and Grady Clay, *Real Places: An Unconventional Guide to America's Generic Landscape* (Chicago: University of Chicago Press, 1994).

35. Light brown markings indicate excavations from the Lohmann Phase (1000–1050); blue gray, Early Stirling (1050–1100); light gray, Late Stirling (1100–1150); dark brown, the Moorehead Phase (1150–1200); charcoal was used to mark post holes.

36. Gerald Hilferty, telephone conversation with author, April 8, 1996, and letter to author, April 9, 1998.

# Bibliography

The best bibliography on Cahokia, and an indispensable research tool, is the online, constantly updated service founded by William I. Woods at Southern Illinois University at Edwardsville and available on the Internet at www.siue.edu/CAHOKIAMOUNDS.

The Cahokia Mounds State Historic Site maintains a Web site, www.cahokiamounds.com, and can also be reached by e-mail at chaokiamounds@ezl.com.

Sally A. Kitt Chappell can be reached by e-mail at schappel@condor.depaul.edu.

Two excellent videos are available to the general public: *Cahokia Mounds: Ancient Metropolis,* at the bookstore of the Cahokia Mounds Museum Society, 30 Ramey Street, Collinsville, IL 62234, and *Cahokia: America's Lost Metropolis*, from the BBC 2 at Box 1001, Manchester M60 3JB, England.

The references listed below deal with Cahokia generally. References of a more specific nature, such as those on the geography of Illinois, are cited in the endnotes and are not repeated here.

_____

Anderson, David G., and Kenneth E. Sassaman, eds. *The Paleoindian and Early Archaic Southeast.* Tuscaloosa: University of Alabama Press, 1996.

Anderson, J. P. "A Cahokia Palisade Sequence." In *Explorations into Cahokia Archaeology,* ed. Melvin L. Fowler, 88–89. Illinois Archaeological Survey Bulletin 7. Urbana: University of Illinois, 1969.

Balesi, Charles J. *The Time of the French in the Heart of North America, 1673–1818.* Chicago: Alliance Française, 1992.

Bareis, Charles J., and James W. Porter, eds. *American Bottom Archaeology.* Urbana: University of Illinois Press, 1984.

Brackenridge, Henry Marie. *Views of Louisiana Together with a Journal of a Voyage up the Missouri River in 1811*. 1814. Reprint Chicago: Quadrangle Books, 1962.

Brose, David S., James A. Brown, and David W. Penney, with photographs by Dirk Bakker (*sic*). *Ancient Art of the American Woodland Indians*. New York: Henry N. Abrams in association with Detroit Institute of Arts, 1985.

Brose, David S., and N'omi Greber. *Hopewell Archaeology: The Chillicothe Conference*. Kent, Ohio: Kent State University Press, 1979.

Brown, James A., ed. *Mississippian Site Archaeology in Illinois*. Illinois Archaeological Survey Bulletin 8. Urbana: University of Illinois, 1971.

———, ed. *Perspectives in Cahokia Archaeology*. Illinois Archaeological Survey Bulletin 10. Urbana: University of Illinois, 1975.

Brown, Margaret Kimball, and Lawrie Cena Dean. *The French Colony in the Mid-Mississippi Valley*. Carbondale, Ill.: American Kestral Books, 1995.

Buisseret, David. *Historic Illinois from the Air*. Chicago: University of Chicago Press, 1990.

Collot, Georges-Henri-Victor. *Voyage dans l'Amérique Septentrionale, ou Description des pays arrosés par le Mississippi, l'Ohio, le Missouri et autres rivières affluentes*. Paris: A. Bertrand, 1826.

Conzen, Michael. *Frontier Farming in an Urban Shadow*. Madison: State Historical Society of Wisconsin, 1971.

Crook, A. R. "Origin of Monks Mound." *Bulletin of the Geological Society of America* 26 (1915): 74–75.

Dalan, Rinita A. "Electromagnetic Reconnaissance of the Central Palisade at the Cahokia Mounds State Historic Site." *Wisconsin Archeologist* 70 (1989): 309–32.

DePratter, Chester B. *Late Prehistoric and Early Historic Chiefdoms in the Southeastern United States*. New York: Garland, 1991.

Emerson, Thomas E. *Cahokia and the Archaeology of Power*. Tuscaloosa: University of Alabama Press, 1997.

———. *Mississippian Stone Images in Illinois*. Illinois Archaeological Survey Circular 6. Urbana: University of Illinois, 1982.

Emerson, Thomas E., and R. Barry Lewis, eds. *Cahokia and the Hinterlands: Middle Mississippian Cultures of the Midwest*. Urbana: University of Illinois Press, 1991.

Fagan, Brian M. *Ancient North America: The Archaeology of a Continent*. Rev. ed. New York: Thames and Hudson, 1995.

Fowler, Melvin L., ed. *The Ancient Skies and Sky Watchers of Cahokia: Woodhenges, Eclipses, and Cahokian Cosmology*. Wisconsin Archeologist 77, nos. 3–4. Madison: Wisconson Archaeological Society, 1996.

———. *The Cahokia Atlas: A Historical Atlas of Cahokia Archaeology*. Studies in Illinois Archaeology 6. Springfield: Illinois Historic Preservation Agency, 1989.

———, ed. *Explorations into Cahokia Archaeology*. Illinois Archaeological Survey Bulletin 7. Urbana: University of Illinois, 1969.

——— ed. *Explorations into Cahokia Archaeology*. 2d rev. ed. Illinois Archaeological Survey Bulletin 7. Urbana: University of Illinois, 1977.

Fowler, Melvin L., and Robert L. Hall. "Late Prehistory of the Illinois Area." In *Handbook of North American Indians*, 15:560–68. Washington, D.C.: Smithsonian Institution, 1978–.

Goddard, George W. *Overview: A Life-Long Adventure in Aerial Photography*. Garden City, N.Y.: Doubleday, 1969.

Goode, J. Paul. *The Geographic Background of Chicago*. Chicago: University of Chicago Press, 1926. This rare book was given to me by William Conger.

Griffin, James B. *Archeology of Eastern United States*. Chicago: University of Chicago Press, 1972.

———. "Changing Concepts of the Prehistoric Mississippian Cultures in the Eastern United States." In *Alabama and the Borderlands*, ed. Reid Badger and Lawrence A. Clayton. University: University of Alabama Press, 1985.

Gums, Bonnie L. *Archaeology at French Colonial Cahokia*. Studies in Illinois Archaeology 3. Springfield: Illinois Historic Preservation Agency, 1988.

Hall, Robert L. *An Archaeology of the Soul: North American Indian Belief and Ritual*. Urbana: University of Illinois Press, 1997.

Hoffmeister, Donald F., and Carol O. Mohr. *Fieldbook of Illinois Mammals*. New York: Dover, 1972.

Holley, George R., Rinita A. Dalan, Neal H. Lopinot, and Phillip A. Smith. *Investigations in the Grand Plaza, Cahokia Mounds Historic Site, St. Clair County, Illinois*. Edwardsville: Office of Contract Archaeology, Southern Illinois University at Edwardsville, 1990.

Hudson, Charles M. *The Southeastern Indians*. Knoxville: University of Tennessee Press, 1976. This book has some excellent passages on the absorption of Indian ways and artifacts into southern culture.

Iseminger, William R. "Looking Back over Twenty Years: Recollections of Cahokia." *Cahokian,* winter 1990 and winter 1991.

———. "Mighty Cahokia," *Archaeology,* May–June 1996, 33–37.

Iseminger, William R., Timothy Pauketat, Brad Koldehoff, Lucretia S. Kelly, and Leonard Blake. "East Palisade Excavations." In *The Archaeology of the Cahokia Palisade,* 35–37. Illinois Cultural Resources Study 14, Thomas Emerson, gen. ed. Springfield: Illinois Historic Preservation Agency, 1990.

Jackson, Kenneth T. *The Ku Klux Klan in the City: 1915–1930*. Chicago: Ivan R. Dee, 1992.

Kelly, J. E. "The Emergence of Mississippian Culture in the American Bottom Region." In *The Mississippian Emergence,* ed. Bruce D. Smith, 113–52. Washington, D.C.: Smithsonian Institution Press, 1990.

Krupp, E. C. "Cahokia: Corn, Commerce, and the Cosmos." *Griffith Observer* 4 (1977): 1–20.

Lepper, Bradley T. "Ancient Astronomers of the Ohio Valley." *Timeline,* January–February 1998, 9. The article draws on the research of astronomer Ray Hively and philosopher Robert Horn of Earlham College in Indiana.

Lopinot, N. H., and W. I. Woods. "Wood Overexploitation and the Collapse of Cahokia." In *Foraging and Farming in the Eastern Woodlands,* ed. C. Margaret Scarry, 206–31. Gainesville: University Press of Florida, 1993.

MacLean, Nancy. *Behind the Mask of Chivalry: The Making of the Second Ku Klux Klan*. New York: Oxford University Press, 1994.

McAdams, William R. "Archaeology." In *Report of the Illinois Board of World's Fair Commissioners at the World's Columbian Exposition 1893,* ed. H. W. Rokker. Springfield, Ill., 1895.

Milner, George R. "Mississippian Period Population Density in a Segment of the Central Mississippi River Valley." *American Antiquity* 51 (1986): 227–38.

Milner, George R., Eve Anderson, and Virginia G. Smith. "Warfare in Late Prehistoric West-Central Illinois. *American Antiquity* 56 (1991): 581–603.

Mink, Claudia Gellman. *Cahokia, City of the Sun: Prehistoric Urban Center in the American Bottom*. Collinsville, Ill.: Cahokia Mounds Museum Society, 1992.

Moorehead, Warren K., ed. *The Cahokia Mounds*. University of Illinois Bulletin 26, no. 4. Urbana: University of Illinois, 1929.

———. *The Cahokia Mounds: A Preliminary Report*. University of Illinois Bulletin 21, no. 6, pt. 1. Urbana: University of Illinois, 1923.

Pauketat, Timothy R. *The Ascent of Chiefs: Cahokia and Mississippian Politics in Native North America*. Tuscaloosa: University of Alabama Press, 1994.

Pauketat, Timothy R., and Thomas E. Emerson. *Cahokia: Domination and Ideology in the Mississippian World*. Lincoln: University of Nebraska Press, 1997.

Peet, S. D. "The Great Cahokia Mound." *American Antiquarian* 12 (1891): 352–56.

Pfeiffer, John. "Indian City on the Mississippi." In *Nature/Science Annual*. New York: Time-Life Books, 1974. Also see Pfeiffer's "America's First City," *Horizon* 16, 2 (1974): 58.

Phillips, James L., and James A. Brown. *Archaic Hunters and Gatherers in the American Midwest*. New World Archaeological Record. New York: Academic Press, 1983.

Plotkin, Mark J. *Tales of a Shaman's Apprentice*. New York: Viking Press, 1993.

Putnam, F. S., and J. J. R. Patrick. *Twelfth Annual Report of the Peabody Museum*. Cambridge: Harvard University, 1880.

Rau, C. "A Deposit of Agricultural Flint Implements in Southern Illinois." In *Annual Report of the Smithsonian Institution,* 401–7. Washington, D.C.: Smithsonian Institution, 1868.

———. "Indian Pottery." In *Annual Report of the Smithsonian Institution,* 346–55. Washington, D.C.: Smithsonian Institution, 1867.

Ridgley, Douglas C. *The Geography of Illinois*. Chicago: University of Chicago Press, 1921.

Rogers, J. Daniel, and Bruce D. Smith, eds. *Mississippian Communities and Households*. Tuscaloosa: University of Alabama Press, 1995.

Rolingson, Martha Ann. "Elements of Community Design at Cahokia." In *The Ancient Skies and Sky Watchers of Cahokia: Woodhenges, Eclipses, and Cahokian Cosmology,* ed. Melvin L. Fowler, 84–96. Wisconsin Archeologist 77, nos. 3–4. Milwaukee: Wisconsin Archeological Society, 1996.

Schuberth, Christopher J. *A View of the Past: An Introduction to Illinois Geology*. Springfield: Illinois State Museum, 1986.

Segrave, Kerry. *Drive-in Theaters: A History from Their Inception in 1933*. Jefferson, N.C.: McFarland, 1996.

Shaffer, Lynda Norene. *Native Americans before 1492: The Moundbuilding Centers of the Eastern Woodlands.* Sources and Studies in World History Series, ed. Kevin Reilly. Armonk, N.Y.: M. E. Sharpe, 1992.

Silverberg, Robert. *Mound Builders of Ancient America: The Archaeology of a Myth.* Athens: Ohio University Press, 1986.

Skele, Mikels. *The Great Knob: Interpretations of Monks Mound.* Studies in Archaeology 4. Springfield: Illinois Historic Preservation Agency, 1988.

Smith, Bruce D. *The Emergence of Agriculture.* New York: Scientific American Library, 1995.

———, ed. *Mississippian Settlement Patterns.* New York: Academic Press, 1978.

Smith, Harriet M. "The Murdock Mound: Cahokia Site." In *Explorations into Cahokia Archaeology,* ed. Melvin L. Fowler, 49–88a. Illinois Archaeological Survey Bulletin 7. Urbana: University of Illinois, 1969.

Squier, E. G., and E. H. Davis. *Ancient Monuments of the Mississippi Valley: Comprising the Results of Extensive Original Surveys and Excavations.* Smithsonian Contributions to Knowledge 1. New York: Bartlett and Welford, 1848. Reissued, with an introduction by David Meltzer, Washington, D.C.: Smithsonian Institution Press, 1998.

———. *Ancient Monuments of the Mississippi Valley, Comprising the Results of Extensive Original Surveys and Explorations.* With a new introduction by James B. Griffin. New York: AMS Press for Peabody Museum of Archaeology and Ethnology, Harvard University, 1973.

Stoltman, James B., ed. *New Perspectives on Cahokia: Views from the Periphery.* Monographs in World Archaeology 2. Madison, Wis.: Prehistory Press, 1991.

Struever, Stuart, and Felicia Antonelli Holton. *Koster: Americans in Search of Their Prehistoric Past.* Garden City, N.Y.: Anchor/Doubleday, 1979.

Walthall, John A., ed. *French Colonial Archaeology: The Illinois Country and the Western Great Lakes.* Urbana: University of Illinois Press, 1991.

Walthall, John A., and Elizabeth Benchley. *The River L'Abbe Mission: A French Colonial Church for the Cahokia Illini on Monks Mound.* Studies in Illinois Archaeology 2. Springfield: Illinois Historic Preservation Agency, 1987.

Walton, Clyde C. *John Francis Snyder: Selected Writings.* Springfield: Illinois State Historical Society, 1962.

Watters, H. W. "Field School Maps Mound Group." *Cahokian,* summer 1997, 9–10.

White, Richard. *The Middle Ground.* Cambridge: Cambridge University Press, 1991.

Wild, J. C. *The Valley of the Mississippi Illustrated in a Series of Views.* Edited by Lewis Foulk Thomas. St. Louis, Mo.: Chambers and Knapp, 1841.

Wittry, Warren. "The American Woodhenge." In *Explorations into Cahokia Archaeology,* ed. Melvin L. Fowler, 43–48. Illinois Archaeological Survey Bulletin 7. Urbana: University of Illinois, 1969.

———. "Cahokia Woodhenge Update." *Archaeoastronomy* 3 (1980): 12–14.

Woods, W. I. "ICT-II Phase II Testing" and "ICT-II: Testing and Lithics." In *Archaeology of the Cahokia Mounds,* ed. Thomas E. Emerson. Illinois Cultural Resources Study 9. Springfield: Illinois Historic Preservation Agency. 1993.

Young, Biloine Whiting, and Melvin L. Fowler. *Cahokia: The Great Native American Metropolis.* Urbana: University of Illinois Press, 2000.

# Credits for Illustrations

Full citations of credited publications will be found in the bibliography.

FIG. 1. Anglo-Australian Telescope Board
FIG. 2. National Aeronautics and Space Administration
FIG. 3. National Aeronautics and Space Administration
FIG. 4. National Aeronautics and Space Administration
FIG. 5. Cahokia Mounds State Historic Site, photo by William R. Iseminger
FIG. 6. Tracing from Johns Hopkins University Press, graphic addition by author
FIG. 7. American Museum of Natural History, New York
FIG. 8. Illinois State Geological Survey
FIG. 9. Conservation Research Institute, drawing by Heidi Natura
FIG. 10. Illinois State Geological Survey
FIG. 11. Illinois State Geological Survey
FIG. 12. Illinois State Geological Survey
FIG. 13. Illinois State Geological Survey and Northern Illinois University.
FIG. 14. Cahokia Mounds State Historic Site and Mikels Skele
FIG. 15. Cahokia Mounds State Historic Site and Mikels Skele
FIG. 16. Map by John E. Kelly, adapted from Ronald E. Yarbrough
FIG. 17. Illinois Natural History Survey, map by Kate Hunter
FIG. 18. Cahokia Mounds State Historic Site, painting by Susan Walton, photo by Art Grossman
FIG. 19. Photo by Pete Bostrom, from the collections of James Maddok, Calvin Howaard, and Floyd Ritter
FIG. 20. Cahokia Mounds State Historic Site, painting by Lloyd K. Townsend

FIG. 21. Drawing by Jon E. Gibson

FIG. 22. Gordon Hart Collection, photo © 1985 Dirk Bakker, The Detroit Institute of Arts

FIG. 23. National Museum of the American Indian, photo © 1985 Dirk Bakker, The Detroit Institute of Arts

FIG. 24. Cahokia Mounds State Historic Site, drawing of canoe construction by Susan Walton, close-up of adze by William R. Iseminger

FIG. 25. Painting by Jay Matternes

FIG. 26. Cahokia Mounds Museum Society, photo by Art Grossman

FIG. 27. Map by John E. Kelly

FIG. 28. Courtesy of American Museum of Natural History Library

FIG. 29. Drawing by Jon E. Gibson

FIG. 30. Thomas Gilcrease Institute of American History and Art, photo © 1985 Dirk Bakker, The Detroit Institute of Arts

FIG. 31. Thomas Gilcrease Institute of American History and Art, photo © 1985 Dirk Bakker, The Detroit Institute of Arts

FIG. 32. Ohio Historical Society

FIG. 33. Ohio Historical Society

FIG. 34. Ohio Historical Society, from Squier and Davis, *Ancient Monuments of the Mississippi Valley*

FIG. 35. Drawing by Jason Scarpelo

FIG. 36. Ohio Historical Society, from Squier and Davis, *Ancient Monuments of the Mississippi Valley*

FIG. 37. Aerial photo and plan Ohio Historical Society, from Squier and Davis, *Ancient Monuments of the Mississippi Valley*

FIG. 38. Maps by John E. Kelly

FIG. 39. Cahokia Mounds State Historic Site, photo by William Fecht

FIG. 40. Painting by Susan Walton

FIG. 41. Cahokia Mounds Museum Society, painting by L. K. Townsend, photo by Art Grossman

FIG. 42. Map by John E. Kelly

FIG. 43. Arkansas Archaeological Survey, map by Martha Ann Rolingson

FIG. 44. Arkansas Archaeological Survey, map by Martha Ann Rolingson

FIG. 45. Arkansas Archaeological Survey, map by Martha Ann Rolingson

FIG. 46. Cahokia Mounds Museum Society, painting by Michael Hampshire, photo by Art Grossman

FIG. 47. Reprinted with the permission of the University Press of Florida

FIG. 48. Cahokia Mounds Museum Society, painting by Michael Hampshire, photo by Art Grossman

FIG. 49. Cahokia Mounds State Historic Site

FIG. 50. Cahokia Mounds Museum Society, drawing by Karen Corley

FIG. 51. Cahokia Mounds State Historic Site, painting by Don Vonderbeck

FIG. 52. Cahokia Mounds State Historic Site, drawing by George Bloodsworth

FIG. 53. Cahokia Mounds Museum Society, painting by L. K. Townsend, photo by Art Grossman

FIG. 54. Cahokia Mounds State Historic Site, illustration by Paul Bradford

FIG. 55. Cahokia Mounds Museum Society, illustration by Albert Meyer

FIG. 56. *Wisconsin Archeologist,* United States Geological Survey map, with graphic additions by Melvin L. Fowler

FIG. 57. Cahokia Mounds Museum Society, photo by Art Grossman

FIG. 58. Cahokia Mounds Museum Society, photo by Art Grossman

FIG. 59. Angel Mounds State Historic Site, Evansville, Indiana, photo by Larry Cohen

FIG. 60. Cahokia Mounds Museum Society, painting by Michael Hampshire, photo by Art Grossman

FIG. 61. Frank H. McClung Museum, University of Tennessee, photo © 1985 Dirk Bakker, The Detroit Institute of Arts

FIG. 62. Peoria 1691 Foundation, painting by Lonnie Eugene Stewart

FIG. 63. American Resources Group, adapted from Charles Balesi

FIG. 64. Andreas, *History of Chicago from the Earliest Period to the Present,* 1:43

FIG. 65. Andreas, *History of Chicago from the Earliest Period to the Present,* following 1:48

FIG. 66. Illinois State Historical Society, drawing by Gordon Peckham

FIG. 67. American Resources Group, photo by Jim Balsitis

FIG. 68. Illinois Historic Preservation Agency, from Walthall and Benchley, *River L'Abbe Mission,* drawing by Carla Zedialis.

FIG. 69. Illinois Historic Preservation Agency, from Walthall and Benchley, *River L'Abbe Mission*

FIG. 70. George Rogers Clark National Historic Park, National Park Service

FIG. 71. Newberry Library, from Collot, *Voyage dans l'Amérique Septentrionale*

FIG. 72. American Resources Group, photo by Ken Seeber

FIG. 73. American Resources Group, photo by Ken Seeber

FIG. 74. American Resources Group, photo by Ken Seeber

FIG. 75. St. Louis Art Museum, Eliza McMillan Fund

FIG. 76. Cahokia Mounds State Historic Site. Peale obtained data from Stephen H. Long, from *Annual Report of the Smithsonian Institution,* 1861, 386

FIG. 77. Joslyn Art Museum, Omaha Nebraska, gift of Enron Art Foundation

FIG. 78. Joslyn Art Museum, Omaha Nebraska, gift of Enron Art Foundation

FIG. 79. Smithsonian National Museum of American Art, gift of Mrs. Joseph Harrison Jr.

FIG. 80. Edward E. Ayer Collection, the Newberry Library, from Wild, *Valley of the Mississippi Illustrated,* plate 10

FIG. 81. Edward E. Ayer Collection, the Newberry Library, from Wild, *Valley of the Mississippi Illustrated,* frontispiece

FIG. 82. Edward E. Ayer Collection, the Newberry Library, from Wild, *Valley of the Mississippi Illustrated,* plate 9

FIG. 83. Edward E. Ayer Collection, the Newberry Library. Illinois Central Railroad Company broadside, undated

FIG. 84. Edward E. Ayer Collection, the Newberry Library. Illinois Central Railroad Company brochure, undated

FIG. 85. *Illustrated Encyclopedia and Atlas of Madison County (Illinois)* (St. Louis: Brink, 1873)

FIG. 86. Smithsonian Institution

FIG. 87. *Harper's Weekly,* 1860s

FIG. 88. Southern Illinois University–Edwardsville

FIG. 89. Illinois State Historical Society

FIG. 90. Illinois State Historical Society

FIG. 91. Cahokia Mounds State Historic Site

FIG. 92. Cahokia Mounds State Historic Site

FIG. 93. Cahokia Mounds Museum Society, photo by Peter Bostrom

FIG. 94. Missouri Historical Society, St. Louis, daguerreotype by Thomas M. Easterly

FIG. 95. Missouri Historical Society, St. Louis, daguerreotype by Thomas M. Easterly

FIG. 96. Cahokia Mounds State Historic Site

FIG. 97. Archeological Research Laboratory, University of Wisconsin–Milwaukee

FIG. 98. Southern Illlinois University–Edwardsville

FIG. 99. Cahokia Mounds State Historic Site

FIG. 100. Cahokia Mounds State Historic Site

FIG. 101. Cahokia Mounds State Historic Site

FIG. 102. Cahokia Mounds State Historic Site, photo by Edward George Ihmels

FIG. 103. Ohio Historical Society

FIG. 104. Ohio Historical Society

FIG. 105. University of Wisconsin–Milwaukee

FIG. 106. Cahokia Mounds State Historic Site

FIG. 107. Cahokia Mounds State Historic Site

FIG. 108. Cahokia Mounds State Historic Site

FIG. 109. Illinois State Museum

FIG. 110. United States Geological Survey

FIG. 111. Illinois Archaeological Survey, drawings by Harriet Smith

FIG. 112. Cahokia Mounds State Historic Site, photos by Richard Y. Norrish

FIG. 113. Photo by Alex S. MacLane/Landslides

FIG. 114. Map by John E. Kelly

FIG. 115. Cahokia Mounds State Historic Site

FIG. 116. Cahokia Mounds Museum Society, drawing by Albert Meyer

FIG. 117. Cahokia Mounds State Historic Site, drawing by William R. Iseminger

FIG. 118. Cahokia Mounds State Historic Site, painting by William R. Iseminger

FIG. 119. Cahokia Mounds State Historic Site, painting by Lee Woolery

FIG. 120. Cahokia Mounds Museum Society, drawing by William R. Iseminger

FIG. 121. Cahokia Mounds State Historic Site, photo by James P. Anderson

FIG. 122. Cahokia Mounds Museum Society, drawing by Albert Meyer

FIG. 123. Cahokia Mounds Museum Society, photo by Art Grossman

FIG. 124. Cahokia Mounds State Historic Site

FIG. 125. Cahokia Mounds State Historic Site

FIG. 126. Cahokia Mounds State Historic Site, photo by William R. Iseminger

FIG. 127. Cahokia Mounds State Historic Site, photo by William R. Iseminger

FIG. 128. National Aeronautics and Space Administration

# Index

Page numbers in italics refer to illustrations.

Accault (Ako), Michel, 80
Adena culture, 41
adzes, 31, *32*
aerial photographs, 140–42, *141*
agriculture: bottle gourds, 39; communal construction associated with, 64, 67–68; glaciation and, 10, *11;* large-scale Mississippian, 46, 48; by Late Woodland people, 46; Mississippians changing from digging stick to hoe, 47–48; plant cultivation at Poverty Point and Koster, 39; pumpkins, 39; risk sharing in, 24; squash, 39; steel plow, 108–9; Trappist, 90. *See also* corn
airmail, 148
airports, 147–50
Ako (Accault), Michel, 80
Altithermal (Hypsithermal) Climatic Interval, 33
Alton (Illinois), 18, *107*
*American Antiquarian* (magazine), 117, 118–19
American Bottom, 18–25; floods, 19–22; physical regions, *22;* soil, 12; and UNESCO World Heritage List application, 173
American Indian Movement, 180

American Indians against Desecration, 180
Amerindians. *See* Native Americans
Amiel, Henri-Frédéric, 55
Anderson, James P.: and Cahokia Mounds Museum Society, 171; and Master Management Plan, 171; overseeing Cahokia site, 153, 154–58; stockades excavated by, 140, 168; in UNESCO World Heritage List application, 172
Angel site (Indiana), 48
animals: biodiversity of American Bottom, 24–25. *See also* birds; mammals
animal skins, 69
Antiquities Act (1906), 128
Archaeological and Historic Preservation Act (1974), 171
archaeology: Brackenridge and Mississippian, 97–99; contributors to Cahokian, 166–70; first published aerial photographs, 140; Fowler's work, 160–66; "highway salvage archaeology," 158; Long's expedition, 99–101; Moorehead's survey, 130–32, *131, 132;* postwar changes in, 150–51; and preservation, 123, 158;

professional archaeologists hired at Cahokia Mounds State Park, 153, 154–58; of Rau, 110–12; Smith's work at Murdock Mound, 142, 144, *145;* of Snyder, 115–17; St. Louis world's fair arousing interest in Cahokian, 128; Wittry excavating solar calendar, 158–62

Archaic period, 30–39

Architectural Associates, 182

architecture: celestial phenomena in Native American, 55–56; cosmic landscape architecture at Cahokia, 51–75; French traditions in Illinois, 82, *82;* height as metaphor for power, 57; innate evocative powers of, 4; Mississippian, 49; multilayered values in, 3; optical illusion in, 144. *See also* construction techniques; earthworks

arthritis, 74

Aten, Larry, 172

atlatls, 28, 30–31, *30*

authority, symbols for legitimating, 64–65

Aztalan (Wisconsin), 48

bannerstones, 31, *31,* 36

Bareis, Charles J., 167–68, 201n. 9

bark, 70, 71

bear claws, 68

beavers, 25, 60, *60,* 97–98

Bell, Wood, 179–80

Beloit College, 167, 201n. 9

Benchley, Elizabeth, 86, 168, 182

Bennett, John, 167

Berkeley, George, 103

Big Bang, xiv, *xv*

Big Mound (St. Louis), 106, 112, 113, 119–20, *120*

"birdman tablet," 118, *119*

birds: flyways, 19; in Mississippi Valley, 25. *See also* waterfowl

Black Hawk, 82, 103

Blake, Leonard, 170

Bodmer, Karl, 101–3, *102,* 108

bottle gourds, 39

Boucher, Pierre, 77

bow and arrow, 46

Brackenridge, Henry Marie, 97–99

Brady, Thomas, 88

Brooks Pasture, 130

Brown, Margaret Kimball, *93,* 182, 186

burial: in Big Mound, 113; cemeteries, 36, 66; in Mound 72, 165, *166;* mounds for, 40–41; in Powell Mound, 67

Burlington chert, 39

Bushnell, David I., 128

Cahokia (village): founded as Indian mission, 81; St. Louis Downtown Airport, 148

"Cahokia and the Surrounding Mound Groups, The" (Bushnell), 128

"Cahokia: Corn, Commerce, and the Cosmos" (Krupp), 159–60

Cahokia Creek, 19, 23, 30, 90, *164*

Cahokia Diversion Canal, 23

Cahokia Illini: Fox attacking Cahokia Mounds settlement in 1752, 86; French mission to, 80–81; hostilities between French and, 83–85; La Salle mentioning, 79; Mississippian Cahokians distinguished from, 5, 197n. 3; move into Cahokia area, 71

Cahokia Mounds

archaeology at: aerial photographs, 140–42, *141;* "Cahokia baseline," 164, 165; contributors to, 166–70; Fowler's work, 160–66; Moorehead's survey, 130–32; Patrick's work, 117–18, 160; Peet's work, 118–19; professional archaeologists hired at, 153, 154–58; Rau's work, 110–12; Smith's work, 142, 144, *145;* Snyder's work, 115–17

Cahokian construction and occupation of, 51–75; abandonment of, 71–75, 185–86; agriculture, 12, 13, 15, 24, 47–48; animated landscape of, 55–57; cardinal directions marked in, *50,* 51, *53;* chunkey, 60, 61, 70, 165; as city, 5; dawn at equinox, *6;* exalted world created by mounds, 58–59; harvest festival, 54; houses, 65, *66,* 142, *175,* 184–85; labor involved in public works, 62–65; as landscape cosmogram, 55; as microcosm on earth, 59–65; natural materials used, 68–71;

ordinary life, 65–68; Pacific Climate Episode affecting, 72; population, 2, 46, 193n. 1; pottery, 35, 36, 40, 70, 110–12, *112;* public works and organizational control, 63–65; ridge-topped mounds and plan of, 67, *68,* 163–64, *164;* sacred order preserving social order, 60–61; shared vision at, 65–71; site planning, 144–46; as solar calendar, 52, *53,* 158–62; trade, 71, *72,* 73, 165; urban renewal, 61–62; vertical and horizontal cosmography reflected in, 59–60; warfare, 74; world center shrine in, 56–57. *See also* ruling class

components of: Grand Plaza, 22, *52, 53,* 64, 146, 184; Kunnemann Mound, 53, *131,* 155, 191; Murdock Mound (Mound 55), 142, 144, *145,* 200n. 33; North Plaza, 52, *53;* Powell Mound (Mound 86), 67, 137, *138,* 163, 164; Rattlesnake Mound, 97, *131,* 155, 163, 164; Twin Mounds, *52,* 101, *102,* 156, 184; Woodhenge, 52, 159, 160, 173, 184; woodhenges, 51, 63, *63,* 64, 160. *See also* Monks Mound; Mound 72; stockades

in early twentieth century, 125–51; new buildings encroaching on, 146–50, *147;* at St. Louis world's fair of 1904, 126–28; urbanization, 129–30; during World War I, 130

French presence, 77–93; Cantine Mounds, 87–88; Collot's survey of region, 91–92, *92;* first Christian chapel on Cahokia, 84–86, *84, 85;* France cedes to England, 87; French and Indians living in harmony, 80–83; hostility between French and Indians, 83–84; Trappist monks at, 88–91

modern, 153–87; aerial view at early dawn, *152;* maps comparing Amerindian times with 1966, *124. See also* Cahokia Mounds State Historic Site; Cahokia Mounds State Park

natural setting of, 7–25; on alluvial floodplain, 18; in American Bottom,

18–25; clear days annually, 23–24; earthquakes, 16; equatorial location in distant past, 9, *10;* as favorable for human habitation, 25; five rivers near, 19; floods, 19; four ecologies meeting near, 7; lakes and swamps near, 22; loess near, 13; longitude and latitude, 23; rainfall, 23, 24; richness of ecological area, 189; soil, 12; as transportation nexus, 23, 97, 115; waterways converging near, 7

in nineteenth century, 95–123; archaeological work, 110–12, 115–19; Brackenridge's description of, 98; drainage projects, 23, 112; Indians removed from lands around, 103; journalists and travel writers discover, 104–6; Long's description of, 99; in Maximilian von Wied's illustrated book, 101–3; National Road through, 97; urban expansion and industrialization near, 112–15; and World's Columbian Exposition, 120–23

preservation efforts: bill to make national park of, 129; Historic Sites Act of 1935 applied to, 142; Moorehead's campaign, 134–35, 137, 151; as National Historic Landmark, 166; National Trust for Historic Preservation supporting, 174; private efforts, 129; as state park, 130, 135–36, 190; UNESCO World Heritage List designation, 2, 172–74, 190

successive values of, 190–91

threats to: double threat in early twentieth century, 129–30; Downtown Airpark, 147–50, 155; railroads, 97, 112–15, *113, 114,* 198n. 19; roads, 97, 146, 158

Cahokia Mounds Museum Society (CMMS): in Cahokia preservation movement, 201n. 9; and Contract Archaeology Program at SIU, 169; expansion of, 176–77; founding of, 171; Houser as founding member, 154; lectures and conferences of, 181; publications of, 177

Cahokia Mounds State Historic Site: Cahokia Mounds State Park becomes, 150–51, 171, 190; Collinsville annexing, 148; lectures and conferences, 181–82; Master Management Plan, 171–72, *172;* as meaning of "Cahokia," 5; Native Americans in programs, 179–81; new visitors' center, 174, 182–86, *183;* volunteer program, 177–79

Cahokia Mounds State Park: creation of, 135–36; Department of Conservation managing, 155; drive-in theater annexed to, 147; expansion of, 136, 155, *156;* Flagg's bill calling for, 130; old museum, 137, 140, 154–55; professional archaeologists hired, 153, 154–58; reclassified as State Historic Site, 150–51, 171, 190; recreational use leaving its scars, 156; in USGS map of 1974, 142, *143*

*Cahokian* (newsletter), 177

Cahokia Slough, 23

calendar. *See* solar calendar

canoes, dugout, 31–32, *32*

Canteen Creek, 19, 23, 30, *164, 190*

Cantine Mounds, 87–88

Cap au Gres Faulted Flexure, 16

Capitol (Washington, D.C.), 145–46

Capitoline Hill (Rome), 144–45

Catlin, George, 103, *104*

cemeteries, 36, 66

Cemetery Mound (East St. Louis), 112

"Centeola: The Maid of the Mounds" (Thompson), 104

Central Mississippi Valley Archaeological Research Institute (CMVARI), 167, 169

Charles IV (king of Spain), 96

chert: for arrowheads, 165; Burlington chert, 39; Mill Creek chert, 48; for tools, 70

Chicago: Ku Klux Klan membership in, 200n. 12; World's Columbian Exposition of 1893, 116, *118,* 120–23, 129

chunkey, 60, *61,* 70, 165

Circle and Octagon (Great Circle Earthwork, Newark Works, Ohio), 42, *43*

civil unrest, 74

Clark, George Rogers, 87, *87*

Clark, William, 97

Cleveland, Claude, 150

climate: Altithermal (Hypsithermal) Climatic Interval, 33; Ice Age, 9–12; of Illinois, 8, 15, 23–24, 194n. 22; Pacific Climate Episode, 72; rainfall, 8, 15, 23, 24, 194n. 22

clothing, animal skins for, 69

Clovis people, 28

CMMS. *See* Cahokia Mounds Museum Society

CMVARI (Central Mississippi Valley Archaeological Research Institute), 167, 169

coal, 9, 90, 198n. 19

Collier, John, 142

Collins, James, 169

Collinsville (Illinois), 134, 148

Collinsville bluffs, 18, 19, 22

Collinsville Road, 97, 137, 146

Collot, Georges-Henri-Victor, 91–92, *92,* 198n. 24

Columbia Bottom, 18

conical (rounded) mounds, 66, 67, *67*

construction techniques: at Cahokia Mounds, 65–66; of Mound Builders, 3; traditional French, 85; wattle-and-daub construction, 65

"Contested Grounds" symposium (1999), 75

continuing education, 177

Contract Archaeology Program (Southern Illinois University at Edwardsville), 169, 171, 182

Cooley, Charles, 23

copper, 122

corn: dietary stress from reliance on, 73; Late Woodland people growing, 46; mineral-rich Illinois soil for, 15; Mississippian large-scale cultivation of, 48, 67; Pacific Climate Episode affecting, 72; preparation of, 70

Corn Belt, 12

cornmeal, 70

creation myths, 60

Crook, A. R., 113, 131

Cushing, Frank Hamilton, 57

Cutler, Hugh, 170

Dalan, Rinita A., 64, 169, 195n. 27, 196n. 11

Dartaguiette, Pierre, 84

Davis, E. H., 199n. 30

deer, 25, 33, 34, 68, *68*

Deere, John, 108

deforestation, 73
Denny, Sidney, 171
Department of Conservation (DOC), 155,
    171, 172, 174
Deuel, Thorne, 137
dietary stress, 73
digging sticks, 47–48
Dillow, Don, 177–79
disease, 73
DOC (Department of Conservation), 155,
    171, 172, 174
Downer, Alan, 172, 201n. 23
Downtown Airpark, 147–50, 155
drainage: Illinois's natural, 12; projects near
    Cahokia, 23, 112
drive-in theaters, 146–47, *147*
dugout canoes, 31–32, *32*
Dupo (Illinois), 18, 91
Duvall, R. E., 135

Eagan, John J., 94
Eagle Mound (Great Circle Earthwork,
    Newark Works, Ohio), 42, *43*
Early Archaic Amerindians, 30–33
Early Woodland period, 39–46
earth, xviii, *xix*
earthquakes, 16–18, *16*
earthworks: Monks Mound as largest
    totally earthen structure in New World,
    160; mud for, 21; Native Americans ele-
    vating to high art, 3. *See also* mound
    building
Eastern Woodlands, 7, 8, 46
East St. Louis (Illinois): Cemetery Mound,
    112; flood of 1993, 19; Hardy on develop-
    ing, 130; Ku Klux Klan membership in,
    200n. 12; race riot of 1917, 134; as rail-
    road center, *114*
Edelhardt meander, 22
effigy mounds, 43–46, *44*
elite: as allying itself with power of sky,
    64–65; charnel houses for dead, 65; di-
    etary stress in, 73; houses for, 65; stock-
    ade separating lower classes from, 163;
    whelk shells for jewelry, 70
Emerson, Tom, 170
equinoxes, *6*, 37, 52, *53*, 158, 186, 191
Etowah (Georgia), 48

fabrics, 70–71
Fagan, Brian M., 51, 195n. 2
Falcon drive-in theater, 146–47, *147, 155*
Falling Gardens (near St. Louis), 99–101
farming. *See* agriculture
Federal-Aid Highway Act (1956), 158
Federal Flood Control Act (1928), 194n. 15
Federation of Women's Clubs (Granite City,
    Illinois), 129
Fekete, Thomas, 135
fences, 82, *82*
"Field for Archaeological Research in Illi-
    nois, The" (Snyder), 117
fish, in Mississippi Valley, 25
Fisk, Bill, 150
Flagg, Norman G., 130, 199n. 3
flint hoes, 47–48, *48*
flint knapping, 70
floods, 19–22, 137, 194n. 15
flyways, 19
forced perspective, 144–45
forests, 24
Fort Ancient (Ohio), 45, 108, 117, 128
Fort de Chartres, 83, *83*, 92, *93*
"Fort Hill" (Ohio), 42
Fowler, Melvin L.: aerial photography by,
    141; Anderson and Iseminger studying
    with, 154; in Cahokia Mounds preserva-
    tion movement, 201n. 9; interpretive
    center site testing, 182; mapping entire
    site, 160; Mound 72 excavations, 61,
    165–66, *165*; on ridge-top mounds and
    plan of Cahokia, 67, *68*, 163–64; on sa-
    cred landscape and social hierarchy,
    64–65; on second-level communities, 99;
    skeletons found by, 61, 165; stockades ex-
    cavated by, 140, 161–63
Fox Indians, 83, 86
French and Indian War, 87
French presence, 77–93; Cantine Mounds,
    87–88; Collot's survey, 91–92, *92;* first
    Christian chapel on Cahokia Mounds,
    84–86, *84, 85;* hostilities between French
    and Indians, 83–85; Indian customs
    adopted, 81–82; Marquette-Jolliet voy-
    age, 78–79; marrying Indian women, 80,
    81; Trappist monks, 88–91
Fritz, Gayle, 170

Gartner, William G., 55
Gerhard, Frederick, 110
glacial till plain, 10
glaciers, 9–12, *11*
Goddard, George W., 140
Gonville (Rupulay), Jean B., 88
Goode, J. Paul, 108
Grand Plaza, 22, *52, 53,* 64, 146, 184
grasslands (prairie), 24, 33, 59
"Great American Pyramid, The" (Smith),
    122–23
"Great Cahokia Mound, The" (Peet), 118–19
Great Circle Earthwork (Newark Works,
    Ohio), 42, *43*
Great Depression, 137
Great East Side Electric Railway System,
    126, *126*
Great Serpent (Ohio), 43–46, *45*, 123
Greer, Billy H., 149
grids, 96
growing season, 24
Guillet, Dom Urban, 88–89, 91

Haiti, 96
Hall, Robert L., 56–57, 158, 160, 166, 168
Halley's Comet, *45, 188,* 191
Harding, Fred, 130
Harding Brothers Syndicate, 130
Harding Mound, *132*
*Harper's Monthly*, 122–23, 126
Helton people, 34
Hiatt, Ettus, 186
Hilferty, Gerald, 182, 184, 186
Hill, T. Ames (Amos), 108, 110, 156, 190
Hilligoss, Marvin, *93*
Hinkle, Philip, 136
Historic Sites Act (1935), 142
Hiwasee Island (Tennessee), 48
hoes, 47–48, *48,* 70
Holder, Preston, 167, 168
Holley, George, 169
Holmes, William, 46
Holocene Epoch, 16
Hopewell culture, *37,* 41–46, *43,* 108
Hopewell Culture National Monument
    (Hopewell Mound City), 42, *44*
Houser, Jim, 154
houses, 65, *66,* 142, *175,* 184–85

Hoxie, Frederick E., 103
Hudson, Charles M., 60, 180–81
Hughes, Robert, 103
human sacrifice, 61, 67
hunting: atlatls in, 28, 30–31, *30;* by Ca-
    hokians, 68; of mammoths and
    mastodons, 28, 29, *29;* by Middle Ar-
    chaic people, 33; on waterways, *26*
Hypsithermal (Altithermal) Climatic Inter-
    val, 33

Ice Age, 9–12, *11*
Illini. *See* Cahokia Illini
Illinoian glacial stage, 10
Illinois: biodiversity, 24–25; climate, 8, 15,
    23–24, 194n. 22; coal deposits, 9, 90,
    198n. 19; in Corn Belt, 12; Department
    of Conservation, 155, 171, 172, 174;
    drainage, 12; Early Archaic Amerindians
    in, 30–33; early settlers in, 108–10; earth-
    quakes, 16–18, *16;* flatness, 10, 12, 194n.
    6; French strain in, 92; geology, 8–18;
    glacial till plain, 10; during Ice Age,
    9–12, *11;* internal improvement bill of
    1837, 109; Jolliet's map of waterways of,
    *80;* Ku Klux Klan membership in, 200n.
    12; Late Archaic Amerindians in, 36;
    limestone layers underlying, 9; loess,
    12–15, *13, 14,* 194n. 8; Middle Archaic
    settlements in, 33–36; minerals, 15; in
    New France, *78;* in Precambrian Era, 9;
    statehood for, 110; "The Stone Age in
    Illinois" at World's Columbian Exposi-
    tion, 121–22; vegetation, 24, *24;* water,
    vegetation, and urbanized regions, *20*
*Illinois as It Is* (Gerhard), 110
Illinois Central Railroad, 109, *109,* 190
Illinois County Airport Law (1945), 149
Illinois Geological Survey, 113
Illinois Historic Preservation Agency, 171,
    174
Illinois River, 19
Illinois State Historical Society, 117, 128,
    129
Illinois State Museum: ceasing to sponsor
    Cahokia, 171, 176; Deuel work at Powell
    Mound, 137; East Stockade excavations,
    168; in joint management of Cahokia

Mounds State Park, 155; Moorehead sur-
    vey, 130–31, 134; Wittry excavations, 158
Illinois State Museum Society, 154, 171, 201n.
    9
Indian Removal Act (1830), 102–4
Indians. *See* Native Americans
interpretive (visitors') center, 182–86; diora-
    mas of seasons, 185; drive-in movie
    mock-up, 185; exterior, 183–84, *183;*
    house foundations incorporated in,
    184–85; interior, 184–86; patio, 184; spec-
    ulations on demise of site, 185–86;
    sunken well diorama, 185; theater for
    orientation program, 184; Townsend
    mural, 184
Interpretive Center Tract I (ICT-I), 182
Interpretive Center Tract II (ICT-II), 182
Iseminger, William R.: on abandonment of
    Cahokia, 72; on contributors to Cahokia
    archeology, 167–70; on labor required
    for stockade building, 163; and Master
    Management Plan, 171; overseeing Ca-
    hokia site, 153, 154–58; on slumping in
    Monks Mound, 174–76; on trade at Ca-
    hokia, 73; in UNESCO World Heritage
    List application, 172

Jackson, Andrew, 103
Jackson, J. B., 181
Jarrot, Nicolas, 88, 89
Jefferson, Thomas, 96, 99
jerky, 34
jewelry: natural materials for, 68; whelk
    shells for, 70; in Woodland burials, 41,
    *41*
Jolliet, Louis, 78–79, *80,* 197n. 2

Kaskaskia (Illinois), 87
Kaskaskia River, 19
Kelly, A. R., 137
Kelly, John E., 55, 57, 128–29, 167, 169
Kelly, Lucretia, 170
Kickapoo Club (Bloomington, Illinois), 130
Kinley, David, 130
Koldehoff, Brad, 170
Koster (Illinois), 30, 32, 33–36, 39
Kreider Truck Company, 174
Krupp, E. C., 159–60

Ku Klux Klan, 132–34, *133,* 200n. 12
!Kung San people, 39
Kunnemann Mound, 53, *131,* 155, 191

labor: for building stockades, 62–63, 162,
    163; to build Monks Mound, 63, 196n.
    11; in Cahokia Mounds public works,
    62–65; in hunter-gatherer societies, 39;
    specialization of, 40
La Croix, Jean-Baptiste, 87–88, 197n. 13
Lakeside (Nickols) airport, 147–48
land: European division of, 96; Native
    American attitude toward, 82, 103
Land Grant Act (1850), 109
Land Ordinance Act (1785), 96
La Salle, René-Robert Cavelier de, 79–80
Late Archaic Amerindians, 36–39
Late Woodland period, 46
Latrobe, Charles Joseph, 104
La Violette, Jacques, 80
Lawrence, Donna, Productions, 184
Lee, Richard B., 39
L'Enfant, Pierre-Charles, 145–46
levees, 19, *21,* 194n. 15
Levy, Isaac, 87–88, 197n. 13
Lewis, Meriwether, 97, 99
Lincoln, Abraham, 108
Lisa, Manuel, 97
loess, 12–15, *13, 14,* 194n. 8
Long, Stephen H., 99–101, *100*
Lopinot, Neal H., 169, 170, 171
Louis XIV (king of France), 77
Louisiana Purchase, 96–97
Louisiana Territory, 96–97
lower world, symbols of, 60
Lunsford-Pulcher site, 91, *92*

mall (Washington, D.C.), 146
mammals: beavers, 25, 60, *60,* 97–98; deer,
    25, 33, 34, 68, *68;* mammoths, 27, 28, 29;
    mastodons, 27, 29, *29;* in Mississippi
    Valley, 25
mammoths, 27, 28, 29
Manifest Destiny, 103
Marquette, Jacques, 78–79
Master Management Plan, 171–72, *172*
mastodons, 27, 29, *29*
Mastodon State Park, 29

Maximilian von Wied, Prince, 101–3, 198n.
  13
McAdams, William, 117, *118*, 120–23
McKeithen site (Weeden Island, Florida), 55,
  *55*
McKern, Will, 137
McKinley, Ashley C., 140
mealtimes, 34
Mehrer, Mark, 170
Mephan, George S., 136
Meramec River, 19
Mercier, Jean-Paul, 83, 84–85
Michelangelo, 144–45
Middle Archaic Amerindians, 33–36
Midyett, Omar, 148
Mill Creek chert, 48
Mills, William C., 128
Milner, George, 170, 196n. 11
minerals, 15
Mississippians: architecture, 49; arts and
  crafts, 25; Brackenridge and archaeology
  of, 97–99; characteristics of tradition,
  49; emergence of, 46–49; hoe replacing
  digging stick, 47–48; and Hopewell cul-
  ture, 46; languages, 48; large-scale agri-
  culture, 46, 48; Long's measurements of
  sites, 99–101; political systems, 49; settling at Cahokia, 19; sites of, *47;* standard planning devices employed by, 4;
  Stone Age technology of, 2, 3; stratified
  society of, 2; trade, 46, 48, 71. *See also*
  Cahokia Mounds
Mississippi Valley: Archaic peoples in, 30;
  biodiversity, 25; curve of river near Cahokia, 18–19; Eagan's *Panorama of the
  Monumental Grandeur of the Mississippi
  Valley, 94;* five rivers near Cahokia, 19;
  French explorers, 78–79; Marquette's
  map of river, *79;* Paleo-Indian life in,
  29–30; settlement of, 110; in temperate
  zone, 7, 8; tributaries of river, 8, *8;*
  Wild's *The Valley of the Mississippi Illus-
  trated,* 105–6, *107*
Missouri Fur Company, 97–98
Missouri River, 19
Mitchell site, 113, 167
Monks Mound: "birdman tablet" from, 118,
  *119;* Bodmer's drawing of, 101, *102;*

Brooks Pasture near, 130; and cardinal
  directions, 51, 52, *52, 53;* as critical in creating integrated community, 64; drive-in
  theater near, 146–47, *147,* 155; entire site
  oriented with respect to, 142, 144, 145;
  Hill's access trail to, 156; Hill's farm on,
  106, 108, 190; home of great chief on,
  66; in interpretive center mural, 184; Ku
  Klux Klan rally on, 132–34, *133;* labor required to build, 63, 196n. 11; as largest
  totally earthen structure in New World,
  160; McAdams's drawing of, 117, *118;*
  Mound 72 aligning with, 164; on natural
  levee, 22; new values accruing to, 127;
  Patrick's measurement of, 117, *118;* as
  platform mound, 67; railroad near, 97,
  *113;* Ramey's complex on, 110; Ramey
  subdivision near, 150, 155; St. Louis
  world's fair excursions to, 126–27;
  slumping in, 174–76; Smith's "The Great
  American Pyramid," 122–23; Snyder's
  study of, 115–16; stairs to top of, 176; as
  state park, 117, 135–36, 190; State Park
  Place near, 136–37, *138, 139;* subdivisions
  planned near, 129; as tallest structure in
  United States, 2, 67; threat to make beer
  garden of, 128–29; Trappist Monastery
  on, 89, 91; trees growing on, 108, 156–57,
  *157;* in UNESCO World Heritage List
  application, 173; vertical dimension provided by, 57; Wild's depiction of, 104,
  *105,* 108
Monks of Cahokia, 117, 129
Moorehead, Warren K., 129; campaign to
  preserve site, 134–35, *135,* 137, 151; *Primitive Man in Ohio,* 129; survey of site,
  130–32, *131, 132*
Mormons, 75
Morris, Charles, 182–83
mound building: ceremony for, 66; common human motive in, 49; by Early
  Woodland people, 40–46; height created
  by, 57; by Hopewell culture, *37,* 41–43,
  *43;* in Middle Archaic period, 36;
  mounds as mass, 58; mounds seen as
  natural phenomena, 113; at Poverty
  Point, Louisiana, 37–39, *38;* speculation
  on identity of builders, 104; in stages, 61;

types of mounds, 66, *67. See also* Ca-
  hokia Mounds
Mound 55 (Murdock Mound), 142, 144, *145,*
  200n. 33
Mound 72: Anderson in excavation of, 154;
  burials in, 165, *166;* celestial orientations
  from, *53;* cross section of, *166;* Fowler excavating, 165–66, *165;* and orientation of
  Cahokia Mounds, 163–64; skeletons
  found in, 61, 165; in UNESCO World
  Heritage List application, 173
Mound 86 (Powell Mound), 67, 137, *138,*
  163, 164
Moundville (Alabama), 48
mud, 21
Mule, Jay, *179*
Mullanphy, John, 89
Murdock Mound (Mound 55), 142, 144, *145,*
  200n. 33

Napoleon, 91, 96, 97
Nassaney, Michael, 182
Natchez Indians, 83
National Congress of American Indians, 103
National Park Service, 172
National Road, 97, 146
National Trust for Historic Preservation, 174
Native American Graves Protection and
  Repatriation Act (1990), 180
Native Americans, 27–49; Archaic period,
  30–39; in Cahokia Mounds State Historic Site programs, 179–81; celestial
  phenomena in life of, 55–56; cosmic
  models for communities, 55; Early Archaic period, 30–33; Early Woodland period, 39–46; emerging interest in culture
  of, 127; French adopting customs of,
  81–82; Indian Removal Act of 1830,
  102–4; land as viewed by, 82, 103; Late
  Archaic period, 36–39; Late Woodland
  period, 46; Middle Archaic period,
  33–36; as overlooked by other Americans, 180–81; Paleo-Indians, 27, 29–30;
  routes to North America, 27; succession
  of creative adaptations by, 75; villages
  perceived as center of world, 57. *See also*
  Cahokia Illini; Mississippians
Nauvoo (Illinois), 75

needles, 68

Newark Works (Ohio), 42, *43*

New Madrid earthquakes of 1811–12, 16–17, 91

Nickols (Lakeside) airport, 147–48

Niiregead, Orif, 117

North Plaza, 52, *53*

Notre Dame de Bon Secours (Our Lady of Good Help) monastery, 89

nutritional stress, 73

Octagon State Memorial (Ohio), 42

Office of Contract Archaeology (Southern Illinois University at Edwardsville), 171, 182

Ohio Hopewell, 42–46

Olivier, Donatien, 90

optical illusion, 144, *145*

Our Lady of Good Help (Notre Dame de Bon Secours) monastery, 89

Pacific Climate Episode, 72

Page, Daniel, 110

Paleo-Indians, 27, 29–30

palisades: French, 82, *82,* 88. *See also* stockades

Pallozola, Chris, 177

*Panorama of the Monumental Grandeur of the Mississippi Valley* (Eagan), *94*

Parker, Katie, 170

Parmalee, Paul, 170

Patrick, John J. R., 117–18, 160

Pauketat, Timothy R., 63–64, 168

Peabody, Charles, 129

Peale, Titian Ramsay, *100*

Peet, Stephen, 118–19

Peoria Indians, 83

Pershing, John J., 141

Pfeiffer, John, 52, 54

pigments, 68

platform mounds, 66–67, *67*

pollution, 74

population density, 73

Porter, James, 167

*poteaux en terre,* 85, 190

*poteaux sur sole,* 85

pottery, 35, 36, 40, 70, 110–12, *112*

Poverty Point (Louisiana), 37–39, *38;* dimensions of, 38; solar calendar at, 37, *38,* 55

Powell Mound (Mound 86), 67, 137, *138, 163,* 164

prairie (grasslands), 24, 33, 59

Prairie du Rocher (Illinois), 90, 92

prairie grasses, 12, *13,* 71, 137

"Prehistoric Mounds of Illinois, The" (Snyder), 117

preservation: Antiquities Act of 1906, 128; Archaeological and Historic Preservation Act of 1974, 171; and archaeology, 123, 158; Big Mound demolition as rallying point for, 119–20; bill to make Cahokia national park, 129; Historic Sites Act of 1935, 142; Illinois Historic Preservation Agency, 171, 174; Moorehead's campaign, 134–35, 137, 151; National Historic Landmark status, 166; national movement focusing on buildings, 174; National Trust for Historic Preservation, 174; Powell Mound demolition, 137, *138;* Snyder as early preservationist, 117, 123; state park created at Cahokia, 135–36; state support required for, 128–29; UNESCO World Heritage List, 2, 172–74, 190

Preston, Douglas, 28

*Primitive Man in Ohio* (Moorehead), 129

property rights, French concern with, 82

Pulcher Mound group (Square Mound Farm), 115, *116*

pumpkins, 39

Putnam, F. W., 129

railroads, 97, 112–15, *113, 114,* 198n. 19

rainfall, 8, 15, 23, 24, 194n. 22

ramadas, *71*

Ramey, H. K., 140

Ramey, Thomas, 110, 115

Ramey family, 128, 129, 130, 131, 136

Ramey subdivision, 150, 155

Randall, E. O., 199n. 3

Rattlesnake Mound, 97, *131,* 155, 163, 164

Rau, Charles, 110–12, *112,* 199n. 30

rawhide, 69, 71

Reed, Nelson, 65, 167, 201nn. 9, 19

Reelfoot Rift, 18

Reeves, Dache M., 140

Regan, Ben, 148–49

*Reise in das innere Nord-America in den Jahren 1832 bis 1834* (Maximilan von Wied), 101

"ridge and swale" topography, 12, 22

ridge-topped mounds, 66, 67, *67, 68,* 163–64

Ridgley, Douglas C., 194n. 6

riots, 74

roads: Collinsville Road, 97, 137, 146; encroaching on Cahokia Mounds, 97, 146, 158; "highway salvage archaeology," 158; National Road, 97, 146

Robertson, Bea, 154

rounded (conical) mounds, 66, 67, *67*

ruling class: as allying itself with power of sky, 64–65. *See also* elite

Rupulay (Gonville), Jean B., 88

Rust, Dale, 150

sacrifice, human, 61, 67

Ste. Anne's Militia, 92, *93*

St. Louis (Missouri): Big Mound, 106, 112, 113, 119–20, *120;* growth as threat to Cahokia Mounds, 130; growth of, 87; Ku Klux Klan membership in, 200n. 12; Long's measurements of mounds north of, 99, *100;* settlers converging on, 97; Trappists and, 89, 90; world's fair of 1904, 126–28, *126*

St. Louis Downtown Airport, 148

Salzer, Robert, 167, 201n. 9

Save the Mounds (Edwardsville), 130

Schubert Club (East St. Louis), 129

Schuberth, Christopher J., 16, 17, 194n. 8

Shannon, C. H., 117

shellfish, 70

Silverberg, Robert, 42, 104

skins, animal, 69

Smith, Bruce D., 40

Smith, Harlan Ingersoll, 122–23, 126

Smith, Harriet M., 142, 144, *145,* 146, 163, 200n. 33

Smithsonian Institution, 134, 141

smog, 72

snake rattles, 68

Snyder, John Francis, 113, 115–17, *116,* 118, 123

solar calendar: at Cahokia Mounds, 52, *53,* 158–62; at Poverty Point, Louisiana, 37, *38,* 55 solstices, 52, *53*, 158, 159

Southern Illinois University at Edwardsville, 169, 171, 176, 182

specialization of labor, 40

Spiro (Oklahoma), 48

Springfield Plain, 12

Square Mound Farm (Pulcher Mound group), 115, *116*

squash, 39

Squier, Ephraim G., 42, *43*, 199n. 30

State Park Place (housing development), 136–37, *138, 139*

stockades, *162;* aerial photography revealing, 140, *141;* anatomy of, *161;* design evolution, *62;* as evidence for war, 74; Fowler excavating, 140, 161–63; labor required for building, 62–63, 162, 163; organized workforce required to build, 163, *163*

"Stone Age in Illinois, The" (World's Columbian Exposition), 121–22, *122*

Stone Mountain (Georgia), 134

stone tools: adzes, 31, *32;* flint hoes, 47–48, *48;* McAdams on, 121; Mississippian, 70

Struever, Stuart, 30, 32, 33–36

sun, xvi, *xvi*

swamps, 22

tanning, 69

Terry, Robert S., 167

Thomas, Louis Foulk, 104–8

Thompson, Daniel Pierce, 104

Thompson, James R., 174, 182

Titterington, P. F., 137

Tonti, Henri de, *76*

tools, 70–71

Townsend, L. K., 184

trade: among Mississippians, 46, 48, 71; in Archaic period, 31–32; at Cahokia, 71, 72, *73*, 165; at Cantine Mounds, 87–88; between Illinois and Ohio Hopewell, 45–46; by Poverty Point people, 39

transportation: breaks in, 23; Cahokia as nexus of, 23, 97, 115; Cahokia Mounds impeding modern, 130, 146; railroads, 97, 112–15, *113, 114,* 198n. 19. *See also* roads; waterways

Trappist monks, 88–91

Treaty of Paris (1763), 87

trees: Cahokians using, 71; forests in Illinois, 24; on Monks Mound, 108, 156–57, *157*

Trubitt, Mary Beth, 169

Twin Mounds, *52,* 101, *102,* 156, 184

UNESCO World Heritage List, 2, 172–74, 193n. 3

University of Illinois, 130–32, 167, 201n. 9

University of Wisconsin-Milwaukee (UWM), 160, 168, 182, 201n. 9

upper world, symbols of, 60

urban sink, 74

urban stress, 74

*Valley of the Mississippi Illustrated, The* (Wild), 105–6, *107*

Venus, xvi, *xvii*

Virgin Mary, cult of, 81

visitors' center. *See* interpretive (visitors') center

Walthall, John A., 197n. 3

war, 74, 163

Washington, D.C., 145–46

Washington University, 167, 201n. 9

waste disposal, 73

waterfowl: abundance near Cahokia, 19; Middle Archaic hunting of, 33, 34; in Mississippi Valley, 25

water spiders, 60, *60*

waterways: Cahokia in nexus of, 23; five rivers near Cahokia, 19; hunting and fishing on, *26;* inland, *21;* Jolliet's map of Illinois, *80;* woodlands near, 24

wattle-and-daub construction, 65

Wells, Harold R., 140

West, Eliott, 75

Wheatley, Paul, 55

whelk shells, 70, 165

White, Richard, 81

Wiant, Michael, 196n. 11

Wild, J. C., 104–8, *105, 107,* 108

Wildcat, Tommy, 179, 180

Williams, Ken, 168

Wilson, Thomas, 129

Wittry, Warren, 158–60, 167

women: Frenchmen marrying Indian, 80, 81; work of, 69–70, *70*

wood: overexploitation of, 73; uses for, 68–69, 71

Woodhenge, 52, 159, 160, 173, 184

woodhenges, 51, 63, *63,* 64, 160

Woods, William I.: on additions to Monks Mound, 175–76; and Contract Archaeology Program, 169, 171; on deforestation at Cahokia, 73; drilling into Monks Mound, 176; French chapel excavated by, 86; interpretive center site excavated by, 169, 182; on loess at Cahokia, 12; online bibliography of, 194n. 7

World's Columbian Exposition (1893), 116, *118,* 120–23, 129

world's fairs: St. Louis fair of 1904, 126–28; scientific meetings associated with, 122; as showcases of art and scholarship, 120–21; World's Columbian Exposition of 1893, 116, *118,* 120–23, 129

World War I, 130

Worthen, Amos, 113

Wydick, Sue, 171

Yarbrough, Ronald E., 22, 194n. 15

Zuni, 57